NUMBERS

and

DEUTERONOMY

for

EVERYONE

Also available in the Old Testament
for Everyone series by John Goldingay

Genesis for Everyone, Part 1
Genesis for Everyone, Part 2
Exodus and Leviticus for Everyone

NUMBERS
and
DEUTERONOMY
for
EVERYONE

JOHN
GOLDINGAY

WESTMINSTER
JOHN KNOX PRESS
LOUISVILLE • KENTUCKY

First edition
Published by Westminster John Knox Press
Louisville, Kentucky

10 11 12 13 14 15 16 17 18 19—10 9 8 7 6 5 4 3 2 1

Cover design by Eric Walljasper, Minneapolis, MN

Library of Congress Cataloging-in-Publication Data

Goldingay, John.
  Numbers and Deuteronomy for everyone / John Goldingay.
      p. cm. — (The Old Testament for everyone)
  ISBN 978-0-664-23377-8 (alk. paper)
  1. Bible. O.T. Numbers—Commentaries.   2. Bible. O.T. Deuteronomy—
Commentaries.   I. Title.
BS1265.53.G65   2010
222'.14077—dc22

                                                              2010017890

CONTENTS

CONTENTS

CONTENTS

© *Karla Bohmbach*

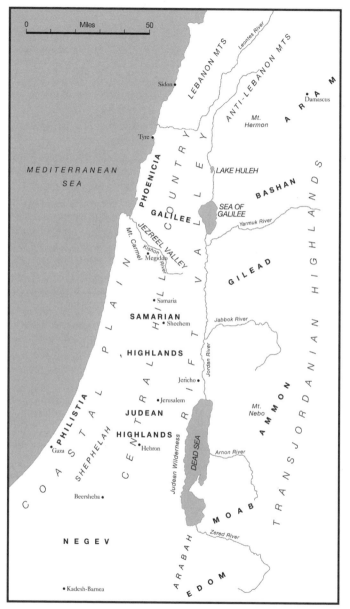

© *Karla Bohmbach*

ix

ACKNOWLEDGMENTS

The translation at the beginning of each chapter (and in other biblical quotations) is my own. I have stuck closer to the Hebrew than modern translations often do when they are designed for reading in church so that you can see more precisely what the text says. Thus, although I prefer to use gender-inclusive language, I have let the translation stay gendered if inclusivizing it would make unclear whether the text was talking in the singular or plural—in other words, the translation often uses "he" where in my own writing I would say "they" or "he or she." Sometimes I have added words to make the meaning clear, and I have put these words in square brackets. Space confines do not allow for including the whole of the biblical text; where there is insufficient room for that, I make some general comments on the material I have had to omit. At the end of the book is a glossary of some terms that recur in the text (mostly geographical, historical, and theological expressions). In each chapter (though not in the introduction) these terms are highlighted in **bold** the first time they occur.

The stories following the translation often concern my friends as well as my family. None are made up, but to be fair to people, they are sometimes heavily disguised. Sometimes I have disguised them so well that when I came to read them again, it took me time to remember who it was they were describing. In these stories, my wife, Ann, frequently appears. Just before I began writing this book, she died after negotiating with multiple sclerosis for forty-three years. Our shared dealings with her illness and disability over these years contribute to everything I write, in ways you will be able to see but also in ways that are less obvious. I thank God for her, and I am glad for her sake, though not for mine, that she can now sleep till resurrection day.

I am grateful to Matt Sousa for reading through the manuscript and spotting unclarities and slips and to Tom Bennett for checking the proofs.

INTRODUCTION

As far as Jesus and the New Testament writers were concerned, the Jewish Scriptures that Christians call the "Old Testament" *were* the Scriptures. In saying that, I cut corners a bit, as the New Testament never gives us a list of these Scriptures, but the body of Scriptures that the Jewish people accept is as near as we can get to identifying the collection that Jesus and the New Testament writers would have worked with. The church also came to accept some extra books, the "Apocrypha" or "deuterocanonical writings," but for the purposes of this series that seeks to expound the "Old Testament for Everyone," by the Old Testament we mean the Scriptures accepted by the Jewish community.

They were not "old" in the sense of antiquated or out-of-date; I sometimes like to refer to them as the First Testament rather than the Old Testament, to make that point. For Jesus and the New Testament writers, they were a living resource for understanding God and God's ways in the world and God's ways with us. They were "useful for teaching, for reproof, for correction, and for training in righteousness, so that the person who belongs to God can be proficient, equipped for every good work" (2 Timothy 3:16–17). They were for everyone, in fact. So it's strange that Christians don't read them very much. My aim in these volumes is to help you do that.

My hesitation is that you may read me instead of the Scriptures. Don't do that. I like the fact that this series includes the biblical text. Don't skip over it. In the end, that's the bit that matters.

An Outline of the Old Testament

The Jewish community often refers to these Scriptures as the Torah, the Prophets, and the Writings. While the Christian

Old Testament comprises the same books, it has them in a different order:

> Genesis to Kings: A story that runs from the creation of the world to the exile of Judahites to Babylon
>
> Chronicles to Esther: A second version of this story, continuing it into the years after the exile
>
> Job, Psalms, Proverbs, Ecclesiastes, Song of Songs: Some poetic books
>
> Isaiah to Malachi: The teaching of some prophets

Here is an outline of the history that lies at the background of the books (I give no dates for events in Genesis, which involves too much guesswork).

1200s	Moses, the exodus, Joshua
1100s	The "judges"
1000s	Saul, David
900s	Solomon; the nation splits into two, Ephraim and Judah
800s	Elijah, Elisha
700s	Amos, Hosea, Isaiah, Micah; Assyria the superpower; the fall of Ephraim
600s	Jeremiah, Josiah; Babylon the superpower
500s	Ezekiel; the fall of Judah; Persia the superpower
400s	Ezra, Nehemiah
300s	Greece the superpower
200s	Syria and Egypt, the regional powers pulling Judah one way or the other
100s	Judah's rebellions against Syrian power and gain of independence
000s	Rome the superpower

The Torah

Humanly speaking, the dominant figure in Numbers and Deuteronomy is Moses, and the King James Bible calls these books the Fourth and Fifth Books "of Moses." They do refer to Moses' writing some things down but not to his writing the books themselves; they speak about Moses in the third person, rather giving the impression that someone else is writing about him. Like most of the Bible, the books themselves are anonymous; they don't tell us who wrote them. One of the characteristics of Numbers and Deuteronomy is that they give us another run at topics already handled in Exodus and Leviticus. For instance, Deuteronomy gives another set of instructions about the treatment of servants to follow on the two sets that have already appeared in Exodus and Leviticus. All of these come from a time before the people are settled and thus in a position where they need to use even one set. They give us another set of instructions about celebrating the festivals in spring, summer, and fall, to follow on the three that have appeared in Exodus and Leviticus.

It seems that over the centuries beginning with Moses, God was continually guiding the community in how to live their lives in connection with their worship and everyday life. God's guidance took different shape as different social contexts required it to do so, and Numbers and Deuteronomy, like Exodus and Leviticus, brought together the fruit of this guidance as part of the great work of teaching that constitutes the five books of the Torah. The book of Ezra speaks of Ezra's bringing the Torah to Jerusalem from Babylon in 458 BC, some time after the exile, and maybe this indicates that the process of assembling the Torah (and thus Numbers and Deuteronomy) is now reaching its completion. So the books will incorporate material that accumulated over the best part of a millennium, from Moses to Ezra.

The King James Bible did not invent the idea of linking the first five books with Moses; it was around by Jesus' time, and the New Testament presupposes the link. But it is doubtful whether people simply meant to imply Moses actually wrote the books. They had other books and traditions that were associated with Moses, even though people knew they came from their own day. Calling something "Mosaic" was a way of saying, "We accept this as the kind of thing Moses would approve."

None of the opening five books is really a work on its own, complete in itself. Thus Numbers and Deuteronomy do not have a proper beginning of their own but presuppose the story in

Genesis to Leviticus. There, God's promises to Abraham found partial fulfillment within Genesis, but the book ends with the family of Jacob in the wrong country because of a famine. Exodus 1–18 takes up this story by getting Jacob's descendants out of Egypt and on their way to Canaan, but then for a long time the story stands still. They spend the whole of Exodus 19–40 and Leviticus at Mount Sinai. The time involved is only two years, but the space given to this time shows how much importance was attached to Israel's stay there and to Israel's working out its implications over subsequent centuries. So at the end of Leviticus the people are still on the way; Numbers and Deuteronomy take them from Sinai to the edge of the promised land.

The five books are a bit like the five seasons of a TV series, each ending with questions unresolved so that you return for the next one. Indeed, the series goes on for another six seasons (making it some sort of record) as the story continues though Joshua, Judges, 1 and 2 Samuel, and 1 and 2 Kings. Numbers and Deuteronomy are part of a gargantuan story running from Genesis right through to the books of Samuel and Kings. We know it does end then because turning over the page takes us to a kind of spin-off, a new version of the entire story, in First Chronicles. So Genesis to Kings tells a story that takes us from creation via the promise to Israel's ancestors; the exodus; the meeting with God at Sinai; the people's journey in Canaan; the dramas of the book of Judges; the achievements of Saul, David, and Solomon; and then the division and decline that end up with many people from Judah transported to Babylon.

As we have it, then, this huge story belongs in the period after the last events it records, the exile of people from Judah to Babylon in 587 BC. I don't assume it was written from scratch then, but strenuous effort to work out the stages whereby it reached its eventual form has not produced any consensus on the process whereby this happened. So it's best not to fret about the question. But the way the story extends from the beginning of the world to the end of the Judahite state does invite us to read the beginning in light of the end, as with any story, and this sometimes helps us to notice points about the story that we might otherwise miss and to avoid misunderstanding points that would otherwise be puzzling.

4

Numbers and Deuteronomy

Looking at Numbers and Deuteronomy in one volume of the Old Testament for Everyone means considering the whole account of Israel's journey from Sinai to the edge of the promised land. Numbers begins with the people still at Sinai and with Moses still giving them instructions from God, as in Leviticus, but the focus of the instructions changes. They now concern the journey the people are about to begin. The first third of Numbers relates these instructions, given over the last three weeks at Sinai. The middle third tells of the journey, which turns out to take forty years. For the last third they are in the Vale of Moab, east of the Jordan and the Dead Sea, and the story prepares the way for their arrival in Canaan. Through this last two-thirds of the book, instructions on various matters interweave with stories about particular events.

Throughout Deuteronomy the people remain on the edge of Canaan as the book relates Moses' last address to Israel. He reviews the journey they have made, challenges this new generation about the attitudes to God that need to characterize their lives, and gives them detailed instructions about issues they will need to handle there. He urges them to stay in covenant relationship with God, appoints Joshua as his successor as leader, gives them God's blessing, and climbs a nearby mountain for a look at the country the people are about to enter, before he himself dies.

Both Old and New Testaments assume that the stories and the teaching are significant for their own readers. Psalm 95 holds stories and teaching together: Israel needs to pay heed to God's instructions and learn the lessons from what happened on this tumultuous journey if they are not to get into a mess in the way Israel often did. It is often helpful to imagine the story being told or read to Israelites in succeeding centuries. First Corinthians 10 shows how Paul reckons it was vital for the Corinthians to learn from these stories, while the story of Jesus' temptations in the wilderness shows how he, too, assumes that Deuteronomy needs to determine the shape of his life.

NUMBERS 1:1–2:34

Finding Yourself in Your Family Story

[1]Yahweh spoke to Moses in the Sinai wilderness in the meeting tent on the first day of the second month in the second year after they came out of Egypt: [2]"Make a count of the whole Israelite community by their kin groups, by their fathers' households, with a list of the names of every male, one by one, [3]from the age of twenty and up, everyone in Israel who can go out with the army. You are to record them by their troops, you and Aaron. [4]Someone from each clan is to be with you, each the head of his father's household. [5]These are the names of the men who are to stand with you: for Reuben, Eliezer ben Shedeur; [6]for Simeon, Shelumiel ben Zur-shadday; [7]for Judah, Nachson ben Amminadab; [8]for Issachar, Nethanel ben Zuar; [9]for Zebulun, Eliab ben Helon; [10]for the sons of Joseph: for Ephraim, Elishama ben Ammihud, for Manasseh, Gamaliel ben Pedahzur; [11]for Benjamin, Abidan ben Gideoni; [12]for Dan, Ahiezer ben Ammishadday; [13]for Asher, Pagiel ben Ochran; [14]for Gad, Eliasaph ben Deuel; [15]for Napthali, Ahira ben Enan. [16]These are the people nominated from the community, the leaders of the ancestral clans, the heads of the companies of Israel.

[The rest of the chapter gives the count for each clan, to a total of 603,550; this omits the Levites, whose task was to look after the sanctuary. Chapter 2 sets out how the clans are to take their position as they march.]

My son Mark just came across a photo from exactly twelve years ago. My wife, Ann, and my mother are sitting at a picnic table; I am lying on the grass ("typically," Mark said; I am not sure what to make of that). Somewhere in the vicinity are our other son, Steven, and his wife, Sue, because it is a family farewell party on the Sunday before Ann and I undertake the biggest move of our lives. Three days later (twelve years ago tomorrow, as I write), we will get on the plane for that strange flight that starts in mid-afternoon and leaves you in Los Angeles still in the early evening even though it is eleven hours later. Among the poignancies of the moment is the fact that Ann's being wheelchair-bound means we will not be making the trip back across the Atlantic as other people do, and my mother's being nearly ninety means she will not be making the trip to see us, so we have had to face the fact that we are unlikely all to be together again. Behind us in the photo is our house, in which you could see the marks of preparation for this move. We have pointed out to our sons that this is the time they have to collect any of the belongings they left there when they moved out, and what they did not collect has gone to the thrift store. Most of the belongings we intend to take were shipped some weeks ago so they would get there before us (they didn't, but that's another story). Now, we simply have to pack our actual suitcases.

At the beginning of Numbers, the Israelites encamped at Mount Sinai are about to resume the biggest move of their lives. It should take about eleven days to complete it, rather than eleven hours. Actually it will take astonishingly longer, for reasons that will emerge. The first ten chapters of the book concern preparations for this move.

The story so far has established that the move may involve some battles. They didn't have to fight the **Egyptians**, and God has said nothing about fighting the **Canaanites**; God has taken responsibility for seeing the Canaanites off. But Abraham once had to go to battle to rescue Lot when he got taken captive in the context of war, and Moses and Joshua had to lead Israel in defending themselves against the Amalekites on the way from Egypt to Sinai. God sometimes enables the people of God to live in the world on the basis of extraordinary divine interventions but sometimes lets them live in that world on a basis not so different from the one everyone else uses. Jesus will both urge his disciples to be peacemakers and at the Last Supper tell them to buy a sword. It won't be surprising if the Israelites need to fight again. So they are going to march as a fighting force.

It might still seem odd that the first thing Moses and Aaron do in preparing to leave Sinai is count their fighting men. In 2 Samuel 24 David gets in trouble for doing this, a difference that reflects how people are sometimes expected simply to rely on God (counting soldiers thus suggests lack of trust) but on other occasions to take responsibility for their destiny in the way other people do. And it is significant that here God, not Moses, commissions the count.

The story has another implication for people listening to it. Like most citizens of the United States or any other country, most of the listeners will never be involved in fighting wars. The kinds of wars Numbers will relate belong in the distant past, as the battles involved in conquering North America and gaining independence lie in the distant past for people in the United States. Yet they are part of the story that defines the nation as a whole.

Although Moses' count involves only the fighting force, it is described as a count of the whole community. The people who belong to the twelve clans are not just the soldiers but the people of every age and both sexes. The whole community is about to undertake this journey, and there is another sense in which people listening to the story find themselves here not because they belong to a fighting force but because it is their family story. They all belong to Reuben, or Zebulun, or Dan, or one of the other clans. When they hear the name of their clan, it enables them to nudge one another and say, "That's us!" It is their story.

Maybe there is another hint of this being their family story in a puzzling feature of the story. The fighting force comes to 603,550. With the women, the young people, and the old people, that implies a total community of two or three million. That is about the population of the whole of Egypt at this time. Canaan's population was maybe 200,000. Never until the twentieth century did Palestine's population come to two or three million. If the Israelites had proceeded like a wagon train, it would have been 2,500 miles long. Even with wagons ten abreast, it would be 250 miles long.

The problem here is not that God could not have provided such a large company with food and water; God could have done so. The problem is that the numbers are out of all proportion with the numbers of peoples in the area at this time. One reason may be that the numbers have come to be misunderstood. The word for thousand is also the word for company in Numbers 1:16, and elsewhere it can denote a family. If the community was about six hundred *families*, this would make more sense. Yet six hundred *thousand* would cover the Israelites over quite a number of generations, and the people listening to the story could see the figure as also covering them. It is as if they were there, taking part in the exodus, the **covenant** making, and the journey to Canaan.

They are described as clans, kin groups, and households. The clans are often referred to as tribes, but this term is misleading. *Tribes* suggests separate peoples (Israel itself is more like a tribe). The twelve clans are the descendants of the twelve sons of Jacob, who was also called Israel—physical descendants or people adopted into these clans. Each clan divides into kin groups, and each kin group, into households (I avoid the word *family*, which can also be misleading). A "father's household" would be my wife and me, our two sons and their wives, and their children. Israelites might have more sons, though they would likely have lost some in childbirth or infancy (daughters would have married into other families). We would not be living eight thousand miles apart but in adjacent houses in the same village, farming our plot of land nearby. A "kin group" would include the households headed up by my brothers (if I had any). The village as a whole might include a couple of other kin groups from my clan, from whom my sons would have found their wives.

NUMBERS 3:1–5:4

God's Claim on Levi

¹This is the line of Aaron and Moses at the time Yahweh spoke with Moses on Mount Sinai. ²These are the names of Aaron's sons: Nadab, the firstborn, and Abihu, Eleazar, and Ithamar. ³These are the names of Aaron's sons, the anointed priests whom he ordained to serve as priests. ⁴But Nadab and Abihu died before Yahweh when they presented foreign fire before Yahweh in the Sinai Wilderness. They had no sons, so Eleazar and Ithamar served as priests in the lifetime of their father Aaron.

⁵Yahweh spoke to Moses: ⁶"Bring the clan of Levi forward and have them stand before Aaron the priest to assist him. ⁷They are to look after responsibilities for him and for the whole community before the meeting tent by doing service for the dwelling. ⁸They are to look after all the accoutrements of the meeting tent, the responsibility of the Israelites, by doing service for the

9

dwelling. [9]You are to give the Levites to Aaron and his sons; they are totally given to him from among the Israelites. [10]Aaron and his sons you are to appoint to look after their priestly work; the outsider who comes near is to be put to death."

[11]Yahweh spoke to Moses: [12]"Now. I myself am taking Levi from among the Israelites in place of all the firstborn, the first issue of the womb from the Israelites. The Levites are to be mine. [13]Because every firstborn is mine. At the time I struck down every firstborn in Egypt I consecrated to myself every firstborn in Israel, human and animal. They are to be mine. I am Yahweh."

[Numbers 3:14–4:49 goes on to record the various kin groups within Levi, with their numbers and their specific tasks in looking after the meeting tent and its transporting on the journey. Numbers 5:1–4 then deals with some taboos that the Levites and Israelites in general have to be aware of.]

Last night I was watching the "Extras" on the DVD of a movie called *The Soloist*, whose background is Skid Row in Los Angeles, ten minutes away from where I sit. It noted the contribution made by volunteers (of the kind I could be) to the needs of homeless people there. Just now I read an e-mail from our pastor reminding us that Saturday is another "work day" when members of the congregation are cleaning up the grounds around our church, disposing of weeds and brush, and so on, and I am wondering whether I should take part rather than sit at home writing *Numbers and Deuteronomy for Everyone* (you can e-mail me to tell me the answer). At least I shall take part when our church makes dinner at a local homeless shelter next week, and I shall thus miss the Episcopal party at the Dodgers game. And on Sunday I shall preside at the Eucharist; does that constitute my alternative contribution to the church's work? And what about the coffee sign-up—should I put my name down for one Sunday? Another congregational e-mail exchange this week discussed the appropriate salary for our organist; and while members of churches sometimes fulfill the duties of janitors, secretaries, and receptionists, often churches employ people to do them.

There is so much to do, not just for the individual but for the church and the rest of the local community. So we allocate tasks to different people or groups. That is part of the background to the position of the Levites. As the **Torah** tells the story, the community has just built an elaborate meeting tent or portable sanctuary, a dwelling or place for God to stay in Israel's midst. The story came in Exodus 35–40, many chapters ago but only a month ago chronologically. Building the sanctuary there was an odd thing to do, because now they have to carry it two hundred miles to **Canaan**. Fortunately God has thought of that. The Levites are going to carry it. Oh, thanks, say the Levites.

That is only a temporary task, though less temporary than they think. Fifteen miles a day, three weeks? No problem. It will turn out actually to be forty years, and rather more miles. But this is to get ahead of ourselves. The task will still be temporary, and the transportation task is not where Numbers starts. For the community listening to this story, the Levites' role is the subsequent, ongoing one, looking after the sanctuary that has become the fixed temple in Jerusalem, not the moveable dwelling. The community might have looked after it by allocating each clan one month on duty; conveniently, there are twelve clans. Or it could have relied on volunteers or people who "feel called." The building of it did rely on people volunteering and on the utilizing of gifts that God's **spirit** had given people. But for taking care of the sanctuary and leading in worship, God has told Israel to set one clan aside.

This presupposes a principle running through Israel's relationship with God. Everything belongs to God: place, people, time, things. Israel acknowledges this by directly giving over part of all these things to God: they give to God (and therefore hold back from) every seventh day, every seventh year, a tenth of the harvest, and the firstborn of the flocks. It would be appropriate to give their human firstborn, but instead God takes one of the clans, and does so for this task of looking after the sanctuary. There turn out to be 273 more Israelite firstborn than there are Levites, so Israel makes up for the difference by paying five shekels each (maybe six months wages for a laborer) to "redeem" them, to buy them back for ordinary life. That also conveniently gives the priesthood some resources for its work. The criterion for choosing Levi, the violence of their commitment to God when Israel made the gold calf (see Exodus 32) will seem strange to us, but that history might remind one not to mess with them, or rather not to mess with God. This chapter's opening allusion to the Nadab and Abihu story (Leviticus 10) would issue the same reminder and remind the Levites themselves that leaders tend to fall into sin and that the bigger they are, the harder they fall.

Levi himself had three sons, Gershon, Kohath, and Merari, who gave their names to the three major kin groups within the clan. Kohath's descendants included Amram, Moses, and Aaron's father. The priestly work in the narrow sense is the responsibility of Aaron and his descendants (elsewhere the Old Testament gives different impressions about this, reflecting how things transpired at different points in Israel's history). Levi's other descendants are responsible for other aspects of looking after the sanctuary and its worship.

Meanwhile, God prescribes how the Levite kin groups are to camp around the sanctuary, thus guarding against other Israelites coming too close after having one drink too many. God also prescribes how the kin groups are to look after the transporting of the sanctuary when it has been dismantled, again to protect it from them and them from it. The summary statements in Numbers 5 about keeping the camp free of the **taboo**s brought by eruptions and discharges and by contact with death relates to the broader need to keep the community a place where God can properly be present.

NUMBERS 5:5–31

Breaking Faith

⁵Yahweh spoke to Moses: ⁶"Tell the Israelites: 'If a man or woman does anything wrong to someone, thus breaking faith with Yahweh, the person is liable. ⁷They are to confess the wrong they did, make reparation for the amount involved, add one-fifth to it, and give it to the person wronged. ⁸If the person does not have a restorer to make reparation to, the reparation that is made belongs to Yahweh, to the priest, as well as the expiation ram with which he makes expiation for him. ⁹Every

offering of all the sacred things that Israelites present to the priest is to be his. [10]While for each person, his sacred things are to be his, what the person gives the priest is to be his.'"

[11]Yahweh spoke to Moses: [12]"Speak to the Israelites and tell them, 'When a man's wife goes off and breaks faith with him, [13]and someone has slept with her but it was concealed from her husband and she has kept it secret, so she has defiled herself but there is no witness against her and she was not caught; [14]or a jealous spirit has come over him and he has become jealous in respect of his wife when she has defiled herself; or a jealous spirit has come over him and he has become jealous in respect of his wife when she has not defiled herself: [15]the man is to bring his wife to the priest and bring as an offering for her one tenth of a measure of barley flour. He is not to pour oil on it or put frankincense on it, because it is a grain offering of jealousy, a grain offering of mindfulness, which produces mindfulness of waywardness.'"

[The chapter goes on to detail the ritual, which involves the woman's drinking a mixture of sacred water and dirt from the sanctuary floor and praying that if she is innocent, no harm will come to her, but if she is guilty, she may suffer internal sickness.]

I remember having a slight fit of jealousy (it was twenty years ago, but I still remember!) when my wife started talking to the man next door. He was another priest, my colleague and friend, but that didn't make much difference. He was a wise and spiritual man, and Ann would go and talk to him about issues between her and God, and most of me was really glad she did, but a bit of me was jealous. Shouldn't she be able to talk to me about such things? Wasn't I supposed to be everything to her? The answer, of course, is "No," and at head level I knew that, but at gut level I felt guilty that she needed to talk to him, and a bit resentful, and—jealous. In another context, a friend described someone's close relationship to someone other than his wife as "spiritual adultery." I'm not sure I believe in that, but I recognize the reality of spiritual jealousy. I can't imagine what it's like to know your spouse has committed physical adultery, or to suspect it.

I can imagine how horrendous could be the consequences for a wife whose husband suspects her in this way. It would not be surprising if she got physically abused or simply thrown out.

In a modern Western context she might be able to cope with being thrown out, as a wife may be able to cope if the shoe is on the other foot and she therefore walks out on her husband. In a traditional society it would likely mean social death and/or prostitution and/or physical death.

So the test for adultery covers several possible situations: A woman may have actually committed adultery, or a husband may be irrationally suspicious, or he may have reason for suspicion. Perhaps a sparkle has come into her eyes; this can happen to people who fall in love with someone new. Maybe she is pregnant and he thinks the child might not be his. Or maybe he just wants an excuse to get rid of her.

A test to determine the actual situation is in her interests as well as in his. For both, it involves trust in God. It's not like a DNA test or a pregnancy test. If Numbers left prayer out of the picture, it would count as magic or superstition. Instead, it constitutes an appeal to God to make a ritual an effective way of establishing the truth. It will have nasty physical consequences for the woman if it indicates she is guilty; the language may refer to her losing a baby or not being able to conceive in the future. It would discourage her from maintaining a lie if she was actually guilty.

What about a test for adultery by a husband? That would be fair. Maybe God is working with the human community's common double standard for adultery; men get away with things that women do not. Maybe the community and God recognize that it is the woman who actually gets pregnant. It is important to know who has responsibility for her child; her husband should not get out of it if it is his. Maybe God recognizes that a wife's need for protection from her husband's jealousy is greater than a husband's need for protection from his wife's jealousy.

The test for adultery follows on the rule about making restitution, which is a footnote to earlier rules in Leviticus 5–6. Their presupposition is that stealing or damaging something obliges you to put things right with the other person. Your offenses are not crimes against the state; Israel has no system for paying fines or going to prison. But you have done wrong against God as well as the other person. Any wrong against another person involves ignoring God's instructions; it may specifically involve lying under oath (the reference to confession may presuppose a prior denial). So as well as making restitution to the other person (and paying a little extra), you make restitution to God. The particular concern of this footnote is, "What happens if the wronged person has died and has no **restorer** or near relative through whom you could make restitution to the person's family?" The answer is that it also goes to the priest as a way of its going to God. The rule explicitly applies both to men or women. The rules in the **Torah** in general apply to everyone, but from time to time they incorporate a reminder that women and men are equally responsible before God and equally able to relate to God.

NUMBERS 6:1–27

The Lord Bless You and Keep You

[1]Yahweh spoke to Moses: "Speak to the Israelites as follows: 'When a man or woman makes an extraordinary vow, as a dedicated person, to dedicate himself to Yahweh, [3]he shall not drink wine or strong drink, or vinegar made from wine or strong drink, or drink any grape juice, or eat grapes, fresh or dried. [4]The entire period of his dedication he shall not eat anything made from the grapevine, even seeds or skin. [5]The entire period of his dedication vow, no razor is to pass over his head; until the completion of the period that he dedicates himself to Yahweh, he is to be holy, letting the locks of the hair of his head grow. [6]The entire period of his dedication to Yahweh he shall not go near a dead person. [7]For his father, mother, his brother or sister, he shall not defile himself when they die, because his dedication to God is on his head. [8]The entire period of his dedication, he is sacred to Yahweh.'"

[Verses 9–21 prescribe the offerings that dedicated people are to make if they accidentally come in contact with a dead person, and the offerings they are to make at the end of the dedication period.]

[22]Yahweh spoke to Moses: [23]"Speak to Aaron and his sons: 'This is how you are to bless the Israelites, saying to them:
  [24]"Yahweh bless you and keep you!

> [25]"Yahweh shine his face to you and be gracious to you!
> [26]"Yahweh lift his face to you and make things go well for you!"'
> [27]So they are to put my name on the Israelites so that I myself bless them."

"Bless you," we say when someone sneezes. "Blessings," we put at the end of e-mails. "God bless," my father would say as we went to bed. "It was a time of blessing," someone may say at the end of a service. "Bless my soul," we may say as an exclamation. "Bless you," I sometimes say at the end of a phone conversation. "It was a blessing in disguise," we may say when something unpleasant turns out to be beneficial. And at the end of a church service, I proclaim, "The blessing of God Almighty, the Father, the Son, and the Holy Spirit, be among you and remain with you always." What do we mean by blessing?

The Aaronic blessing links this important word with several other important words. "Blessing" itself has a prominent place in Genesis 1 and in later stories; it denotes the bestowing of fruitfulness. God's initial promise of blessing has been mightily fulfilled in the world, but humanity's fruitfulness and Israel's fruitfulness are not things to take for granted. They come about only as God makes them come about. Further, Israel needs keeping as well as blessing. Epidemic could imperil Israel. So could other peoples' attacks. So could its own stupidity.

Less prosaically, the blessing then speaks of God's face shining on us. When the sun shines on us, we feel good. When someone who loves us smiles at us, we feel good. The smile is a sign of love. It is linked with grace, another key theological term. There is something unpredictably and mysteriously gracious about being loved; you know that any attractive attributes you have (counterbalanced by your less attractive features) cannot explain this love. It is undeserved, inexplicable, yet real.

Lifting the face suggests someone with power and authority raising the eyes to look with favor on a suppliant. Such a person has the power to make things go well for you. More literally God "establishes well-being for you." Translations often have **peace** for this word *shalom*, but it suggests a much broader reality than this: not peace of mind but life working out well.

16

The priests' blessing is God's blessing. It is one of the many ways that (for reasons God never explains) God acts via other human beings in relating to us, speaking to us, and working in us. The priests declare God's name over the people. A person's name stands for the actual person, so God's name being over us suggests God's being over us. The priests' declaring the blessing means people become aware of God's intention to bless them, but it does more than that. The priests are God's means of conveying the blessing. When pastors say, "I baptize you in the name of the Father, the Son, and the Holy Spirit," they are not providing a running commentary on the event but making it happen. The priests' words are more than informative. They are performative; they make the blessing happen. Yet they do so only because God wills to have things work this way. "I myself" bless them, God says. That both qualifies the preceding words (don't think the priests have a strange power they could misuse) but also underlines them (God really will bless you).

The earlier part of the chapter concerns the way people may especially dedicate themselves to God for a period of time. Once again Numbers makes clear that this can apply to women as well as men. A "dedicated person" is a *nazir*, so this is a "Nazirite vow." The marks of dedication are ones of self-denial. You promise to forgo alcohol and anything that is anywhere near being alcohol. You let your hair grow; there is no explanation of why this should be an expression of consecration, but anyone who was alive in the sixties or who has read 1 Corinthians 11 knows that hair is very important to us. Further, you avoid contact with death. Death always makes people **taboo**, because one of the essential things about **Yahweh** is to be the living God. When you need to have contact with death (for instance, by burying a family member) you solve that by a **purification** ceremony, but someone taking a vow of dedication forgoes even that. Making the vow means making hard choices. Thus Jesus tells people they cannot follow him unless they are prepared to repudiate their parents and choose (if necessary) between following him and burying their parents.

Numbers does not tell us why someone might make a dedication vow of this kind; it is more concerned to put constraints around it and stop people from undertaking a vow too casually (which is again part of Jesus' concern with people who want to become disciples). It was the only way a person could make a commitment to God simply by choosing to. Whereas you could not choose to be a priest or a prophet, someone with religious inclinations could choose this way to manifest a special dedication to God. Another aspect of its significance is that people could make such solemn promises in connection with their prayers. It is as part of a prayer that Hannah promises to dedicate her son to God (1 Samuel 1).

NUMBERS 7:1–8:4

Provision for the Sanctuary

¹On the day Moses finished setting up the dwelling, he anointed it and consecrated it and all its accoutrements, and the altar and its accoutrements. When he had anointed and consecrated them, ²the Israelite leaders, the heads of the fathers' households (they were the leaders of the clans, who were in charge of the people who were enrolled) presented ³and brought their offering before Yahweh: six covered wagons and twelve oxen, a wagon for two leaders and an ox for each. When they had presented them before the dwelling, ⁴Yahweh said to Moses, ⁵"Receive them from them so they can do service for the meeting tent. Give them to the Levites, each as required for his service." ⁶So Moses received the wagons and the oxen, and gave them to the Levites. ⁷Two carts and four oxen he gave to the Gershonites as required for their service. ⁸Four carts and eight oxen he gave to the Merarites as required for their service, under the direction of Ithamar, son of Aaron, the priest. ⁹To the Kohathites he did not give any, because the service of the sanctuary rested on them; they would carry it on their shoulders. ¹⁰The leaders presented offerings for the dedication of the altar on the day it was anointed. When they presented the offerings before the altar, ¹¹Yahweh said to Moses, "They are to present their offerings for the dedication of the altar one leader each day."

[Verses 12–88 relate how each leader duly presents a silver bowl and a silver basin filled with shekels, a gold ladle filled with incense, three bulls, six rams, six lambs, and six goats.]

18

[89]When Moses went into the meeting tent to speak with him, he heard the voice speaking to him from above the atonement cover on the declaration chest, from between the two cherubs. He spoke to him.

[8:1]Yahweh spoke to Moses: [2]"Speak to Aaron as follows: 'When you put up the lamps, the seven lamps are to give light in front of the candelabrum.'" [3]Aaron did so. He put up its lamps in front of the candelabrum, as Yahweh commanded Moses. [4]This is how the candelabrum was made: it was hammered work of gold; the hammered work extended to its stem and its petals. According to the description Yahweh had given Moses, so he made the candelabrum.

We want to build a "proper chapel" at our seminary. We outgrew the original chapel decades ago, and for services we use an auditorium or a church adjacent to the campus. Now, one of the great cultural strengths of the United States is the generosity of its philanthropists, people who make a lot of money and are prepared to be openhanded with it. The seminary benefits considerably from this; it has enabled us to build a new library. To build a place of worship, members of the seminary community will make their own contributions, but these will resemble the copper coins an impoverished widow put into the temple treasury, which count hugely to God, because of the sacrifice they involve, but are little help to the priests managing the temple's budget.

God has given Israel instructions for building a magnificent portable sanctuary on the basis of people's gifts, and Moses has overseen the building of it (see Exodus 25–40). It needs further provisions for it to begin its work, and it needs means of transporting it through the wilderness to the country the people are journeying to.

Exodus did not tell us whether some Israelites were in a position to be more generous than others in contributing toward the actual building. It would not be surprising if this was so; the giving of others would have more the significance of the widow's coins. Numbers 7 emphasizes that each clan made the same contribution. That ignores the fact that (say) **Judah** was more than twice as numerous as Manasseh. God did not say all the clans had to make the same offerings. They do so, implying a mutual recognition that all had the same status.

For people reading this story, that would not be so. Judah and **Ephraim** became the clans that counted. Who cares about far-off clans like Asher or Naphtali, and about the northern kingdom's having been put out of existence by **Assyria**? Numbers 7 invites the people to look at things a different way. It details the contributions of each of the twelve clans, made over twelve days, and does so by repeating the same paragraph twelve times with a different clan name and leader's name at the beginning. This makes the chapter the longest in the entire Bible apart from Psalm 119. If you belong to a far-off clan that doesn't obviously count any longer as "Israel," it reminds you that you do. Your leader took part in this story, and you made as big a contribution as (say) Judah. If you belong to Judah, it reminds you not to overestimate your importance and not to underestimate the significance of clans that seem to be lost.

We have noted that six hundred families rather than two or three million people is closer to the actual number of people involved. The quantities involved in the clan offerings would also need to be scaled down in a literal historical account. Presumably the meeting tent itself, to which Moses resorted with frequency when he needed to receive God's guidance in connection with his leadership (and to which God would summon him in that connection) was a simpler affair than the one whose construction has been described in Exodus; Exodus and Leviticus give the background information about the tent, the **altar**, the chest that contained God's declaration (that is, the Ten Commandments), the atonement cover on top of it, and the cherubs standing over it. While the **Torah** is concerned about real history, it is not preoccupied by literal history. It likes to glorify the magnitude of events as a way of expressing their true significance for Israel and for us. Here we are, three thousand years later, thinking about the adventures and generosity of some ancient clans about to begin a journey through an isolated Middle Eastern wilderness. Yes, these events were more important than anyone could have dreamed at the time. The numbers give expression to that fact.

NUMBERS 8:5–9:14
God's Flexibility

[5]Yahweh spoke to Moses: [6]"Take the Levites from among the Israelites and cleanse them. [7]This is what you are to do to them to cleanse them. Sprinkle purification water on them. They are to pass a razor over their whole body and wash their clothes. Then they will be cleansed. [8]They are to get a bull from the herd with its grain offering, choice flour mixed with oil, and you are to get a second bull of the herd for a purification offering. [9]You are to present the Levites in front of the meeting tent and assemble the whole Israelite community, [10]and present the Levites before Yahweh. The Israelites are to put their hands on the Levites [11]and Aaron is to put them forward as a presentation offering before Yahweh from the Israelites, so they may be there to do service for Yahweh."

[The rest of Numbers 8 elaborates on this instruction and describes its fulfillment.]

[9:1]Yahweh spoke to Moses in the Sinai Wilderness on the first month of the second year after they came out of Egypt: [2]"The Israelites are to observe Passover at its set time. [3]You are to observe it on the fourteenth day of this month at twilight, at its set time in accordance with all its rules and decisions." [4]So Moses told the Israelites to observe Passover [5]and they observed Passover in the first month on the fourteenth day of the month at twilight, in the Sinai Wilderness. Just as Yahweh commanded Moses, so the Israelites did. [6]There were some men who were taboo because of someone's body and could not observe Passover that day, so they appeared before Moses and Aaron that day. [7]These men said to him, "We are taboo because of someone's body. Why should we hold back from presenting Yahweh's offering at its set time among the Israelites?" [8]Moses said to them, "Stay here so I can listen to what Yahweh commands about you." [9]Yahweh spoke to Moses: [10]"Speak to the Israelites: 'When anyone is taboo because of a body or is on a long journey, of you or your future generations, and he is to observe Passover for Yahweh, [11]they are to observe it in the second month on the fourteenth day at twilight.'"

[Verses 12–14 add some other reminders about Passover.]

A woman came to talk to me after church two weeks ago. In the sermon I had described the way the Psalms invite us in prayer to appeal to God's compassion, grace, and steadfast love, especially when we know we are in the wrong in relation to God. She could not really believe God is like that. From childhood God had been portrayed to her as holy, strict, and hard-nosed. With God, you couldn't get away with anything. We stood outside church on the main street with cars and buses passing, and she wept at the idea of God's being compassionate, loving, and merciful, as the Old Testament says.

The Passover story provides another example. The **Torah** has given many detailed instructions about how the Israelites must do this and that and get every detail right. You could get the impression that God is really anal. Then along comes a situation when following God's instructions raises problems. When someone died just before Passover and the family had to bury him, they had the taint of death on them and could not go straight into worshiping the living God. What are they to do?

Moses would take such a conundrum to the meeting tent to consult God. Meanwhile the family wait to discover what they are to do. Why will this take some time? Perhaps we should not be too supernaturalist about the process. While Moses sometimes hears a supernatural voice, I doubt whether we need to assume this always happens. Decisions perhaps come by similar processes to ours. Moses asks Aaron what he thinks and goes to the meeting tent and sits and thinks about the pros and cons of various possibilities ("Should they ignore the **taboo** rule? Hardly. Could we have a special **purification** process in the circumstances? Would that work? Should they watch the Passover observance from a distance? That would seem phony.") He asks God to guide his thinking, then makes a decision in the conviction that God is doing so. One way or another, God says, "Don't worry, it's not a problem. I'm not legalistic. They can celebrate Passover next month."

"They do need to keep the rest of the rules," God adds. "Being flexible because of circumstances doesn't mean you can ignore them. They're there for a reason. They aren't arbitrary." Thus on other occasions God comes down like a ton of bricks on someone who ignores the rules (Numbers 15 provides a scary example). It's possible to project legalistic attitudes onto God when really we are the legalistic ones, like the people who gave that misleading impression of God to the woman I spoke of. We'd like life and our relationship with God to be governed by totally clear rules. It isn't. That's a mercy, because life is messy. We need the kind of flexibility God is prepared to show.

The Levites' dedication to God's service raises overlapping issues. While they don't get ordained like the priests (see Leviticus 8–9), they do go through a multifaceted process that takes them from being ordinary Israelites to being people who give their lives to their work, which they will do on behalf of the entire people. The Israelites put their hands on them as a gesture indicating that the Levites do represent them and take their place, and that they associate themselves with them. Their commissioning involves a process of cleansing that suggests removing anything that clashes with who God is, and it involves offerings that seal this removing. This enables them to spend their time in close proximity to God in a way that would imperil ordinary people; it would be too "hot." God knows people need to be aware of the difference between God and them, but also makes provision to ensure this does not make them unable to relate to God. The Levites act as a buffer zone, a pair of oven gloves, an equivalent to the vest you wear when someone has an x-ray. The people can then come into God's presence with safety.

One of the Levites' ongoing duties will be to ensure people don't come too near the sanctuary in a taboo state or drunk. In the immediate context, their work will involve demanding physical service, carrying the parts of the dwelling while the people are on their journey. That will continue after their arrival and until the time of David, as the portable sanctuary seems to move around. Only when Solomon built a fixed temple did it stop doing so. They do this from the age of twenty-five to the age of fifty (if seventy is now the new sixty, in a society with poor health resources and diet, fifty is the old sixty).

As with other aspects of this story, the actual history of the role of the Levites in Israel was more complicated than this orderly narrative paints it. What Leviticus and Numbers give to Israel is a theological scheme for understanding how things turned out to be.

NUMBERS 9:15–10:36

The Journey Actually Begins

[15]On the day the dwelling was set up, the cloud covered the dwelling (the declaration tent). In the evening it would be over the dwelling, with an appearance like fire, until morning. [16]That is how it would continually be: the cloud would cover it, and there would be an appearance like fire at night. [17]At the prompting of the cloud's lifting from over the tent, after this the Israelites would move on, while at the place where the cloud would stop, there the Israelites would camp. [18]At Yahweh's word the Israelites would move on, and at Yahweh's word they would camp; through all the time the cloud would dwell over the dwelling, they would camp. [19]When the cloud stayed over the dwelling for a long time, the Israelites would keep Yahweh's mandate and not move on. [20]When there were times that the cloud would be over the dwelling for a number of days, at Yahweh's prompting they would camp and at Yahweh's prompting they would move on. [21]When there were times the cloud was there from evening to morning, as the cloud lifted in the morning they would move on. Day or night, when the cloud would lift, they would move on.

[Numbers 9 continues to underline this point. Numbers 10 then relates the making of two trumpets for signaling the time to move on, and also for signaling the imminence of battle or the celebration of festivals. It then relates how the people duly set out for the first time.]

[10:33]They moved on from Yahweh's mountain three days' journey, with Yahweh's covenant chest moving on ahead of them on the three days' journey to spy out a stopping place for them, [34]and with Yahweh's cloud over them by day as they moved on from the camp. [35]When the chest moved on, Moses said, "Up, Yahweh, your enemies are to scatter, your foes to flee before you!" [36]When it stopped, he would say, "Return, Yahweh, to the countless thousands of Israel!"

Although I make decisions easily (though this does not mean I make them wisely), when it was a question of deciding to take my disabled wife six thousand miles from Britain to California to a place we had visited only once and where we couldn't be sure everything would work out, even I could recognize that the move contained an element of risk. Undoing the decision and the move, however, would be horrendously complicated. I was therefore grateful when God provided unasked-for signs that it was the right decision. One day a student at my seminary sensed God saying to her, "Tell John 'Judges 18:6.'" Neither of us knew what the verse said. The TNIV has "Go in peace. Your journey has the Lord's approval"; the NRSV has "Go in peace. The mission you are on is under the eye of the LORD." God had taken the verse entirely out of context, as God often does. Because God gave such assurances of involvement with us in this journey, I would say to people that I wasn't worried about whether things would work out. It was God who was going to look stupid if they didn't. (Things have worked out, and God doesn't look stupid.)

In the West, it feels important to us as individuals that our life journeys work out. In Scripture, God focuses more on the life journey of Israel, assuming that much of our significance comes from our belonging to a people. God does not regularly give individuals direct guidance of the kind I have just described; this has happened to me only at two crucial decision-making points in my life. Neither does God regularly give Israel or the church direct guidance of that kind. Perhaps God wants us to run our own lives as responsible people, not to be little children whose decisions are taken by a parent. From time to time God sends prophets to give Israel instructions in a particular context, but God mostly leaves Israel to make its decisions in light of what God has already done and revealed. Churches often ask for God's guidance but then make decisions the same way as any other body does; and that is OK.

At this crucial time in Israel's life God made a commitment to seeing that Israel reached its destiny in the country it was promised. That would encourage Israelites reading the story as my experience of God's giving a sign would encourage me if things went wrong. When **Ephraimites** and then also **Judahites** were eventually thrown out of their country, they could recall how God made sure of their ancestors' mile-by-mile journey to the country in the first place; surely God would not be totally abandoning the people later?

There is another side to the question, or another issue it raises. While emphasizing God's clear guidance, Numbers also emphasizes Israel's systematic responsiveness. God made clear when Israel was to move; Israel followed. Even more significant and challenging, God made clear when Israel was to stay, and Israel stayed.

Another implication is this. Whereas the journey to **Canaan** should have taken a mere ten days or so, actually it is going to take decades, as a result of acts of rebellion we shall shortly read about. Setting off from Sinai, Israel does not know about that, but the people reading this story know about it. They also know about their own subsequent rebellions and abandonments by God, and about the paradoxical way God stays with them even as they live with the consequences of rebellion and with abandonment. The guidance that Numbers here describes will be required only because Israel will take so long over its short journey. God is like a parent confining a child to its room as a punishment but saying, "I'll come and sit with you, though."

Perhaps that relates to another surprising element in the story of their departure. Moses asks his Midianite father-in-law to accompany them on their journey because he is well-acquainted with the wilderness and can guide them on the way. Excuse me; I thought God was going to guide them. Maybe this part of the story shows that Israel also operated with those two ideas of God's guidance. It was God that guided, but God guides through "natural" human processes and gifts. Of course, Moses may be using that as an argument to support the real concern he speaks of first. He wants his extended family, people who were not Israelites, to accompany Israel in order to enjoy Israel's blessings in Canaan. His father-in-law is initially unwilling (perhaps he is being polite and wonders if he is really wanted), though we know he agrees because we hear of his family in Canaan later.

Moses' "prayer" presupposes that Israel's rebelliousness isn't the only problem God will face on the journey. There will be peoples opposing the fulfillment of God's intentions. Moses' prayer is a kind of encouragement to the people to trust that God can deal with the obstacles standing between them and their destiny, but more directly it is an encouragement to God to make that happen. It is okay to urge God to do the things that God is committed to and can do and that we need God to do.

A nice Jewish tradition suggests that the reason Israel marched on for three days from Sinai apparently without stopping is that they are relieved to be leaving the place where God gave them so many rules; they are like a schoolboy running out of class when the teacher dismisses it, in case the teacher has a change of mind and calls it back. If so, Israel will be disappointed. They will find God can keep speaking to them in the wilderness.

NUMBERS 11:1–35

On Missing Garlic

[1]Now the people lamented their troubles in Yahweh's hearing. Yahweh heard, his anger flared, and Yahweh's fire burned among them and consumed the edge of the camp. [2]The people cried out to Moses and Moses pleaded with Yahweh, and the fire died down. [3]That place was called Burning because Yahweh's fire had burned among them.

[4]When the other people they had collected in their midst were full of longing, the Israelites also again wept and said, "If only someone would give us meat to eat! [5]We remember the fish we could eat in Egypt for free, the cucumbers, the melons, the leeks, the onions, and the garlic, [6]but now our throats are dry. There is nothing at all to see but this 'stuff.'" [7]The "stuff" was like coriander seed; in appearance it was like resin. [8]The people went about and gathered it, ground it with millstones or pounded it in a mortar, and cooked it in a pot or made it into loaves. Its taste was like rich cream. [9]When dew fell on the camp at night, the "stuff" would fall on it.

[10]Moses heard the people weeping, in their kin groups, each person at his tent doorway. Yahweh's anger flared right up, and Moses was troubled. [11]Moses said to Yahweh, "Why have you brought trouble on your servant? Why have I not found favor in your eyes, that you have put the burden of this entire people on me? [12]Am I the one who conceived this entire people or am I the one who birthed it, that you should say to me, 'Carry it in your arms, the way a nurse carries a baby,' to the country you promised to its ancestors? [13]Where could I get meat to give this

entire people when they weep at me and say, 'Give us meat to eat'? [14]I can't carry this entire people on my own. It's too heavy for me. [15]If this is how you are going to deal with me, will you simply kill me if I have found favor in your eyes so that I may not have to look at my troubles?"

[16]Yahweh said to Moses, "Gather for me seventy of the senior people in Israel, people you know are both senior members of the people and leaders. Take them to the meeting tent. They are to stand there with you. [17]I will come down and speak with you there, and withdraw some of the spirit that is on you and put it on them so they may carry the burden of the people with you and you will not carry it on your own. [18]You are to say to the people, 'Sanctify yourselves for tomorrow. You shall eat meat, because you have been weeping in Yahweh's ears and saying, "If only someone would give us meat to eat, because it was better for us in Egypt."'"

[The rest of the chapter relates how God does these two things.]

My mother didn't know about garlic. This is not unreasonable; she had learned to cook in the days when British cooking was boring, before Elizabeth David introduced us to proper cooking (she was our Julia Child) and before immigration from the Indian subcontinent turned chicken tikka masala into our national dish. My mother didn't even know about onions or leeks; only from my wife (who came from another part of the country) did I discover that onions are the most important vegetable in the world. And I don't think any of us ate melon until the first time we visited Israel. (We did know about fish, but mostly as in fish and chips. We certainly knew about cucumbers, though growing these is a bit of a challenge in the British climate.)

So I could go a long way with these Israelites as cooks. They know about garlic and onions and fish. And I could sympathize with them for missing these in the wilderness when all they have is this "stuff." It's what we usually refer to as "manna," which more or less simply transliterates a word that readers might otherwise take to mean "What?"—hence the Israelites' question "What is it?" (Exodus 16:15). It seems to be a resinlike substance present in the morning on certain trees in Sinai that you can indeed treat in the way described.

28

Why are the Israelites so worked up when only three days have passed and in a few days they are due to be in the land flowing with milk and honey? Why do they make a fuss about meat when they have flocks and herds with them? What is the point of the reference to the people they had collected (the word comes only here, but it presumably denotes people from other ethnic groups who joined in the exodus, according to Exodus 12:38)? Why is Moses so worked up? Why is God so worked up?

It is not the first time these dynamics have appeared in the story as a whole—hence in part those last questions. The opening verses relate an earlier incident that Moses handles in a more even-keeled way and that God handles by firing a warning shot across the people's bows. This wasn't the beginning. Back on the way from **Egypt** to Sinai (a lot of chapters ago, but only a few months ago) the people had already behaved in the same fashion. Such stories have a prominent place in this middle section of Numbers. The **Torah** works by telling a sequence of parallel stories all making similar points. They are not identical, but they overlap, like healing stories or parables in the Gospels. Accumulating similar stories underlines the points they make.

Here are some of the points from these two stories:

1. Disappointments often come to the people of God, things you might have thought clashed with God's nature and God's promises.
2. These often affect basic physical needs such as health or having something reasonable to eat.
3. Taking too much notice of people on the edge of the community may lead the community astray.
4. These troubles test the people of God, bringing to the surface who they really are.
5. They can make us look wistfully to the past and make us wish God had never taken hold of us.
6. The people of God are then inclined to complain to one another or to their leader or to no one in particular rather than to talk to God about their troubles.
7. The disillusion can then be contagious, hard to dissociate oneself from.

8. God overhears, finds it annoying, and reacts by sending more trouble.
9. The job of leaders is to plead with God on the people's behalf, not least when the people won't turn to God themselves.
10. The complaints often get the leaders down as they feel responsible for the people, as if they actually are responsible for their welfare and happiness.
11. It's okay for leaders to bring their complaints to God in the most confrontational terms rather than complaining to someone else as the people did, even if the leaders' complaints actually imply they are assuming they have more responsibility than they do.
12. God responds to such prayers and cries.

God did put onto seventy senior Israelites some of the **spirit** that was on Moses (which need not imply he had less). The sign is that they "prophesy," which means something like speaking in tongues, a sign for them and the community that God's spirit has come upon them and that they can share in Moses' responsibility. Amusingly, this even affects two of the seventy who had not come to the meeting tent. Joshua is worried about this, but Moses is fine about it. Maybe that says something to the later Israelite community and its leadership about not feeling the need to control everything that God's spirit may do.

Then a supernatural wind deposits quail three feet deep all over the camp, which seems like an answer to prayer but turns out to be something more complicated, because God subsequently strikes down some of the people. Perhaps they had eaten bad quail, but Numbers comments that nevertheless it was God who struck down the victims. If we are inclined to think this doesn't fit with the New Testament, we mustn't miss Paul's emphasis on learning from these stories (1 Corinthians 10:1–13). While these stories were written for later Israel, not for the people who experienced the events, and several psalms already appeal back to them and reckon Israel needs to heed their warnings, Paul adds that they were written for Christian congregations to learn from.

NUMBERS 12:1–15

Miriam the Prophet, Aaron the Priest, Moses the Teacher

[1]Miriam and Aaron spoke against Moses in connection with the Ethiopian wife he had taken: "He has taken an Ethiopian wife!" [2]They said, "Has Yahweh really spoken only through Moses? Has he not also spoken through us?" Yahweh heard. [3]Now the man Moses was very abased, more so than anyone on the face of the earth. [4]Yahweh suddenly said to Moses, Aaron, and Miriam, "Go out, you three, to the meeting tent." The three of them went out, [5]and Yahweh came down in the cloud column, stood at the tent doorway, and summoned Aaron and Miriam. The two of them went out [6]and he said, "Will you listen to my words? If there is a prophet of yours, a prophet of Yahweh, I will make myself known to him in a vision, I will speak to him in a dream. [7]Not so my servant Moses. In my entire household he is trustworthy. [8]I speak to him mouth to mouth, with clarity and not in enigmas. He beholds Yahweh's form. Why were you not afraid to speak against my servant Moses? [9]So Yahweh's anger flared against them. He went away, [10]and as the cloud was moving away from the tent, there— Miriam was scaly, like snow. Aaron turned to Miriam—there, she was scaly. [11]Aaron said to Moses, "My lord, please, do not hold against us the offense that we committed, acting foolishly. [12]Please, she must not be like someone dead, who has come out of his mother's womb and his flesh is half eaten away." [13]So Moses cried out to Yahweh, "God, please, heal her, please!" [14]Yahweh said to Moses, "If her father actually spat in her face, would she not be in disgrace for seven days? She is to shut herself outside the camp for seven days, and then come back." [15]So Miriam shut herself outside the camp for seven days, and the people did not move on until Miriam came back. [16]Then the people moved on from Hazeroth and camped in the Paran wilderness.

The movie *Live and Become* is the story of a boy among the Ethiopian Falasha Jews airlifted to Israel at the time of the Marxist revolution in the 1980s. Except that Schlomo (Solomon) is not a Jew but a Christian. His parents had died, and his adoptive mother thought he would have more future in Israel than in an Ethiopian refugee camp. In Israel, among the people suspicious about his Jewishness are his girlfriend's racist father, who doesn't want his "white" daughter involved with a black guy. It is in this connection that Schlomo gets to take part in a debate on the interpretation of the **Torah** with another teenager, who also turns out to be racist in the way he seeks to demonstrate that Adam was white and that black people were destined by Noah to be the slaves of white people. Schlomo wins the debate in the synagogue by demonstrating that Adam was neither white nor black; if anything, he was red (in Hebrew, the words for Adam, earth, and red are similar).

Racism is where Numbers 12 starts, though it is only one of a complex set of questions washing around in the story. Moses has married another wife; perhaps Zipporah has died, or perhaps this is a second wife (having more than one wife is a sign of status, so leaders commonly take extra wives). Miriam and Aaron are not protesting that; they are complaining about her being an Ethiopian and therefore black. Viewing people as inferior on the basis of their skin color is a rather modern phenomenon, but there are one or two hints of it in the Old Testament. Then there is Miriam's being Moses' sister; does this new wife push Miriam further away from Moses?

One can imagine Moses groaning. The people complained against him in **Egypt**; they complained against him at the Reed Sea; they complained against him on the way to Sinai, and they have complained against him on the way from Sinai. He has already told God that it is all too much. Now his sister and brother have turned against him. It is plausible to describe him as the most unpopular person in all the world. (Translations have him as the "meekest" man in the entire world, which is not obviously true, and the word nowhere else means "meek"; it means afflicted.)

Explicitly, Miriam and Aaron's question concerns Moses' status as someone through whom God speaks. It is a classic example of a story that becomes clearer when we put ourselves in the position of later Israelites reading it. A question running through their story as we read it in later Old Testament books is the relationship between Moses' teaching and the messages given through prophets, who were often associated with and supported by priests. Many prophets and priests said things in conflict with Moses' teaching. They encouraged people to worship other gods, assured the community that things were fine between them and God when they were not, and encouraged them to make images of God as aids to worship. Further, the living voice of prophecy with its priestly support could seem more impressive and relevant than mere "Mosaic" traditions passed on from the past.

Numbers 12 affirms that God speaks through prophets, though it suggests that this speaking falls short of what people gain through paying attention to Moses' teaching. There is something straightforward and direct about that speaking; it is not a matter of dreams and visions whose meaning is often enigmatic. That is a fair characterization. Three thousand years later, individual aspects of the Torah are puzzling to us, but its nature is to be concrete and clear. Prophets are like poets; they speak in metaphors and images. For Israel as God's household, the clear teaching of Moses needs to have priority over arguable interpretations of prophetic oracles. You can always trust Moses.

So when Miriam tries for equal status, God puts the prophet in her place. God chastises her in particular because it is her position as prophet that is the issue. She comes first at the opening of the story; Aaron has more of a supporting role. Her chastisement is a temporary attack of what translations traditionally called leprosy, but the word does not refer to the disabling disease that we denote by that name but to a skin disease that (as Aaron notes) makes the skin seem to be decomposing and makes a person corpselike. Moses prays an urgent five-word prayer (five words in Hebrew as in English), a model of praying for someone (not least someone who has done wrong to you). As often happens with prayers in the Old Testament, God doesn't fully say "Yes," but neither does God say, "No." What comes about is the necessary compromise between the demands of love and the demands of justice. Scaliness is viewed as having similar implications to contact with actual death, which makes it impossible to come into the sanctuary that belongs to the living God. Miriam therefore withdraws outside the camp until the affliction disappears, and the people wait for her.

At the end of the story, they are getting near the country they are bound for.

NUMBERS 13:1–14:38

A Spy Story

[Numbers 13 begins by relating how God bids Moses to send men from each clan to scout out the land of Canaan, from where they cut down a huge bunch of grapes and some pomegranates.]

3:25They came back from investigating the country at the end of forty days. 26They went straight to Moses and Aaron and the entire Israelite community at Kadesh in the Paran wilderness and brought back word to them and the entire community, and showed them the fruit of the country. 27They told them, "We came to the country that you sent us to. Yes, it flows with milk and sweetness, and this is its fruit. 28Only, the people that lives in the country is powerful and the cities are fortified, very large. Moreover we saw the Anakites there. 29The Amalekites live in the Negev region, the Hittites, Jebusites, and Amorites live in the mountains, and the Canaanites live by the sea and by the side of the Jordan." 30But Caleb hushed the people before Moses. He said, "Let's definitely go up and take possession of it, because we can definitely do it." 31But the men who went up with him said, "We can't go up against the people, because they are stronger than us."

[The argument continues for a while until God intervenes.]

14:11Yahweh said to Moses, "How long will this people disdain me? How long will they have no faith in me for all the signs I have done in their midst? 12I will strike them with an epidemic and dispossess them and make you into a greater and more powerful people than them." 13Moses said to Yahweh, "But the Egyptians will hear, because you brought this people up by your might from their midst, 14and they will tell the inhabitants of this country who have heard that you, Yahweh, are in the midst of this people, you Yahweh who have appeared in plain sight with your cloud standing over them, you who go in front of them in a cloud column by day and a fire column by night."

[Moses goes on to try some other arguments on God.]

²⁰Yahweh said, "I pardon, in accordance with your words. ²²Yet as I live and as Yahweh's splendor fills the entire world, ²²none of the people who have seen my splendor and my signs that I did in Egypt and in the wilderness and tested me these ten times and not listened to my voice ²³will see the country I promised their ancestors. None who disdained me will see it."

[Verses 24–38 expand on this.]

I like to raise student eyebrows by pointing out occasions when God has abandoned segments of the church. In the first Christian centuries, the eastern Mediterranean (Turkey, the Levant, Egypt, North Africa) was full of lively Christian churches, but now there are hardly any Christians there. In sixteenth-century Europe, the only question was whether the churches would be Catholic, Reformed, Lutheran, or whatever, but now the continent is post-Christian. And (I go on to say) that is how the United States will be in ten years. God will never abandon the church, but God can abandon whole areas or generations of it. (Of course, we can trust that God will not abandon an area or a generation except where it has already abandoned God.)

That pattern goes back to this story. Its first puzzling feature is the very fact that God commissions Moses to scout out the country. Why would God do that? That question will be complicated when Deuteronomy 1 reports Moses as declaring that the scouting was the people's idea, not God's. We likely have another indication that the **Torah** combines more than one version of the story, as it does with the creation story, the flood story, and so on. (If you read the full version of Numbers 13–14, you will spot repetitions and seams that reflect this.) So what is the significance of including the two angles on who wanted the scouting to happen? The Israelites might want some reassurance about the nature of the country and its people, so that would make them keen on the scouting. At the same time God might want to encourage them by reports of how fine a country it was. But God's agenda for the scouts includes whether the people there are few or many, strong or weak, even though the Israelites are not supposed to have responsibility for defeating them; God is committed to driving them out. If the scouts discover that they are many and strong, is that to encourage the Israelites to rely on God?

Concrete evidence of the country's attractiveness (especially compared with the Sinai wilderness) is the giant cluster of grapes the scouts bring back; the image still provides the symbol for the Israel ministry of tourism. The country flows with milk and sweetness: that is, there is lots of pasturage for sheep, goats, and cattle, and there are lots of fruit trees. The usual English phrase is "flowing with milk and honey," but the "honey" is not bees' honey but syrup made from fruit such as figs, the main source of sweetness in the Middle East.

The trouble is that the scouts spend more time talking about the frightening prospect of having to dislodge the country's present occupants. There is a neat irony about Caleb's being the one scout who is convinced it can be done. Caleb represents **Judah**, but Numbers 32:12 will later note that his father was actually a Kenizzite, not physically an Israelite, but evidently someone who had become part of Israel. Further, it is appropriate that his kin group comes to possess land around Hebron from where the scouts brought their concrete evidence of the country's fruitfulness. We later learn that Joshua (who represented **Ephraim**) agrees with Caleb, so their two clans (later the leading clans) can listen to the story with some satisfaction, though the vast bulk of their clans agreed with the other scouts rather than with their famous representatives.

The people are convinced by the majority of the scouting party who declare that Israel cannot possibly overcome the country's inhabitants. As they have done before, they rail at Moses and Aaron (this is easier than railing at God) and determine to head back to **Egypt**. Joshua and Caleb attempt to change their minds. Joshua comes first at this point, no doubt because of his importance later on—and he is the leader who has to put his money (or rather his troops) where his mouth is. But they only find the people starting to stone them for their trouble, until God appears and declares the intention to cast off the people altogether and start again with Moses. As well as pointing out the disadvantages in that strategy, Moses includes in his "prayer" a reminder of what God said at Sinai when the same dynamics appeared (Exodus 32–34): **Yahweh** is, after all, the God who claims to be long-tempered and full of commitment, and one who carries people's waywardness and rebellion, even though also one who does not acquit the guilty. God is always having to handle the question of how to deal with both parts of that self-description. Here, God does so in a different way from the one adopted at Sinai, by reaffirming the need to take action against the entire current generation of Israel but also by agreeing to keep faith with Israel in the long run. The next generation will enter **Canaan**. This generation will live and die out like Bedouin in the wilderness.

It is astonishing that Moses is so courageous in speaking like this to God and that God agrees that Moses is right. It would be a shame if we assumed the church does not have the same freedom and might sometimes win the same response. It might even lead God not to cast off the church in the United States.

NUMBERS 14:39–15:41

The Intentional and the Unintentional

[39]When Moses spoke these words to all the Israelites, they went into great mourning. [40]Early next day they went up to the mountain ridge, saying, "Yes, we will go up to the place Yahweh said, because we did wrong." [41]But Moses said, "Why are you transgressing Yahweh's word when that will not work? [42]Don't go up, because Yahweh is not in your midst. Otherwise you will tumble before your enemies, [43]because the Amalekites and the Canaanites will be there in front of you and you will fall by the sword. Because of the fact that you have turned away from Yahweh, Yahweh will not be with you." [44]They insisted on going up to the mountain ridge, but Yahweh's covenant chest and Moses did not move from the midst of the camp, [45]and the Amalekites and the Canaanites living in the mountains came down and struck them down as far as Hormah.

[Numbers 15:1–29 then lays down a series of rules that supplement, reprise, or clarify ones in Leviticus. They concern details of how to bring offerings and how to handle a situation when you accidentally fail to observe one of the rules.]

[30][Yahweh said to Moses,] "The person who acts with hand upraised, whether native born or resident alien: Yahweh is the one he is reviling. That person will be cut off from the midst of his people. [31]It is Yahweh's word he has scorned. It is Yahweh's command he has broken. That person will definitely be cut off. There is waywardness on him."

[32]When the Israelites were in the wilderness, they found someone collecting wood on the Sabbath day. [33]The people who found him collecting wood brought him before Moses, Aaron, and the entire community, [34]and placed him in custody because it had not been specified what should be done to him. [35]Then Yahweh said to Moses, "The person must definitely be put to death by the entire community stoning him outside the camp." [36]So the entire community took him outside the camp and stoned him to death as Yahweh commanded Moses.

[37]Yahweh said to Moses, [38]"Speak to the Israelites and tell them they are to make themselves a fringe on the corners of their clothes, throughout their generations. They are to put a purple cord on the fringe at each corner. [39]You will have the fringe and see it, and be mindful of all Yahweh's commands, and you will observe them and not explore the promptings of your mind and eyes, the things you lust after; [40]so you will be mindful and observe all my commands, and be holy to your God. [41]I am Yahweh your God who brought you out from Egypt to be God for you. I am Yahweh your God."

In our church we usually douse the candles during the final hymn, before the ministers process down the aisle and walk outside into the main street, back into the outside world, to say goodbye to the congregation. One Sunday a few months ago, our final hymn was "This little light of mine, I'm going to let it shine," and our rector suddenly realized that there was something symbolically wrong about dousing the candles as we claimed we were going to take our light out into the world. So he got the acolytes (people who share in the leading of the service) to carry the candles in the procession instead of dousing them. Practices such as lighting (and dousing) candles bring home to us something of the significance of Christian faith. They don't do anything in themselves, but they outwardly express and symbolize things that are important.

Numbers 14 has related how the Israelites have gotten into trouble "investigating" the country they are destined to enter because they ended up "lusting" or being unfaithful. At the end of Numbers 15 God sets up a practice designed to discourage them from "investigating" and "lusting." In our culture, freedom is an ultimate value. Whenever someone wants to limit people's right to say things that would offend other people or lead young people astray, other people will protest that their First Amendment rights are being compromised and that they have a right to freedom of speech. Freedom of thought is similarly vital to academics. Here God urges people voluntarily to limit their freedom of thought and their freedom of action, and provides them with a practice to aid this. There might seem little connection between fringes or tassels and obedience to God's commands, though purple fringes might suggest there is something royal and priestly about the people who wear them. That connects with God's closing comment: this is all about being holy. The fringes remind people of their status and calling. In later Jewish practice, in the context of persecution the fringes came to be attached to an undergarment; then they came to be part of a prayer shawl. Practices do change. The important thing about the fringes was that the wearer could see them and be reminded of the need to commit oneself to doing what God said.

What comes between the main story of the exploration of **Canaan** and this paragraph about fringes illustrates that further. First there is the account of the Israelites deciding to advance up the mountain ridge toward Hebron and the heart of the country they will eventually occupy, as God had intended them to do. One can imagine Moses tearing his hair. When they are supposed to go, they won't. Now they are not supposed to go, but they insist on doing so! (Hormah is in the wilderness between where the mountain ridge begins and where Israel is camped).

There follows a series of miscellaneous rules about the grain offerings and libations that accompany sacrifices, about the way resident aliens can and must follow the same practices, about offering some of the first of your baking to God, and about the way to make up for it when you unintentionally fail to keep one of the rules (for instance, if you forget to make some offering at the right time). Placed at this point in the story, these rules constitute good news in two ways. First, they presuppose that the story is going to continue. Israel is going to get into Canaan and implement them there. Israel is going to be making offerings. The stupid unwillingness to continue the journey when God commissions it and the stupid attempt to continue it when God forbids it do not mean the story derails. The other good news is that God's taking the drastic action that Numbers 14 describes doesn't mean you have to tiptoe around God afraid that the slightest infraction will get you in hot water. There's a world of difference between outright rebellion and an accidental slip. God isn't legalistic. You can always sort matters out if your failure was unintentional; even if it was intentional, you can throw yourself on God's mercy and find forgiveness.

Outright rebellion does have horrific consequences. You risk being "cut off" from the community. Being cut off isn't something Israel does but something you risk God doing (perhaps by your dying young, or your line dying out). That applies to the individual as well as to the community as a whole. The wood gatherer's disobedience flouts a key command. It relates to another key Israelite practice. For many people listening to the story, living in a context where their neighbors were not Israelites, the Sabbath command was a vital marker of their commitment to God. Keeping Sabbath came to epitomize the **covenant**; ignoring it is equivalent to abandoning the covenant. It is a serious business. The people hearing this story need to recognize how important keeping Sabbath is. A story such as this, like the New Testament story of Ananias and Sapphira dying because they falsified their pledges, makes one glad one did not live in biblical times. Yet apparently Israelites were able to live with such stories without being totally fazed. They knew God was one who showed mercy to people who sought mercy. The fringes are designed to help them live in obedience rather than risk ending up like the wood gatherer.

NUMBERS 16:1–17:13

Dealing with Ambition

¹Korah, son of Izhar son of Kohath son of Levi, along with Dathan and Abiram sons of Eliab and On son of Peleth, the

Reubenites, took himself [2]and stood up before Moses with two hundred and fifty Israelite men, leaders of the community, commissioned by the assembly, men of repute. [3]They assembled against Moses and Aaron and said to them, "You have too much, when the entire community are holy, all of them, and Yahweh is in their midst! Why do you raise yourselves above Yahweh's assembly?" [4]When Moses heard, he fell on his face. [5]He spoke to Korah and all his group: "In the morning Yahweh can make known who is his and who is holy, and bring him near to himself. The one he chooses is the one he will bring near to himself. [6]Do this. Get yourself censers (Korah and all his group) [7]and put fire in them and lay incense on them before Yahweh, tomorrow. The man Yahweh chooses, he will be the holy one. You have too much, sons of Levi."

[In 16:8–27 Moses continues to upbraid Korah, and Dathan and Abiram critique Moses' leadership. Yahweh threatens to destroy the whole community, but in response to Moses' and Aaron's pleading, Yahweh focuses on Korah, Dathan, and Abiram.]

[28]Moses said, "Because of this you will know that it was Yahweh who sent me to do all these things, because they are not my idea. [29]If these people die the way any human being does and the fate of any human being falls on them, then it was not Yahweh who sent me. [30]But if Yahweh creates something extraordinary, and the ground opens its mouth and swallows them with all who belong to them so that they go down to Sheol alive, then you will know that these men have despised Yahweh." [31]As he finished speaking these words, the ground underneath them split, [32]and the earth opened its mouth and swallowed them and their households, and all Korah's people and all their possessions.

[Numbers 16:33–17:13 goes on to recount the aftermath of the event, which includes the entire people's railing against Moses and Aaron. Yahweh again announces the intention to destroy it and an epidemic starts, but Moses and Aaron make expiation for the community. Yahweh provides for a miraculous sign to confirm the status of Aaron's line.]

I am amazed that anyone seeks a position of leadership. We once had a new principal come to the seminary where I taught in England who unveiled his detailed and carefully thought-out vision for its future. The faculty took one look and said, "Not so much," and the next few years were a struggle as we sought to live together in a Christian fashion and discover how we could work toward a future. Then I myself became the principal, and I had to deal not with this problem but with other issues. In light of the amazement I just mentioned, you might wonder how I came to be principal, but it seemed a good idea at the time, and for much of the period I enjoyed being in that position. I myself enjoyed being able to pursue my own vision, but I was glad to give up the position to come to California with no responsibility but enthusing people about the Old Testament. Here, when I see the president or the provost or the dean going off to face some issue or solve some problem, I can say, "That used to be me, and now it isn't."

Moses continually has to deal with the pressures of leadership, which come sometimes from the people, sometimes from other would-be leaders, and on a bad day from both. In understanding the story, it will again help if we imagine ourselves as the later Israelites for whom it was written, among whom there may well have been tensions over who should have the role of priests. Is this everyone who can claim to be descended from Levi? Levi had three sons; the middle one was Kohath, Moses' and Aaron's grandfather. The **Torah** declared that only Aaron's descendants are priests in the full sense; the other Levites are their support staff. What about the relative positions of Aaron's two sons, Eleazar and Ithamar? Eleazar takes over when his father dies, but subsequently it seems that sometimes the senior priest was a descendant of Ithamar. We can't resolve the historical questions about the relative position of the various groups within the clan of Levi at different periods, but things we learn from the Old Testament do suggest there were conflicts over this. The Old Testament periodically bids the community be charitable to Levites, as it must be charitable to widows and orphans; this suggests they were in a vulnerable position. One can also imagine there being conflicts about the status of different clans. **Judah** and **Ephraim** are the leading clans; they give their names to the states into which Israel divides after Solomon's day. On what basis would they claim leadership? Reuben was Jacob's eldest son: should his descendants be sidelined? The chapter is convoluted and seems to be another where more than one story and more than one version of a story has been combined, hinting at how important these questions were to Israel.

Dathan and Abiram are Reubenites, while Nadab was a grandson of Kohath, like Moses and Aaron, so that by descent he had as much right to leadership as Moses and Aaron. So the story illumines and likely reflects later conflicts in the community. They say that history is written by the winners. I am not sure this is wholly true, but one can ask who are the winners in this story, and the answer is obviously Moses and Aaron. Insofar as it is Aaron, the story will support the later position of Aaron's descendants and in particular to support the idea that they have special forms of priestly responsibility over against other members of the clan of Levi whose task is to be their support staff. Fortunately, the context either side of this story includes plenty of critique of Aaron; it will be unwise for his descendants to make too much of this story, because other people can point to those other elements of the context. The next chapter will also provide some solemn things to think about and will underline how ordinary people are wise to rejoice in being ordinary people. Insofar as the winner is Moses, the story functions as another that urges the later community to continue taking Moses seriously. Moses has no successors; there is no Mosaic office. Taking Moses seriously means paying heed to his teaching rather than to teaching that seeks to displace him.

The descendants of Aaron also have to remember that Korah and his friends are right; the leadership always has to remember that the whole community is holy and God is in its midst. Yet the story presupposes that their arguing for this point is actually self-serving. They are not seeking to introduce democracy, to give actual power to the people. Their claim is that they have as much right to be leaders as Moses and Aaron. People who seek leadership claiming they do so for the people's sake when really it is because they want to exercise power have to remember the story of Korah and his friends. The account of Moses and Aaron's making **expiation** for the people so they are not annihilated also reminds the people's later leaders to be prepared to lean into the wind when people attack them. Such attacks go with the territory. Their vocation is to continue serving them and praying for them, concerned to keep the people in being. They are to do nothing to prove that they are in the right. It is God's job to vindicate them, not theirs.

The description of the rebels' fate includes one of the Torah's few references to Sheol, the place where people go when they die. It is not a place of suffering or punishment or purgatory, but neither does it have the positive connotations of heaven. It's a bit like a waiting room, except that you aren't going anywhere. Burial means we physically end up beneath the ground, so Sheol is also pictured as beneath the ground, and the story vividly portrays the earth opening its mouth so as to swallow up the rebels "alive"—that is, in the midst of life rather than by life gradually ebbing from them. There is also a unique reference to creation. The use of the word reflects how the idea of creation isn't so much that God is acting creatively (as we would say) but that God is doing something powerful, sovereign, and extraordinary. The act of destruction takes the families as well as the menfolk, recognizing that we are not all independent individuals but that our destinies are bound up with our families. The acts of parents do not leave their children unaffected, for good or ill.

NUMBERS 18:1–19:22

Provision and Purification

[1]Yahweh said to Aaron, "You, your sons, and your ancestral household with you carry the waywardness in connection with the sanctuary, and you and your sons with you carry the waywardness in connection with your priesthood. [2]Do bring with you your relatives in the clan of Levi, your ancestral clan, to join you and minister to you, as you and your sons with you are before the declaration tent. [3]They are to take care of responsibilities for you and for the tent as a whole, yet they are not to go near the accoutrements of the sanctuary or the altar, lest both you and they die. [4]They are to join you and look after responsibilities for the meeting tent, relating to all the service of the tent, but no outsider is to come near you. [5]You are to look after responsibilities for the sanctuary and the altar, lest there should again be wrath on Israel."

[Numbers 18 goes on to prescribe how the priests and their families are to receive many of the people's offerings, firstfruits, and firstlings, while the Levites are to live off people's tithes to make up for the fact that their clan is allocated no land.]

[19:1]Yahweh spoke to Moses and Aaron: [2]"This is a rule in the teaching that Yahweh commanded: Tell the Israelites they are to get for you a red cow, complete, one in which there is no defect and on which no yoke has been laid. [3]You are to give it to Eleazar the priest and it is to be taken outside the camp and slaughtered in his presence. [4]Eleazar the priest is to take some of its blood with his finger and sprinkle some of its blood seven times in the direction of the front of the meeting tent. [5]The cow is to be burned in his sight; its hide, its flesh, its blood, with its innards, are to be burned. [6]The priest is to get cedar wood, hyssop, and scarlet yarn, and throw them into the midst of the fire burning the cow. [7]The priest is to wash his clothes and bathe his body in water, and afterwards go into the camp, but the priest is to be taboo until evening. [8]The person who burnt it—he is to wash his clothes in water and bathe his body in water, but be taboo until evening. [9]A man who is clean is to gather the cow's ashes and place them outside the camp in a clean place. The Israelite community is to have them to keep as infirmity water. They are a purification offering.

[Numbers 19 goes on to prescribe how this cleansing process is to work.]

The other day I was visiting a big church in another city. It made for an extraordinary contrast with my little church, where the pastor is the only paid person and the building feels very full if there are seventy people present. This other church had a huge campus with lots of people working there (on a Tuesday!), and a budget that would frighten me. I don't know whether they have had to let staff go in the recession that we are living through as I write, but I do know that one or two churches in my own city have had to do so. Our little church, too, has to work hard to make its budget work. In my classes, potential pastors spend their time discovering the contents of the Bible and the way it may speak to the church in our time, but once they get into the ministry, they may have to spend more time worrying about whether the church's giving will continue to cover their salaries and the salaries of other members of their church's staff.

In an amusing passage in 1 Corinthians 9, Paul supports his argument that it is appropriate for pastors to be paid by referring to a rule in Deuteronomy 25 that prohibits people's muzzling an ox while it is treading out the grain; the ox ought to be free to eat as it works. He also alludes to passages like Numbers 18 that detail how priests and other sanctuary ministers are to be paid. Whereas other clans had an allocation of land so they could grow their food, Levi's task was to focus on looking after the sanctuary rather than on farming. The other clans' farming then supported them. While some offerings that people brought were burned, suggesting their going straight to God, other offerings were made to God but passed to the priests and other Levites. This provided a system for supporting the ministry they undertook on behalf of the whole people and also a system whereby offerings that had been given to God and thus sanctified could be handled in a reverent way.

God begins from the way the priests "carry waywardness"— that is, they bear responsibility for their offenses. Everyone does so in different ways; fortunately God is also prepared to "carry waywardness" for people when they come seeking mercy—"carry" is the word commonly translated "forgive." The trouble is that priests are in more risk of wrongdoing; maybe that is always true of people in ministry. They look after the sanctuary itself and take responsibility for the sacramental acts that happen there, such as the offering of sacrifice, and there are many ways they can accidentally compromise God's holiness. The other Levites are somewhat protected by having to keep their distance from parts of the sanctuary associated with special holiness. Just as priests and Levites are protected from or are free to be involved with aspects of the sanctuary and its work that have a greater degree of holiness, they are also protected from or free to partake from the different offerings in accordance with their varying degrees of holiness. God adds that the Levites themselves need to tithe the tithes they receive.

The ritual involving the red cow takes further a prominent issue in Leviticus. Contact with death (for instance, when you have to bury a family member) means you become **taboo**. The likely background is that death is alien to the living God, so you cannot rush into God's presence when you have just been in contact with death. You have to be cleansed from that contact. Numbers 19 gives the detail on how you achieve that: The water mixed with the red cow's ashes is a means of your cleansing. After that ceremony, you are free to go to the sanctuary again. How did that work? There is a story about a famous rabbi challenged by an unbeliever to explain how it worked, and in the end he confessed he had no idea, but he wasn't bothered. God said it would work, and that was all that mattered.

One implication of the ritual and its background is that most societies have wanted to keep in contact with the world of the dead. One reason is our human grief at the loss of a loved one. Another is a conviction that dead people might know things living people don't know, so it would be nice to be able to consult them. So there are people such as mediums who specialize in making contact with dead people for you. The Old Testament makes clear that Israelites were involved in such practices but also that God forbids them. When you want to know something that is inaccessible to ordinary human knowledge, God and God's agents, such as priests and prophets, are your sources, and you are to live your life in the present with the living God.

NUMBERS 20:1–13

One Fatal Mistake

[1]The Israelites, the entire community, came to the Zin wilderness in the first month, and the people lived at Kadesh. Miriam died there and was buried there.

[2]The community had no water, and assembled against Moses and Aaron. [3]The people argued with Moses and said, "If only we had perished when our relatives perished before Yahweh! [4]Why have you brought Yahweh's assembly into this wilderness for us and our animals to die there? [5]Why did you make us come up from Egypt to bring us to this bad place, a place with no seed or figs or vines or pomegranates, and no water to drink?" [6]Moses and Aaron came from before the assembly to the doorway of the meeting tent and fell on their faces. Yahweh's splendor appeared

47

to them [7]and Yahweh spoke to Moses: [8]"Get the staff and assemble the community, you and your brother Aaron, and speak to a crag before their eyes so that it gives its water, so that you bring water out of the crag for them and provide drink for the community and the animals." [9]So Moses got the staff from before Yahweh as he commanded him, [10]and Moses and Aaron gathered the assembly in front of a crag, and he said to them, "Will you listen, you rebels? Are we to bring water for you out of this crag?" [11]Moses raised his hand and struck the crag with the staff twice. Much water came out, and the community and their animals drank. [12]But Yahweh said to Moses and Aaron, "Because you did not trust me, making me holy in the eyes of the Israelites, therefore you will not bring this assembly into the country that I am giving them."

[13]These are the Argument Waters, where the Israelites argued with Yahweh, and he showed his holiness by means of them.

A few years ago a bright young church leader in England whom I knew slightly made one mistake, and his ministry was finished. It must have been devastating for him; it was devastating for people who had set their hopes on him as a symbol of something God was doing in the church. The mistake arose out of the fact that his wife was chronically ill, which meant he had someone helping him look after her and living in their home. This was really a necessity if he was to fulfill his ministry, but one day there was a scandalized column in a newspaper about there being an improper relationship between the man and the person they employed. I don't know how wrong the relationship actually was; for all I know it may have been pretty innocent, but if that was so, then (more tragically in a way) he had behaved in a way that could give the impression that he was being unfaithful to his wife. One way or the other he made one mistake, and the scandal terminated his ministry.

It ought to have been the case that Miriam, Aaron, and Moses led Israel into the promised land, but they all died before they got there. Indeed, a whole generation of Israel has died; although we would not have worked it out from the way this story begins, decades have passed since God's decree in chapter 14 after the people went on strike. Their children are now the people who have arrived at the staging post for entering Canaan.

So it is also decades since Miriam made the mistake that was related in Numbers 12; her death is not linked to that. Aaron was associated with this incident, but a few months (though a lot of chapters) previously he had made his first mistake in connection with the gold calf, as related in Exodus 32, though his death is not linked with that. He is implicated with Moses, as he had been with Miriam, in Moses' fatal mistake.

Although decades have passed and "the community" or "people" or "assembly" is actually a whole different generation from the one involved in that rebellion, nothing has changed. The Bible story can be depressing; nobody ever learns anything. Or perhaps it can be encouraging in this respect, because we have the same experience in the church; at least it shows us that the problem does not lie merely in us. Again there is no water, and again the community is in a state of panic not just about themselves but about their animals. Again they look back to **Egypt** with rose-tinted spectacles. If we interpret the story literally, by definition this generation had been born after their parents left Egypt, so the spectacles are ones provided by their parents; the parents' sins are indeed visited on the children, and nothing has been gained by waiting a generation. Again they blame their leaders rather than God. Again Moses and Aaron turn to God. Are they distraught, or at a loss, or scared for themselves, or scared for the people? Again God tells them what to do and declares that there will be miraculous provision. Again they do it, and there is.

Yet everything goes wrong. They make their one mistake. How did they fail to trust God and make God holy in the eyes of the Israelites? God instructed them to tell the crag to produce water. What they did was upbraid the people as rebels, and Moses twice hit the crag with his staff. There is some contrast with the story in Exodus 17 where God gave Moses instructions and Moses simply "did so," did as God said (which on that occasion included hitting a rock). It doesn't seem a huge contrast, but God sees it as implying a double failure here, of upbraiding the people and striking the rock.

We commonly assume that the opposite of trusting God is doubting God. In the Old Testament, the opposite of trusting God is trusting something else, such as another god, or political resources, and thus trusting ourselves. (Doubting God doesn't matter so much as long as you are doubting the right God.) When God accuses them of failure of trust, it likely means they are trusting in themselves to solve the problem, and it would link with Moses' taking forceful action, hitting the rock rather than merely addressing it. In turn it would imply failing to make God holy, to recognize and honor God's god-ness. Their action did not involve the precise obedience Moses shows on many occasions, which maybe indicates that something has gone radically wrong with their attitude. But one would never have guessed this was happening if Numbers had not told us. Moses and Aaron made a tiny mistake that had shattering consequences for them both.

Numbers will later record Aaron's death and his son Eleazar's succeeding him as senior priest. It does not say God struck Aaron down; I imagine him getting sick or simply ailing through old age and God making it clear that his time has come. Because of this incident God is not going to make it miraculously possible for him to live on so he is with the people when they enter **Canaan**.

NUMBERS 20:14–21:3

Two Very Different Attitudes to War

[14]Moses sent envoys from Kadesh to the king of Edom: "Your brother Israel has said this: 'You yourself know all the hardship that has befallen us. [15]Our ancestors went down into Egypt and we lived in Egypt for a long time, but the Egyptians did wrong to us and our ancestors. [16]So we cried out to Yahweh and he listened to our voice. He sent an aide and brought us out of Egypt. Now. We're in Kadesh, a city on the edge of your territory. [17]May we pass through your country? We will not pass through fields or vineyards, or drink water from wells. We will go along the King's Road. We will not turn off right or left until we have passed through your territory.'" [18]But Edom said to him, "You are not to pass through my territory or I will come against you with the sword to meet you." [19]The Israelites said to him, "We will go up by the highway. If we drink your water, I and my flocks, I will pay for it. Come on, it's nothing. We are

going to pass through on foot." [20]He said, "You will not pass through." So Edom went out to meet him with a substantial force, strongly armed. [21]Edom refused to let Israel pass through its territory, and Israel turned away from it.

[Verses 22–29 tell of Aaron's death at Mount Hor; his son Eleazar succeeds him.]

[21:1]The Canaanite, the king of Arad, who lived in the Negev, heard that Israel was coming by the Atharim road. He fought against Israel and took some of them captive. [2]Israel made a promise to Yahweh: "If you do give this people into our hand, we will devote their cities." [3]Yahweh listened to Israel's voice and gave the Canaanites over, and they devoted them and their cities. Hence the place was called Devoted.

I write at what we hope is near the end of a war in Iraq but in the midst of a war in Afghanistan whose likely outcome no one can predict; both these wars relate to the attack on the United States of September 11, 2001. Before that there was war in Somalia, and before that Vietnam, and before that Korea, and before that the two World Wars, and before that (for Britain) the Boer War, and before that (for the United States) the Civil War, and before that the Revolutionary War (I understand that Brits prefer to call it the War of Independence). Our history is a history of warfare, though these wars are undertaken for varying reasons and in varying ways.

The same was true for Israel, as Numbers 20–21 illustrate. First there is the war Israel avoids by taking a peacemaking stance in relation to Edom. This will have raised eyebrows among people listening to the story. There was often animosity between Israel and Edom, and Edom eventually took over significant parts of Israel's land. The prophets are particularly fond of declaring that God will bring doom on Edom, and there could be a link between declining to fight Edom and being assured that God will do so. You leave God to sort it out. So here, when the other party is unjustifiably belligerent, you go the long way around to avoid fighting. Further, Edom's ancestor Esau was twin brother to Israel's ancestor Jacob, and you don't fight other members of your family. Moab and Ammon also belonged to Abraham's extended family, and by implication Israel takes the same stance to them as it takes to Edom, skirting their territory.

Then there is the war that comes to Israel. The story about the attack by the king of Arad is odd coming here, because in the context Israel is moving east below the Dead Sea and skirting Edom, whereas Arad is some distance west. Perhaps this incident happened on another occasion, and this was just a convenient place to put it in the story. The king of Arad shares the Edomites' belligerence and does something about it. What, then, are the Israelites to do about the capture of some of their people? Like Abraham going off to rescue Lot, they act to rescue them, but the story escalates, as easily happens in such circumstances. They are not responding to a word from God in taking this action, and they do not consult God about it (but then, neither did Abraham). They do recognize that they need to ask God for help, and in doing so they make a promise.

In Old Testament stories, trouble often comes from making promises in order to get God to do what you need God to do. The Israelites promise to "devote" the cities of Arad to God—in other words, to give them to God as a kind of sacrifice. That means their aim in this battle will not be to gain anything for themselves. They only want their brothers and sisters back. What does "devote" imply? Does it just mean destroying the fabric of the cities? Does it mean sacrificing their animals to God? What will happen to the people there? The next sentence gives the chilling answer. God has said nothing in the **Torah** so far about "devoting" (that is, annihilating) the **Canaanites**, only about throwing them out of the country, but Israel knows this is how war works in its world and assumes it is to operate the same way, and God goes along with that.

NUMBERS 21:4–35

Snakes, and Progress, and Another Attitude to War

[4]They moved on from Mount Hor by way of the Reed Sea to go round Edom, and the people grew impatient on the way. [5]So the people spoke against God and against Moses: "Why did you

bring us up from Egypt to die in the wilderness, because there is no bread and no water and we detest this pathetic food?" [6]So Yahweh sent against the people venomous snakes that bit the people, and many Israelites died. [7]The people came to Moses and said, "We did wrong in that we spoke against Yahweh and against you. Plead with Yahweh to take away the snakes from us." Moses pleaded for the people [8]and Yahweh said to Moses, "Make yourself a venomous [snake] and put it on a standard. When anyone who is bitten looks at it, he will live." [9]So Moses made a copper snake and put it on a standard, and when a snake bit someone, he would look to the copper snake and live.

[10]The Israelites moved on and camped at Oboth. [11]They moved on from Oboth and camped at Iye-Abarim in the wilderness over against Moab on the east. [12]From there they moved on and camped by the Zered wash. [13]From there they moved on and camped beyond the Arnon, in the wilderness that extends from the Amorite border (because the Arnon is the Moabite border, between Moab and the Amorites; [14]that is why it says in the Book of Yahweh's Wars, "Waheb in Suphah and the washes; the Arnon [15]and the slopes of the washes that extend to the settlement of Ar and lie along the Moabite border"). [16]And from there [they moved on] to Well, the well where Yahweh said to Moses, "Assemble the people and I will give them water." [17]Then Israel sang this song:

Come up, well (sing for it), [18]well that the chiefs dug,
That the leaders of the people sank, with their scepters,
    with their staffs.

And from the wilderness [they moved on] to Mattanah, [19]and from Mattanah to Nahaliel, and from Nahaliel to Bamot, [20]and from Bamot to the canyon in the open country in Moab, to the top of Pisgah, which overlooks Wasteland.

[Israel makes the same request of the Amorites as it made of Edom. The Amorites attack, but the Israelites defeat them and take possession of their land. They do the same to the people of Bashan.]

Yesterday in church I was aware, as I sometimes am, that many people make the sign of the cross at certain points in the service. I was never taught to do that, and I would feel self-conscious about trying to do it, but I also feel self-conscious about not doing it, and I wonder if people notice. I like it as an idea. Anything that involves the body and not merely the inner person thereby contributes to involving the whole person. Marking myself with the sign of the cross means I really am marked with the cross. It parallels how God uses the washing rite of baptism in making us part of the church, and uses the practice of giving us bread and wine in applying the benefits of Christ's dying for us and making Christ part of our life. James similarly mentions the elders anointing people with oil when praying for people to be healed (Jesus sometimes uses spit!). Because we are physical people, God uses physical means with us in achieving spiritual ends.

The copper snake works like that. It means that God takes the risk of our turning physical, sacramental signs into super-stitions if we assume they work like magic. Israel did this with the copper snake, burning incense to it as if it were a kind of idol, so King Hezekiah broke it up (2 Kings 18:4). God could heal people without using such means but chooses to use phys-ical means because we are physical people. (In John 3:14, Jesus turns the lifting up of the snake into an illustration. Jesus will be lifted up, on a cross, and people will look to him and find healing.)

There was nothing new about the people's complaining and wishing they had never left **Egypt** and nothing new about God's chastising them for turning their backs on their vocation. Like a parent or a teacher, sometimes God ignores our wrongdoing and treats us with mercy, but God sometimes decides "That's it!" and takes action; you cannot predict when you will get away with things. The snakes as a means of chastisement are a new feature in the story, perhaps because they were a feature of the terrain where Israel was located. (Last week at a faculty retreat not far from my seminary we were told to be wary of bears and rattlesnakes; this was a new warning at a retreat cen-ter for me. Maybe I should have been thinking about the way God might be using bears and rattlesnakes to chastise us.) The place where the Israelites encounter the snakes is also not far from the copper mines at Timna, sometimes dubbed "King

Solomon's Mines," though they were not being worked in his day as they were in Moses' day.

The Israelites move on round the east side of the Reed Sea, avoiding Edom, and Numbers gives us an account of their itinerary and two sidebar notes. The song about the well would testify to God's provision regarding a need that often arose on the journey, not least earlier in this chapter. It would also testify to an Israelite claim to this land east of the Jordan: "*We* dug the well there." The "Book of **Yahweh**'s Wars" is referred to only here, though "Yahweh's Wars" are mentioned later in the Old Testament. It was apparently a collection of celebratory songs relating God's victories over different peoples.

Another such victory follows as the Israelites reach **Amorite** territory, and the story incorporates another celebratory song that the Israelites evidently enjoyed hearing. Again they declare no interest in this territory, but Sihon and his people come out to attack them and find themselves defeated, slaughtered, and dispossessed. Marching north, the Israelites come next to the territory of Og, the king of Bashan, which extends into the modern Golan Heights. This time there is no reference to negotiation. Og simply attacks, and God bids the people not to be afraid; "I hereby give him into your hand." Like Sihon, Og is struck down and dispossessed. So by accident Israel enters into possession of substantial land east of the Jordan, where some of the Israelite clans then decide they would actually like to live.

In these relationships described in Numbers 20–21 Israel is learning to live as a nation in the world as it is, and God is going with Israel through that process. The modern world has at least four attitudes to war: (1) just war, which has criteria for asking whether a war is justified; (2) pacifism, which questions whether war is ever justified; (3) crusade, which makes war in order to put down wrong and in the name of truth; and (4) pragmatism, which makes war when it is in our interests and we think we can win. These last two exercise most influence in Britain and the United States. None of the four is distinctively biblical or is biblical in origin. All can find some support from Scripture.

These stories in Numbers point to other attitudes. You don't fight members of the family; so the modest Mennonite proposal that Christians should decide not to make war against other Christians has some support here (it would have ruled out most wars in U.S. and British history). Your object in making war may be to free people, but you may find it hard to stop there. If you are attacked, it is not obligatory to lie down and die. You don't fight to gain territory, but if you are attacked and you win, it is not necessarily wrong to profit from your victory. And God gets involved with people in a way that interacts with their concerns, ideas, and instincts, and often compromises with these. As Jesus puts it, Moses (and thus God) makes allowance for our human stubbornness and skewed vision, and works with that (see Mark 10). At the same time, the stories are spare in their references to God's involvement. Sometimes you know what God is saying and you see God acting; sometimes you have to act in light of the way you see things.

The stories give us something to think about when we have to make decisions about whether in a particular context war is right.

NUMBERS 22:1–23:4

A Story about Several Asses

¹The Israelites moved on and camped in the Moab steppes across the Jordan from Jericho. ²Balak son of Zippor saw all that Israel had done to the Amorites, ³and Moab was very scared of the people because they were numerous. So Moab was in dread of the Israelites, ⁴and Moab said to the Midianite elders, "The horde will now lick up everything around us the way an ox licks up the grass in the wild." Balak son of Zippor was king of Moab at that time. ⁵He sent envoys to Balaam son of Beor in Pethor, by the River [Euphrates], the country of his kinsfolk, to summon him: "Now. A people has come out of Egypt—it has covered the face of the earth, and it is living next to me. ⁶So now will you come and curse this people for me, because it is too strong for me. Perhaps I shall be able to strike it down and drive it out of the country, because I know that the person you bless is blessed and the person you curse is cursed." ⁷So the Moabite elders and the Midianite elders went with divination [fees] in their hand, came to Balaam and spoke Balak's message to him. ⁸He said to them, "Spend the night here and I

56

will bring back word to you as Yahweh speaks to me." So the Moabite leaders stayed with Balaam.

⁹God came to Balaam and said, "Who are these men with you?" ¹⁰Balak said to God, "Balak son of Zippor, king of Moab, has sent to me: ¹¹'Now. The people that has come out of Egypt— it has covered the face of the earth. Come now and damn it for me. Perhaps I will be able to make war on it and drive it out.'" ¹²God said to Balaam, "You are not to go with them. You are not to curse the people, because it is blessed."

[When Balak receives this reply, he sends an even more impressive group of leaders to lean on Balaam, so Balaam consults God again.]

²⁰God came to Balaam by night and said, "If the men have come to summon you, get yourself off with them, but only do the thing that I tell you. ²¹So Balaam got up in the morning, saddled his donkey, and went with the Moabite leaders. ²²But Yahweh's anger flared because he was going, and Yahweh's aide took his stand on the road as an adversary to him. He was riding the donkey and his two servants were with him. ²³The donkey saw Yahweh's aide standing in the road with his drawn sword in his hand, so the donkey turned off the road and went into the fields. So Balaam hit the donkey to turn it onto the road.

[Eventually the aide stands in the way where the road is very narrow and there is no way past, so the donkey lies down and refuses to budge, and Balaam beats it to try to get it going again.]

²⁸Then Yahweh opened the donkey's mouth and she said to Balaam, "What have I done to you, that you have hit me these three times?"

[After some conversation between Balaam and the donkey, God opens Balaam's eyes so he can see the aide, who also berates Balaam but says it's okay to go as long as he says nothing but what God tells him. He and Balak offer sacrifices and Balaam goes off to wait on God.]

I was once assistant minister in a flourishing suburban church that had a history of having notable rectors, one of whom was by then rector of one of the most high-profile churches in the country. I have never forgotten hearing him say he knew he was not in the place where God really wanted him to be. When he had himself been an assistant minister, God had wanted him to go and serve as a missionary in another country, and he had resisted. He had spent his entire subsequent ministry in what he knew was not God's first intention for his life. It was God's "second best." It was quite a second best! I admired his bravery in not only having faced and come to terms with what had happened but in being willing to talk about it, and I marveled at God's grace in using him powerfully in his ministry even though he could never get back to God's ideal will for him.

There are overlaps between his story and Balaam's. Whereas we may assume that prophecy was a distinctively Israelite phenomenon, a number of Old Testament stories recognize that prophecy, like priesthood and sacrifice, was known among other Middle Eastern peoples, as it is in other cultures. We also know that from material that survives from these peoples themselves. Indeed, a prophet called Balaam appears in an inscription from Old Testament times in a place called Deir Alla a little way north of the Israelites' camp across the Jordan from Jericho. His prophecy speaks of a coming destruction of the country.

Numbers 22–24 assumes that God can work through foreign prophets as well as through Israelite ones. The point is made vividly by having Balaam speak in **Yahweh**'s name; literally he would not have done so, and the Balaam in the Deir Alla inscription does not do so, but this is a way of signaling that he is the means of Yahweh's blessing Israel. The story's further implication is that Israel does not need to be afraid of the power of foreign prophets. Even if they have the power to curse, God can make sure Israel is not imperiled by that power.

When the second embassy arrives offering more impressive rewards than the first to entice Balaam to come and do his stuff, Balaam is dismissive of them; his power cannot be bought. Yet evidently God reckons he should have simply accepted God's original "No" rather than attempting to reopen the question. God's permission to go with the embassy does not indicate this is what God really wants; God is adapting to Balaam. God's willingness to adapt to our inclinations and desires may be good news or bad news.

There turn out to be three donkeys in this story. The first is Balak, who thinks you can buy your way into frustrating God's will for Israel. He makes for a contrast with foreigners such as Jethro (another Midianite) and Rahab; hearing about Israel's escape from **Egypt**, they know it is wise to identify with Israel and submit to Israel's God. The second donkey is Balaam, who thinks God may be willing to have a change of mind about blessing Israel. The third donkey is the donkey that Balaam hits, the character with the most spiritual insight in the story.

The joke is that the donkey can see what Balaam cannot see. She can see when God sends an **aide** to stand in Balaam's way like a highwayman. Though the aide is brandishing a sword, it need not be intended as a threat to Balaam. When such a person appears to Joshua and to David with a sword, it's not a threat but instead a sign that the aide intends to defend Israel. Here it's a reminder that Balaam is off on a venture designed to work the opposite way, which is why God is annoyed with Balaam. The sword is a potential threat to Balaam only if Balaam agrees to try to bring trouble on Israel. God doesn't just strike Balaam dead; God wants to get Balaam on the right side (which is not so different from the aim when Joshua and David have an experience like this).

There is a story about Elisha in 2 Kings 6 that will recall this story and help us see its implications. A Syrian army surrounds Elisha's town, intent on arresting him because he has supernatural knowledge of the Syrians' plans and keeps revealing them to the Israelites. Elisha is relaxed about this, unlike his servant who is understandably in a state of panic. Elisha prays for his servant's eyes to be opened; he then sees the supernatural horses and chariots there to protect him and his master. What we see is not all there is. It will be stupid for Balaam even to think about opposing God's purpose by attempting to curse Israel. Invisible supernatural forces can be involved in events, protecting the people of God. A donkey can see that, even though Balaam cannot.

If you find it hard to believe that a donkey can speak, you can take this as "just a story" and still get its point. The Israelites were very familiar with donkeys and knew that donkeys don't talk. This donkey, however, doesn't talk "naturally." God "opens her mouth." It is God who speaks, using the donkey's mouth. It's what I hope happens every time I climb the pulpit steps. More important than the question of whether a donkey speaks is the question of whether God speaks. If you find that impossible to believe, you have a bigger issue to handle.

NUMBERS 23:5–24

God Doesn't Go Back on a Promise

⁵Yahweh put a message in Balaam's mouth and said, "Go back to Balak and tell him this." ⁶He went back to him. There he was, standing by his offerings, with all the Moabite leaders. ⁷He took up his poem:

> From Aram Balak brought me,
>   Moab's king [brought me] from the eastern mountains:
> "Come, curse Jacob for me;
>   come, doom Israel."
> ⁸ How can I damn what God has not damned,
>   how can I doom what God has not doomed?
> ⁹ For from the top of the crags I see them,
>   from the hills I behold him.
> There: a people that dwells apart,
>   that does not reckon itself one of the nations.
> ¹⁰ Who can count Jacob's dirt,
>   number Israel's dust cloud?
> May I myself die the death of the upright;
>   may my fate be like theirs!

¹¹Balak said to Balaam, "What have you done to me? It was to damn my enemies that I got hold of you. Now. You have simply blessed them!" ¹²He replied, "It is what Yahweh puts in my mouth that I am careful to speak."

[Balak takes Balaam somewhere else to look over Israel and make a declaration about them, and God again gives him a message.]

> ¹⁸ Up, Balak, listen;
>   give ear to me, son of Zippor.

¹⁹ God is not a human person to deceive,
    a human being to relent.
Would he say and not do,
    speak and not fulfill it?
²⁰ Now. "Bless" I received;
    when he blesses, I may not reverse it.
²¹ He has not envisaged harm for Jacob,
    he has not visualized trouble for Israel.
Yahweh their God is with them,
    the acclamation of a king is among them.

[In verses 22–24 Balaam expands further on this vision.]

People in traditional societies know there can be a strange power about blessing and cursing. A Nigerian told me about the way in his society people know that their enemies can use curses to cause harm to them, and the traditional religions of the culture give people charms, rituals, and incantations to counter such curses. Coming to faith in Christ brings both challenge and hope to people. It brings challenge because they can no longer use those traditional devices, but it brings hope because they know that God is greater than anybody's curse.

A similar dynamic about Israel's relationship with God relates to the serious reason God has for confronting Balaam by sending the **aide**. Balaam has manifested some ambivalence about his mission, an ambivalence that connects with some ambivalence about what makes things happen in the world. For modern Westerners, the ambivalence concerns the relationship between what God does and what people such as physicians do. What difference does it make if we pray when someone goes under the surgeon's knife or undergoes chemotherapy? For people in traditional societies, it may concern the relationship between what God does and what curses or blessings do. On one hand, Balaam has earned a reputation as someone whose curses and blessings are effective. That's why Balak paid a lot of money to bring him a long way to do his stuff on the Israelites. On the other hand, Balaam had consulted with God before agreeing to go with Balak, and God had told him he mustn't curse people who are actually blessed. Perhaps people really can have the power to bless or curse, but they are responsible for the proper use of that power. If they misuse their power, it might be effective, but they would be in trouble with God; or it might not be effective, and they would still be in trouble with God. Balaam has told Balak that all the money in the world couldn't make him do the slightest thing contrary to what God says, and he keeps emphasizing this.

But he can ask God whether there might be scope for a change of mind. Certainly you can ask God to relent or have a change of mind when God intends to bring trouble, and God may agree; Moses did so at Sinai (Exodus 32:12–14). Yet getting God to have a change of mind about intending to bless people is a different matter. Human beings may make promises and not keep them; God does not do so. It would count as deception. God doesn't deceive. There is a nice ambiguity about the line that says God has not visualized trouble for Israel. It could alternatively mean that God sees no wrong in Israel; God turns a blind eye to Israel's own wrongdoing, so that it may not deserve blessing but God will still bless it. Both are true. God is in Israel's midst. Israel has no human king like Balak, but it acclaims a greater King, and that is the surest key to its blessing. So alas for Balak, there is no change of mind; indeed, he has paid good money to make the situation worse. The obedient Balaam cannot curse Israel; he can only bless. God has given him a vision of Israel's destiny, of Israel as numerous as grains of dirt or as the particles in a cloud of dust.

The joke is that the Israelites know nothing about this drama unfolding up in the mountains. They are innocently going on with their lives, cooking the dinner and dealing with the children and wondering when they are to cross into the promised land, with no idea that something cataclysmically threatening is going on above their heads. We have no idea how they came to discover what was going on, but we can again imagine later Israel hearing this story, and when they hear about the dirt and the dust cloud their ears prick up, because they know Abraham had once stood on top of the mountains not far from here and had heard God promise that his descendants would become as numerous as earth's grains of dirt (Genesis 13:15). This foreign diviner has seen a vision of God's fulfillment of that promise. How great God's sovereignty is, regarding Israel's destiny and regarding the life and religious activity of someone with no relationship to Israel. The **Torah** from time to time drops these notes about God's involvement with foreigners, which have the potential to make sure Israel doesn't think God's involvement with the world is confined to Israel.

NUMBERS 23:25–24:25

Beautiful Tents, Jacob

[25]Balak said to Balaam, "Don't properly damn them or properly bless them." [26]Balaam replied to Balak, "Haven't I told you, 'Everything Yahweh tells me, I must do?'" [27]Balak said to Balaam, "Will you come so I can take you to another place? Perhaps it will seem right to God to damn them from there." [28]So Balak took Balaam to the top of Peor, which overlooks the wasteland. [29]Balaam said to Balak, "Build me seven altars here and get seven bulls and seven rams ready for me." [30]Balak did as Balaam said and he offered up a bull and a ram on [each] altar. [24:1]But because Balaam had seen it was good in Yahweh's eyes to bless Israel, he did not go as on other occasions to find signs but turned his face to the wilderness. [2]Balaam lifted his eyes and saw Israel dwelling by its clans, and God's spirit came on him. [3]He took up his poem:

"The prophecy of Balaam son of Beor,
    the prophecy of a man whose eye is clear,
[4] The prophecy of one who hears God's words,
    one who sees Shadday's vision, falling, but with eyes open:
[5] How beautiful are your tents, Jacob,
    your dwellings, Israel!
[6] Like valleys that spread out,
    like gardens by a river,
Like aloes that Yahweh has planted,
    like cedars by water.
[7] Water flows from their branches,
    their seed with much water.
Their king will climb above Agag,
    their kingdom will rise high.
[8] God who brought them out of Egypt
    is like a wild ox's horns to them.

> They will devour nations, their adversaries,
>> crush their bones, pierce them with their arrows.
> ⁹ They lie crouching like a lion,
>> like a panther: who would arouse them?
> Blessed are the people who bless you,
>> cursed the people who curse you!"

[Balak loses what remains of his cool and dismisses Balaam, who then delivers yet another prophetic blessing.]

> ¹⁷ "I see them, but it is not now;
>> I behold them, but it is not near.
> A star makes its way from Jacob,
>> a staff arises from Israel.
> It smashes Moab's brow,
>> the skull of all the Sethites.
> ¹⁸ Edom becomes a possession,
>> Seir their enemy becomes a possession.
> Israel gains strength;
> ¹⁹ from Jacob one will rule
>> and destroy what is left of the city."

[Balaam goes on to declare the doom of the Amalekites, the Kenites, and the Kittim, then goes home.]

As a boy I sang in a cathedral choir. One of my favorite anthems was "How Goodly Are Thy Tents, O Jacob," composed by a Victorian composer called Sir Frederick Arthur Gore Ouseley, a professor of music at Oxford, a prolific composer of church music, and a cathedral canon. He inherited his knighthood from his father, a diplomat in Persia and India who published the first translation of the New Testament into Persian. Those were the days. The anthem was a musical setting of words from Balaam's blessing in the King James Version. I don't know what I thought they were about, and I don't know whether Ouseley knew that Balaam's words also come at the beginning of a Jewish prayer used on entering synagogue. They have often been set to music by Jewish composers (the line is also used to commend Jewish summer camps).

Their use to declare God's blessing in the context of Jewish worship is in keeping with their origin. They are apparently the only words by a Gentile that are commonly used in Jewish prayers, which is particularly telling in light of the way Christians have often persecuted Jews, declaring God's curse on them in the way Balak wished rather than declaring God's blessing. It is also apposite that this Gentile blessing comes near the end of the story that takes Abraham's people from the initial promise that they will possess land in **Canaan** to the fulfillment of this promise in their entering into that land. Back in Genesis 12:3 God had promised, "I shall bless people who bless you, but the person who belittles you I will belittle." Now, rather more strongly Balaam declares, "Blessed are the people who bless you, cursed the people who curse you."

Balak has done his best to join the second category, but Balaam has frustrated his desire. Balak is still desperately trying to salvage his project (the point about the offerings is that it is appropriate to worship God before launching into prayer, though Numbers may be being sardonic in noting how many offerings Balaam assumes are necessary). Balaam knows it is useless and inappropriate to try one more time with God. He simply looks down to where Israel is still going about its business in ignorance of this drama. The **spirit** of God comes on him in the manner of the elders in Numbers 11 and of some later prophets. It is a sign of the point he emphasizes; he can only say what God lets him say, and he has no alternative to saying that. He is under compulsion. He is knocked over by God, but his inner eyes are open, and clear in their vision. He sees Israel flourishing like countryside that contrasts with the desolate wilderness where they are encamped. They have God's strength on their side. They will not be defeated by peoples who try to attack or resist them, in the present or in the future. Even if Israel is too feeble to imagine being able to resist them or defeat them, this does not mean they are insecure. God will look after the matter.

For later Israel, and for Jewish people today, Balaam's words constitute an assurance of God's blessing and protection. Over the centuries God has not actually stopped Gentiles from cursing Israel and the Jewish people, yet they have continued in existence, whereas no one today claims descent from the Moabites, Amalekites, or Kenites. The term *Kittim* originally refers to Cyprus, and it is stretched to refer to **Greece** and then Rome; here it may denote people such as the Philistines. In relating the drama unfolding on the mountain ridge above the Israelites in their encampment, the story again reminds its readers that there is more to God's involvement in the world and with Israel or the church than we ever see.

Balaam sees Israel not merely as it is at the moment but as it will be. Agag is an Amalekite king in Saul's day; the Amalekites had attacked Israel on its way out of **Egypt**. Israel's victory over Moab and Edom takes us to David's day; he will be the "star" wielding his staff (I don't see any basis for understanding the expressions messianically). Edom and Moab have been hostile to Israel at this final stage in their journey. If you think it unlikely that Balaam spoke of things God will do only in two centuries' time, you will infer that these are pseudoprophecies back-projected into Balaam's day, though I don't see the need to do that myself. The prophecies lie behind the title of Bar Kokhba, the "son of a star," who led the last Jewish revolt against Rome.

NUMBERS 25:1–26:51

How It All Goes Wrong (Again)

[1]While Israel was living at Acacias, the people began to act immorally with the Moabite women, [2]who invited the people to sacrifices for their god. The people ate and bowed down to their god. [3]So Israel bound itself to the Master of Peor, and Yahweh's anger flared at Israel. [4]Yahweh said to Moses, "Get all the people's chiefs and execute them for Yahweh in the open, so that Yahweh's angry flare-up may turn from Israel." [5]Moses said to Israel's leaders, "Each of you slay his men who bound themselves to the Master of Peor."

[6]And there, an Israelite man came and presented a Midianite woman to his kin in the eyes of Moses and the entire Israelite community; they were weeping at the doorway of the meeting tent. [7]Phinehas son of Eleazar son of Aaron saw it, got up from the midst of the community, took a spear in his hand, [8]went after the Israelite man to the inside chamber, and stabbed the two of them, the Israelite man and the woman, through to her insides. And the epidemic held back from the Israelites, [9]but the

people who died from the epidemic were twenty-four thousand. [10]Yahweh spoke to Moses: [11]"Phinehas son of Eleazar son of Aaron the priest—he has turned my wrath from the Israelites by showing his passion in their midst, so that I did not finish off the Israelites in my passion. [12]Therefore say, 'Now. I am giving him my covenant, friendship. It will be for him and his offspring after him as a permanent priestly covenant, because he was passionate for his God and made expiation for the Israelites.'"

[The chapter's closing verses name the people involved and commission Israel to defeat the Midianites for beguiling them. Chapter 26, verses 1–51, relates a further counting of the people, parallel to that in Numbers 1.]

Numbers cause us some anxiety. I am often discouraged by the numbers of people in our church, afraid it is dying (the average age is quite high). A shrinking church will seem to be a failing church. So from time to time I glance at the attendance figures from a decade or so ago and find that they are not so different from today's figures. We may assume that a healthy church is a growing church, though in the present context of Europe and the United States, simply staying the same is an achievement. On the other hand, a pastor friend of mine grew a church from three figures into four figures but then feared he had merely grown a large club and started insisting that the church do some tougher things, like reaching out to minorities in the area and to needy and homeless people. He soon saw the church shrink in numbers, but in another sense, you could say the church had grown.

There is a reason that the book of Numbers is called Numbers. It starts with God's commissioning Moses to count the Israelites by their clans, and as it draws toward its end, God repeats that commission. The totals for the individual clans vary from the figures in chapter 1; some have shrunk, and some have grown, but the total number is virtually the same as the earlier total. A generation has passed, and God has watched a whole generation die out, which might seem to harbinger the death of the community, but it does not do so. The story thus repeats a point it has made before. Back at Sinai, God first handled the problem caused by acknowledging two obligations. God made a commitment to be Israel's God and to stay in permanent relationship with this people through whom blessing is to come to the world, and thus from now on God has had to do right by this people. God also has a commitment to doing the right thing in another sense; God cannot simply ignore the people's wrongdoing as if it did not matter. One way God squares the circle is through chastening the people even by having a whole generation die out, so that only the next generation will see the promised land. The count recorded in chapter 26 affirms that despite the way death has run through Numbers, God has stayed faithful. Israel's population has not grown, but neither has it shrunk. It has stood still; that is enough.

The unsavory story in chapter 25 meshes with that. It opens up an issue that will recur in Israel's story; one can again imagine Israelites reading it and knowing what they need to learn. In different contexts Israelites were living cheek by jowl with other ethnic groups, and Israelite men sometimes found it natural to marry someone from one of these groups. One reason might be a shortage of women in the Israelite community; another might be the usual process whereby a man meets a woman and falls in love, and her belonging to another ethnic group doesn't seem a big deal.

If that is all that is involved, it is indeed no big deal. Yesterday I listened to a colleague describing the church where he was raised, where a scandal was caused by a white man dating an African American woman. "You are not to be unequally yoked," the pastor reminded people, quoting 2 Corinthians 6:14. "But that refers to being unequally yoked with an unbeliever," my colleague (who was then just a teenager) pointed out. "It's not about race." From then on, he was marked as a dangerous young man.

He was of course right in his comment. Paul is taking up the conviction expressed here in Numbers (though he does not quote this particular passage) about the danger involved in marrying someone who gives allegiance to a different god. Numbers refers to this different God as the **Master** of Peor, which was the name of the mountain where Balak took Balaam to look down on Israel and utter his curse. So "the Master of

Peor" is Baal or the Master as worshiped there (in 31:16 Moses will attribute the Israelites' betrayal to Balaam).

The marriage of two people who serve different gods is like the yoking of a donkey and an ox to pull a cart. They are bound to be pulling different ways. Marrying a foreigner who is prepared to give allegiance to your God is fine. Boaz did this in marrying Ruth. But if the other person isn't prepared to change allegiance, you and your family are implicated in your spouse's allegiance. The immorality from which this story starts is the immorality of being involved with a person who serves another god, not ordinary sexual immorality. The story's focus lies in the men's religious wrongdoing. Their personal relationships involved them in religious relationships.

Once again, God cannot simply ignore that or treat it as something trivial. It constitutes a betrayal of what it means to be Israel. So God insists that Moses takes action. When God speaks of punishment, it is regularly possible for people to repent and for the punishment to be cancelled or ameliorated, but the unfolding of this story suggests a brazenness and willfulness about these men that rules out such repentance.

Some rabbinic writers are uneasy about Phinehas's action, as are some Christian writers. Is it justifiable? Numbers goes on to tell us that God expressed approval, which hints that the Israelites would have been uneasy about it, too. It is not action open to being treated as a precedent, though of course Christians have often assumed it was okay to kill one another in the name of what they saw as the true faith. Their action and that of Phinehas confronts us by raising the question of whether we take with appropriate seriousness our obligation to an exclusive commitment to the one true God, a commitment that overrides (for instance) an inclination to fall in love with someone with a different commitment.

As the Old Testament tells the later story of Israel, there was a period during which the senior priest was not a successor of Phinehas son of Eleazar but a successor of Eleazar's brother Ithamar. One other function of this story is to underline how it is appropriate for Phinehas and his descendants (eventually, the line of Zadok) to be senior priests in succession to Aaron.

NUMBERS 26:52–27:11

Five Pushy Women

⁵²Yahweh spoke to Moses: ⁵³"The country is to be allocated to these people as a share according to the number of names. ⁵⁴To a large group, give a large share and to a small group give a small share. Each is to be given its share in accordance with its enrollment. ⁵⁵Further, the country is to be allocated by lot. By the names of the ancestral clans they are to receive an allocation."

[Chapter 26's closing verses provide information about the Levites and add a conclusion.]

²⁷:¹There came forward the daughters of Zelophehad son of Hepher son of Gilead son of Machir son of Manasseh, of the kin groups of Manasseh son of Joseph. These are the names of his daughters: Mahlah, Noah, Hoglah, Milcah, and Tirzah. ²They stood in front of Moses, Eleazar the priest, the leaders, and the entire community at the doorway of the meeting tent and said, ³"Our father died in the wilderness. He was not one of the group who got together against Yahweh, Korah's group, but died for his own sin. He had no sons. ⁴Why should our father's name disappear from within his kin because he had no son? Give us a holding among our father's brothers." ⁵Moses brought their case before Yahweh, ⁶and Yahweh said to Moses, ⁷"The daughters of Zelophehad are speaking aright. Do give them a holding, a share among their father's brothers. Pass their father's share on to them. ⁸You are to tell the Israelites: 'When a man dies and he had no son, you are to pass his share on to his daughter. ⁹If he had no daughter, you are to give his share to his brothers. If he had no brothers, you are to give his share to his father's brothers. ¹¹If his father had no brothers, you are to give his share to the nearest relative he had from his kin group, and he will own it. It is to be an authoritative rule for the Israelites, as Yahweh commanded Moses.'"

I just came across someone's list of the five feminist biblical scholars who had most influenced him. The idea of "feminist" biblical scholars is that these are people who in their study of Scripture are conscious of their particular identity and experience as women and who know that women are just as fully human as men but also that they have often not been treated in

70

that way. They know that biblical scholarship has been dominated by men, who have not noticed the presence (or absence) of women in biblical stories, or spotted issues raised for women by Scripture, or seen ways in which starting from women's experience opens up aspects of Scripture. (You don't have to be a woman to study Scripture on that basis, but it sure helps.)

Zelophehad's daughters are not the first feminist types in Scripture, but they are the kind of people you notice once you start from such a perspective. Their story comes in this last section of Numbers when Israel is teetering on the edge of its new land, though in terms of the number of pages in the **Torah** it will teeter there for a long time, until the beginning of Joshua. All the stories here relate to this entering into the land and to the life Israel will live there. As usual, then, we may profit from looking at the story from the perspective of the people's life in **Canaan**, and as usual, most Western readers need to remind themselves of how crucial land is to life.

The first verses translated above close the report of the counting of the people and reveal an important aspect of its purpose. It will provide part of the basis for allocating the land when they reach Canaan. Each part of the land will be the possession of one of the twelve clans, of which these women's clan, Manasseh, is one. Each part of a clan's land will be allocated to one of the kin groups within it; within Manasseh, Machir is one, with Gilead as a subdivision; in turn Hepher is a subdivision of that. So Hepher's family (for instance) has a particular allocation of land. Hepher, Gilead, and Machir are also the names of areas in the country, presumably the areas where these kin groups live. The way the names apply to places and not merely persons links with the system's not operating on an exclusively ethnic basis. Non-Israelites can be adopted into a kin group. These particular areas are close to where this story is set; the clan of Manasseh has land east of the Jordan as well as west in the promised land "proper," and that is where Gilead is, just north of where the Israelites are camped.

Whereas God created men and women to exercise authority in the world together, sin in the world led to a situation in which men "rule" (Genesis 3:16), and one illustration of that is that men are assumed to be the heads of kin groups and

71

families. The male head of a family passes on the position to his son when he dies. What if he has no son? Hepher's land would pass to his brother or some other male relative, along lines the story later prescribes. That means it will be absorbed into that other family's land (along with the five women), and Hepher and his family will be forgotten.

Having no son would be an unusual situation, but a high rate of infant mortality, the reality of war and the toll it takes on men, and short life expectancy for other reasons could mean it was by no means a rare one. Having five daughters and no sons would be rare, and in this sense the story has a "just suppose" atmosphere, like the Sadducees' related story about a woman married to seven brothers without ever having a child (Mark 12). Mark's story relates to one way of dealing with the problem of a man's having no son to whom he may pass on responsibility for the family's land, the solution set forward in Deuteronomy 25. It involves one of the man's brothers marrying the widow in the hope that she may have a son by him, who when he grows can assume responsibility for the family land as if he were the dead man's own son. Zelophehad's five feisty daughters have a different solution. Why shouldn't women have that responsibility? In the current Western context that solution does not seem so revolutionary, but not many decades ago it would have seemed so. One can imagine the buzz that went round the Israelite camp as people heard what the famous five were proposing.

The women point out that their father was not implicated in Korah's rebellion (see Numbers 16). If he had been, he would have forfeited his place in Israel and would deserve to be forgotten. It is not quite clear what they mean by his dying for his own sin. Perhaps he died as a sinner like anyone else or because of some specific wrongdoing of his own; maybe the implication is that his sin is the reason he had no son to succeed him. But Moses and Aaron (for instance) die because of their specific wrongdoing, so this is not an argument for the father's being forgotten or for his daughters to lose their identity. Shrewdly, however, they hold back from using this argument. They express concern only for their father's name and thereby confine themselves to an argument with which men such as

Moses, Eleazar, and the other (male) priests may be more comfortable. Let the daughters be treated as if they were their father's brothers. The principle of women inheriting from their fathers is well-known from other Middle Eastern cultures, but they are urban ones, and in the context of a people who still emphasize a clan structure and a concern with what happens to land, it is a brave request.

With Moses, they at least succeed in establishing that this is a possibility worth consulting God about. Maybe one aspect of what then happens is that Moses has a chance to get used to the idea and to imagine living with its revolutionary implications. One can imagine him hearing the voice of his big sister Miriam urging him to accept it. He can also hear God saying, "Yes, they have spoken aright." Not only does it apply to the famous five; it explicitly establishes a precedent that Israel will henceforth follow. Because these women acted assertively, other women will also profit.

The story also establishes a broader principle. In church yesterday we read that frightening passage from James 3 about people who don't have because they don't ask. It's always worth asking God. Maybe God will say no, but maybe God will say yes.

NUMBERS 27:12–23

On Appointing a New Leader

[12]Yahweh said to Moses, "Go up this mountain in the Region Beyond and look at the country I am giving the Israelites. [13]When you have looked at it, you too will join your kin just as Aaron your brother did, [14]just as you rebelled against my word when the community argued in the Zin Wilderness, in connection with making me holy in their eyes by means of the water." (These are the Argument Waters at Kadesh in the Zin Wilderness.) [15]Moses spoke to Yahweh: [16]"Yahweh, the God of the breath of all humanity must appoint someone over the community [17]who will go out ahead of them and come in ahead of them, who will take them out and bring them in, so that Yahweh's community will not be like a flock that has no shepherd." [18]Yahweh said to Moses, "Get yourself Joshua son of Nun, a man who has spirit in him. Put your hand on him. [19]Stand him

in front of Eleazar and the entire community and commission him in their sight. [20]You are to put on him some of your dignity so that the entire Israelite community may listen, [21]but he is to stand in front of Eleazar the priest, and he will ask for the decision of the Urim before Yahweh for him. At his word they will go out and at his word they will come in, he and all the Israelites with him, the entire community." [22]Moses did as Yahweh commanded him. He got Joshua, stood him in front of Eleazar the priest and the entire community, [23]put his hands on him, and commissioned him, as Yahweh spoke by means of Moses.

The rector of a church I know has announced that she intends to retire in a few months, and the church is in the midst of the process for appointing a new rector. The present rector has been there for twenty years and has led the church into a period of great flourishing. They have huge congregations, magnificent premises, and a wide range of ministries. It is an exciting place to visit, let alone to belong to. I find myself thinking, what an act to follow! Who would be so stupid as to want to be the next rector? How do you go about finding a person who can lead the church into its next decade? In our culture, the answer is that you draw up a three-page list of the spiritual and personal qualities, qualifications, and experience the new rector will need to bring, you see how the 118 candidates match up to these, and eventually you whittle the list down to three for interview and thus discover the one person whom God is calling to this ministry.

I imagine that from time to time the search committee wishes that discerning God's will was a bit easier and that we had a process a bit more like the one for appointing Moses' successor. (On the other hand, if people are more involved in the process of discernment, they have responsibility for the outcome, though when a decision goes wrong, we are not very good at remembering that.) Miriam and Aaron are gone; only Moses needs to fade from view before a whole new generation enters **Canaan** under a new leader. He is to climb a nearby mountain in "the Region Beyond" the river Jordan, the region east of the Jordan which is "beyond" the Jordan from a later Israelite perspective (Transjordan, as the approximate area that is now the state of Jordan was once known).

When God reasserts the necessity that Moses should die, Moses' reaction is not to ask God to have a change of mind; asking God to have a change of mind relates to God's intentions for other people, not oneself. Moses is concerned not about his own fate but about his people's. As usual, he has no hesitation about suggesting to God what God could do, and God has no problem about agreeing. As usual, he points out something about God that provides the basis for his prayer, here that God is "God of the breath of all humanity." Back in 16:22 that was a basis for urging God not to cast off the whole community because of the sin of one. Here it suggests similar motivation. "You are the God who puts breath into us. You can't abandon them." Moses has previously protested about the massive demands placed on him by his position of leadership. With some irony, now he insists that some other poor person should have this job.

The alternative is that the people should be like a giant flock without a shepherd. The talk of going out and coming in relates to that image. A flock cannot stay in the fold all day and starve, but when it goes out to find food and water, it needs a shepherd who knows the terrain to lead it to its provision and then bring it home. It is a neat definition of leadership, because there is nothing heroic about this task. It is to make sure that people are provided for and protected, a surprising description in light of what we will remember Joshua for. You could say it is indeed what Moses himself has been doing for the past generation during which Israel has been going nowhere, just marking time. Joshua has a specific task of leadership to undertake in leading the people into Canaan, as Moses had a specific task in bringing them out of **Egypt**. Yet for Joshua and for Moses, the ongoing, everyday task of provision and protection is at least as important.

This consideration may relate to the need for Joshua, as Israel's new leader, to be someone with **spirit** in him. What might that mean? Two stories about him may give us a clue. He first appears as the leader of Israelite forces when Israel was attacked by Amalek (Exodus 17). Then with Caleb he is one of the two Israelite scouts who insist that the people can defeat the Canaanites, because God is with them (Numbers 14). Joshua is a man with guts, another way of saying that he is a man with spirit. As David notes when candidating to fight Goliath, a shepherd needs courage; to provide for his flock and protect it, he has to fight lions and bears (1 Samuel 17). He doesn't need great leadership skills or wisdom (though God will give him the latter). He needs guts. Joshua is that kind of man.

So Moses lays his hands on Joshua, as we say—though the Hebrew word implies an action with more pressure than this English verb implies. It is a sign of identification. Moses is saying, "I identify with this man, he is my man; therefore he does take my place and he has the authority I have exercised in the past." He has something of Moses' dignity; he is to be viewed and treated as they viewed and treated Moses (well, minus the negative aspects). The community is to listen to Yahweh's words and thus in the future listen to Joshua as they listened to Moses. At the same time, Joshua is to stand in front of the priest for this ceremony. Moses and Aaron had stood alongside each other; Joshua and Eleazar will do the same, a little like Britain's queen and the Archbishop of Canterbury. The difference is not one between church and state; Israel is both church and state, and Joshua is responsible to God and responsible for obedience to God. The important thing is that Joshua is not a leader with sole power in Israel. There is a sense in which he is subordinate to the priest. Joshua will lead the people out and in, but he is dependent on Eleazar for God's guidance about when to do so.

NUMBERS 28:1–29:40

Eating with God

¹Yahweh spoke to Moses: ²"Command the Israelites, saying to them: 'At their set times you are to make sure you present to me my offerings, my food, as gifts for me, a nice smell for me.' ³Say to them, 'These are the gifts that you are to present to Yahweh: whole yearling lambs, two each day as regular burnt offerings ⁴(you are to offer one lamb in the morning and offer the second at twilight); ⁵a tenth of a measure of fine flour as a grain offering, mixed with a quarter of a measure of beaten oil ⁶(the regular burnt offering made at Mount Sinai, a nice smell, a gift to Yahweh); ⁷its libation a quarter of a measure for the one lamb (pour it in the sanctuary as a libation of fermented drink to

Yahweh). [8]You are to offer the second lamb at twilight. You are to make the same grain offering as in the morning with its same libation, a gift, a nice smell, to Yahweh. [9]On the Sabbath day: two whole yearling lambs and two tenths of a measure of fine flour as a grain offering, mixed with oil, with its libation, [10]a burnt offering for each Sabbath in addition to the regular burnt offering and its libation.

[The rest of chapters 28–29 gives similar instructions for sacrifices at the beginning of each month; at the festivals of Passover, Flat Bread, and Pentecost; on the first day of the seventh month; on the tenth day (Expiation Day); and (at great length) on the fifteenth day and for seven days following (the Shelters Festival).]

A week ago, our church had a homecoming/harvest barbecue. Alas, I missed it because I had arranged to be elsewhere, but I was there in my imagination, partly because I know these guys know how to barbecue. As I write now, in my imagination I can smell the sausage, ribs, and chicken grilling. To make up for my loss, next Saturday I am holding a beginning-of-the-school-year barbecue for some of my students, and (being a cheat) I shall get some of the excellent prepared and marinated chicken from our Hispanic store and grill it on the new barbecue in our complex. As human beings we do this kind of thing because it tastes nice but also because it does something to personal relationships. We don't just meet in church and in the classroom; eating together adds another dimension to those relationships.

So it is with Israel's relationship with God. It is embodied in the way God and Israel eat together. In this connection, the Old Testament is very bold in the way it pictures God in human terms. Having almost begun with God's taking a walk in the garden in the cool of the evening, the **Torah** often speaks of sacrifices as food for God and of God's inhaling the fine barbecue smell. Christians get worried about this and may critique it as "anthropomorphic," but the critique seems odd as God eventually became a human being. There cannot be so much difference between being God and being human, certainly not an incompatibility between these. Israelites knew that God did not actually eat the sacrifices, though no doubt many people forgot and assumed God did so. Yet God took the risk of speaking in these very human terms. It underlines that God is a real person; not a human person, but truly a person. God is not a principle or a theory, and Israel's faith is not merely a world-view or set of obligations. God is a person, and the Israelites are people; their relationship is a personal relationship. One thing people do is give gifts to one another and eat meals together. So Israel gives God gifts and eats meals with God.

Admittedly its relationship with God is not an egalitarian one like our barbecues, even allowing for the difference between professor and students (though I have had a student throw me in the pool during one of these events). Its sacrifices were more like an event at the White House or Buckingham Palace; the president or the monarch and the ordinary people invited for the event have different status. Or they were like a banquet offered by a Middle Eastern king, to which people come doing obeisance and bearing gifts. We could call them potlucks, except that the host lays down exactly what you are to bring. That again suggests a parallel with a state banquet, when everything has to be done right, people have to sit in the right places, the silverware has to be laid out correctly, and there is appropriate dress to be worn.

Israel's worship thus combined the order of a banquet and the celebration of a barbecue. It also worked according to a schedule. The Torah includes several accounts of this schedule; it evidently worked differently in different centuries. Numbers 28–29 elaborates on Leviticus 23, filling in details about the offerings and adding other material.

First, there are sacrifices each morning and evening. As day dawns, the sacrifice will express the community's giving of itself to God and its seeking of God's blessing and protection for the day. As night falls, it will express the community's thanksgiving for the day and its prayer for protection through the night. The community as a whole would not be present for these sacrifices (most people live much too far away), but everyone would know they were being offered and could be identifying with them.

Second, there are the extra sacrifices associated with the end of the week. Generally the Torah does not stress the worship aspect to the Sabbath, though it is sometimes presupposed elsewhere in the Old Testament, and only here are special sacrifices prescribed. In the Torah the Sabbath's main point is to be the day you stop. Once again, the community would not be present for these sacrifices, but they would mark its gratefulness for the week's work that has passed and its prayer for the week's work that is to follow, and its recognition that this is a day that especially belongs to God. Naturally enough, the daily and weekly offerings involve meat, bread, and wine.

Third, there are sacrifices associated with the beginning of each lunar month. The first day of the month was not mentioned in previous accounts of worship occasions, and here the offerings are more elaborate than those for the Sabbath. On this occasion each month there is to be a **purification** offering, which would mean starting each month by dealing with **taboos** that had accumulated over the previous month and thus giving a clean start to the people's relationship with God for the new month.

Fourth, there are the sacrifices associated with the different occasions of the year, Passover, Flat Bread, Pentecost, the beginning of the seventh month, **Expiation** Day, and Shelters. These remind Israel of God's involvement in its agricultural year and in the one-time events of its story. Passover and Flat Bread remind Israel of the exodus and what they ate then; Shelters reminds them of living in makeshift homes. At the festivals they reenact the event itself in some way. Flat Bread (barley harvest), Pentecost (wheat harvest), and Shelters (fruit harvest) coincide with stages in the harvest and constitute occasions when Israel acknowledges God as lord of the harvest. The first day of the seventh month is now the beginning of the Jewish year and maybe was also so in some contexts in Old Testament Israel. Expiation Day is the annual occasion God provides for removing from the sanctuary the taboos that would make it impossible for God to meet with the people there. Here, the striking feature is the prominence given to Shelters. The bulk of chapter 29 keeps repeating similar information about the offerings for each day of this festival, underlining its importance as *the* worship occasion in the year.

NUMBERS 30:1–16

Negotiations and Love Songs

¹Moses spoke to the heads of the Israelite clans: "This is something Yahweh has commanded: ²When someone makes a promise to Yahweh or takes an oath to impose an obligation on himself, he shall not break his word. In accordance with everything that comes out of his mouth he must act. ³When a woman makes a promise to Yahweh or assumes an obligation when she is in her father's household, in her youth, ⁴and her father hears of her promise or the obligation that she imposes on herself, and her father says nothing to her, all her promises stand and all the obligations she imposed on herself stand. ⁵But if her father restrains her when he hears, none of her promises or the obligations she imposes on herself stand. Yahweh will pardon her because her father has restrained her. ⁶If she does come to belong to a man when there are promises binding her or there is an extravagance that came from her lips that she has imposed on herself, ⁷and her man hears, and says nothing to her when he hears, then her promises stand and the obligation she has imposed on herself stands. ⁸But if her man restrains her when he hears and annuls the promise that was binding her or the extravagance that came from her lips that she had imposed on herself, Yahweh will pardon her. (⁹But the promise of a widow or a divorcee, anything she has imposed on herself, stands in respect of her.) ¹⁰If while in her man's household she makes a promise or imposes an obligation on herself by oath ¹¹and her man hears and says nothing to her, he has not restrained her; all her promises stand and every obligation she has imposed on herself stands. ¹²But if her man does annul them when he hears, anything that came from her lips (her promises or an obligation upon herself) does not stand. Her man has annulled them and Yahweh will pardon her. ¹³Any promise and any sworn obligation to discipline herself, her man may confirm or annul. ¹⁴If her man does say nothing to her from one day to the next, he confirms all her promises or all the obligations that are upon her. He confirms them because he said nothing to her when he heard. ¹⁵If he does annul them after hearing, he bears her waywardness. ¹⁶These are the rules that Yahweh commanded Moses between a man and his woman [and] between a father and his daughter in her youth, in her father's household."

About a year after he got married, one of my students set off from Los Angeles for Chicago, driving the opposite way to the one recommended in the song "Route 66," in order to begin graduate school. Only subsequently in an e-mail did he tell me about how hesitant his wife was about this move. "Some days she just breaks down and starts crying," he said, and added, "There are so many things about marriage that no one ever really talks about! I have learned that making big life decisions is difficult, more difficult when two people are making them together."

Here is God trying to help the Israelites with the process of making some of these life decisions. I wouldn't be surprised if someone had said something to that couple about the trickiness involved in making decisions together and they had nodded sagely. Agreeing in theory and then dealing with things when they happen are very different. Likewise I suspect God is laying these rules down for the Israelites in light of their having discovered they needed some help. The fact that they did need it makes them more like us than often seems the case. The rules presuppose we are independent individuals making independent decisions about what we plan to do; but only in rare circumstances is this so.

In Israel, things might work out as follows. Luke 2 tells us about the prophet Anna, who spent all her time in the temple courts in worship, fasting, and prayer. She could do that because she was a widow. She had no obligations. (Admittedly we don't have her daughter's opinion on this question. I know a rock-star grandmother or two whose daughters complain that their mothers aren't free to look after their grandchildren because they are out playing a gig.) But suppose there is a woman with prophetic gifts who wants to dedicate herself to that kind of life but is not a widow. Suppose there is a household organized for life and work together, everybody having a role to fulfill. Among them is a sixteen-year-old girl who wants to go and live like Anna. Or suppose there is a new wife or mother who wants to do that. Being part of a family, the family in which you were born or the family you joined when you married, means you take on privileges but also responsibilities. You are not free as you would be if you were on your own. Serving God in Anna's way in the sanctuary is not the only way one could imagine someone wanting to make a special commitment to God. In our context, we could think of a person sensing a call to ordained ministry. In the Old Testament, Hannah promises her unborn (indeed, unconceived!) child to God. The **Torah** refers to promises about making a sacrifice in connection with prayers, and keeping the promise would cost the family, not just the individual. There are also unhappy stories about vows by Jephthah and Saul, though the latter makes explicit that you can always come back to God and seek to renegotiate a promise (as the people realize, though Saul did not, and tragically Jephthah did not). The rules here refer also to a wife's wanting to "discipline herself." She cannot unilaterally decide she will fast today and therefore will not cook for the entire family!

Your relationship with your family involves negotiations as well as love songs (to borrow a line from a telling Paul Simon lyric about marriage, "Train in the Distance"). God provides parameters for the negotiations. By no means does God rule out daughters or mothers making promises to God, but fathers or husbands need to be party to them. They have the right to object, and God will excuse the woman from keeping the commitment if they do so. But they have to object now. It is no use objecting in a month or a year's time. If they annul a commitment then, God holds them responsible for the commitment made and not fulfilled.

The rules are expressed in patriarchal terms because the society works that way. (For the same reason, though there is mention of widows and divorcees who would be independent women, there is no mention of adult single women, because there were hardly any such people; virtually every woman would marry.) It is the male head of the household who has to make sure that the family stays viable. If he makes an unwise commitment, he will have to deal with the consequences; if his wife or daughter does so, he will also have to deal with the consequences. In a less patriarchal society, the negotiations will take a different form. At the same time, the rules make use of a regular way of speaking that subverts or takes the edge off of patriarchy. Hebrew has words for husband and wife, which etymologically mean master/owner and someone owned/mastered. They thus imply a patriarchal understanding of marriage and imply that a wife is her husband's property. The Old Testament rarely uses these words. The words usually translated husband and wife are the ordinary words for man and woman. "His wife" is more literally "his woman"; "her husband" is more literally "her man" (compare "Bess, you is my woman now"). A husband and wife are two people who belong to each other. They cannot make promises or undertake obligations that ignore that fact, even promises and obligations to God.

NUMBERS 31:1–34

Unfinished Business

[1]Yahweh spoke to Moses: [2]"Exact redress for the Israelites from the Midianites; after, you will join your kin." [3]Moses spoke to the people: "Some men from among you are to equip themselves for a campaign and go against Midian to bring Yahweh's redress on Midian. [4]You are to send off to war a division for each clan from all the Israelite clans." [5]So from the Israelite divisions, for each clan a division offered themselves, twelve divisions equipped for a campaign. [6]Moses sent them off to the campaign, a thousand for each clan, and also Phinehas son of Eleazar as the priest for the campaign, with the sacred accoutrements and the trumpets to sound in his hand. [7]They campaigned against Midian as Yahweh commanded Moses, slaughtered every male, [8]and slaughtered the Midianite kings: as well as the others who were slain, Evi, Rekem, Zur, Hur, and Reba, the five Midianite kings. They also slew Balaam son of Beor with the sword. [9]The Israelites captured the Midianite women and young people and took as plunder all their cattle, all their herds, and all their wealth. [10]All the cities where they lived and their settlements they set on fire. [11]They took all the spoil and all the gains, human beings and cattle, [12]and brought the captives, the gains, and the spoil to Moses, Eleazar the priest, and the Israelite community at the camp in the Moab steppes across the Jordan from Jericho. [13]Moses, Eleazar the priest, and all the leaders of the community came to meet them outside the camp. [14]Moses was furious with the army officers, the commanders over the thousands and the hundreds, who had come from the military campaign. [15]Moses said to them, "You

have let every female live! [16]Now. At the word of Balaam they were the ones who for the Israelites came to be a means of instigating a trespass against Yahweh in the matter of Peor, so that the epidemic came on Yahweh's community. [17]So now, slaughter every male among the young people and slaughter every women who has had sex with someone, who has slept with a man, [18]but all the young girls who have not had sex with someone, who have not slept with a man—let them live for yourselves."

[The rest of the chapter focuses on how the people were to deal with the plunder in a way that was to avoid bringing taboo into the community, to be fair to combatants and noncombatants, and to recognize the need to give a proportion to God, and how they did so.]

Two or three years ago, out of the blue, I received a phone call from a Jewish lawyer in Los Angeles. He had self-published a book called *Twenty-six Reasons Why Jews Don't Believe in Jesus*, and he wanted me to make sure that his statements about Jesus and about Christian faith were accurate. I was interested to read the book and had little critique of his facts; the difference between us concerned their interpretation. His book is a twenty-first-century example of a genre almost as old as Christian faith. People who believe in Jesus have always wanted to persuade Jews to believe (often the persuaders have themselves been Jews); Jews who do not believe in Jesus have always wanted to persuade fellow Jews to stay loyal to their traditional faith. Over the past fifty years there has been considerable growth in a movement of Jews coming to believe in Jesus, and to them this means becoming "fulfilled Jews," but other Jews are convinced that they have betrayed their Jewishness and that their movement imperils the existence of Judaism. The increasing secularizing of Jews also imperils Judaism, as does the prevalence of Jews intermarrying with gentiles.

A chapter like Numbers 31 is among the hard ones in the Old Testament for modern people (Christians and Jews) to come to terms with. Why would God tell Moses to kill the Midianites, and why would Moses tell the army to treat the women and young people in the same way? Alternatively, why would the Israelites imagine God had done so, and why would God then stand aside while they put into his book a story that said God did so? And how could Jesus then have declared (for instance) that the whole **Torah** is summed up in the idea of treating others as you would like to be treated (Matthew 7:12)?

Let me begin with a crumb of comfort. While the first part of this chapter closes with the instruction to kill the Midianite boys and women, it never says that this happened. In contrast, it goes on to spend most of its time describing what Israel should do with the plunder from the battle, and then says that they did so. The Torah is not squeamish about telling us when people got slaughtered, so this raises the question of whether the slaughter ever happened. Midian's appearing in strength later in the Old Testament (see Judges 6–8) would be odd if they were annihilated in the wilderness. We have an example here of something that appears elsewhere in the Torah; the commission to execute people can be more a statement about the terrible nature of their offense than a prescription for a court to implement.

That is the point of this story. It links with that Los Angeles Jewish lawyer's concern. It is vitally important that Israel continues to exist and does not assimilate to the Gentile world. Perhaps that is why God tells Moses to complete this piece of unfinished business before he dies. It is vitally important that Israelites do not intermarry with other people unless those other people come to share their commitment to **Yahweh**. That is as vital from a Christian as from a Jewish angle, because God had made the destiny of the entire world depend on Israel—not on what Israel would do but on what God would do through Israel. This might seem a weird action on God's part, but it is an action affirmed by both Old and New Testaments. As Jesus put it in John 4, salvation is from the Jews. Therefore, no Jews, no salvation. One can see why this is so: Jesus is Jewish. No Jews, no Jesus. If the Jewish people had gone out of existence, one can imagine God starting again and working instead with (say) the people of Madagascar, but within Scripture, that idea is not on God's horizon. God is committed to working through Israel. Another reason modern people feel unhappy with a story such as this is that it is hard for us to believe that God was committed to bringing to fulfillment the destiny of the whole world through one people. We are ineluctably pluralist in our attitudes. At the instigation of Balaam (we have not been told that before, and the story does not fill out how this happened) both Israel and Midian have imperiled that possibility by their sexual involvement. God has required Moses to punish Israel for this; God now requires him to punish Midian.

It is also hard for modern people to believe that God punishes, but God's punishment is another theme that runs through both Old and New Testaments. Admittedly, translations make it worse by speaking in terms of vengeance rather than redress or punishment. While God has the strong feelings associated with vengeance, the idea underlying God's action is not that Israel is to take revenge for something done to it but that Midian has been imperiling God's own intentions and that it should be punished. If it makes you feel better, you can again infer that it is more a statement of a theological truth than a statement about what God actually commissioned Israel to do. That links with one further difficulty modern people have with the story. It's hard for us to believe that God uses human agents to punish. In this case, there is more distinctiveness about the opening books of the Bible and what comes later. God used Israel to punish rebellious peoples in Exodus through Joshua; God hardly does that later. In the Prophets and in the New Testament God uses imperial powers to punish rebellious people without their knowing. The Bible associates God's using Israel this way only with the beginning of Israel's story. Later Israel never saw God's acts at the beginning of its story as precedents for what it was to do later. There is no basis for (say) Britain or the United States using them in this way, as they have.

It's easy for us to assume that modern views must be right, and we read them into the Bible. One of the functions of the Bible is to remind us that actually they are just the views of our culture, from some of which we need to escape.

NUMBERS 32:1–42

On Mutual Support

¹Now the Reubenites and the Gadites had much livestock, very extensive, and they looked at the country of Jazer and Gilead: this was a place for cattle. ²So the Gadites and Reubenites came and said to Moses, Eleazar the priest, and the community leaders, ³"Ataroth, Dibon, Jazer, Nimrah, Heshbon, Elealah, Sebam, Nebo, and Beon, ⁴the country Yahweh has struck down before the Israelite community, is cattle country, and your servants have cattle." ⁵So they said, "If we find favor in your eyes, may this country be given to your servants as a holding. Do not make us cross the Jordan." ⁶Moses said to the Gadites and Reubenites, "Are your brothers to go to battle while you settle here? ⁷Why would you deflect the heart of the Israelites from crossing into the country Yahweh has given them? ⁸Your fathers did this when I sent them from Kadesh-barnea to look at the country. ⁹They went up to the Eshcol wash and looked at the country but deflected the heart of the Israelites so that they would not go into the country Yahweh had given them. ¹⁰Then Yahweh's anger flared and he swore, ¹¹"If the people who came up from Egypt, twenty years and upward, see the country I swore to Abraham, Isaac, and Jacob, because they did not wholly follow after me, ¹²except Caleb son of Jephunneh the Kenizzite and Joshua son of Nun, because they wholly followed after Yahweh. . . .' ¹³Yahweh's anger flared at Israel and he made them wander in the wilderness for forty years until the whole generation that did wrong in Yahweh's eyes was finished. ¹⁴Now. You have arisen in place of your fathers as a brood of sinners to add further to the flaring of Yahweh's anger toward Israel. ¹⁵If you turn from following him and he once again leaves you in the wilderness, you will destroy this entire people." ¹⁶They came to him and said, "We will build sheepfolds here for our livestock and cities for our young people ¹⁷but we ourselves will equip ourselves as shock troops ahead of the Israelites until we have enabled them to get to their place, while our young people live in the fortified cities, because of the people who live in the country."

[Moses agrees with this plan, which means Gad and Reuben, and also half of Manasseh, will settle east of the Jordan in the country already accidentally captured from the Amorites.]

As I write, my denomination, the Episcopal or Anglican Church, is in a mess over its stance toward same-sex marriage. While that is itself a tricky issue, the situation is at least as troublesome in its effect on the way Anglicans in different parts of the world are relating to one another. On the whole, the church in the United States and Canada is convinced that same-sex marriage is right and that we should proceed to bless same-sex marriages and/or ordain people married to someone of the same sex. On the whole, churches in Africa think this is wrong and that the North American churches ought not to be proceeding in this way, and they have felt free to aid the setting up of alternative Anglican churches in the United States. The poor Archbishop of Canterbury is trying to hold hands with both sides and hold them together within the Anglican Communion.

You could say he is trying to be Moses, though Moses had more authority than the archbishop has and got more cooperation from the Israelite clans. Until recently in this story, it looked as if the country the Israelites would possess lay entirely west of the Jordan, which is a natural boundary. It was not part of the plan to do battle with anyone east of the Jordan, but some peoples there have been unwise enough to attack the Israelites rather than let them pass through, and have paid for it with their lives and their land. Among other things, it illustrates the way the fulfillment of God's intentions interacts with human actions. God had no plan to give Israel land east of the Jordan, but that now becomes part of the "plan."

Moses comes on strong in his reaction to Gad and Reuben, not least in characterizing them as a brood of sinners. He is almost as rude as John the Baptist. He illustrates the way the Bible has little time for Western virtues such as politeness or tolerance. If I had been the head of Gad or Reuben, I would have given Moses a mouthful back; I admire the clans for sticking to the substance of his argument and ignoring the rhetoric. They thereby make it possible to reach a compromise. Gad and Reuben will actually take the lead in the Israelite invasion of **Canaan** so as to share in taking the country, as the other clans have been involved in taking the land where these two clans want to settle. They thus indicate a recognition that the whole people of God stand together and need to be committed to supporting one another. One part cannot say to another, "I need to look after my destiny and do what will enable me to fulfill my calling" or "I do not need you" (1 Corinthians 12). It has to be prepared to argue, negotiate, and compromise. It cannot take unilateral action.

One can imagine Israelites in (say) the time of Elijah asking, "Why do those clans live across the Jordan? Does that really count as Israel? Do they really belong with us?" This story gives them an answer. It would also constitute a challenge to the eastern clans to keep maintaining the kind of commitment they promise here.

NUMBERS 33:1–34:29

Land, Promises, and Politics

[1]This is the route of the Israelites who came out of Egypt by their troops under the direction of Moses and Aaron. [2]Moses wrote down their starting points on their route at Yahweh's word.

[There follows a list of places on the route from Egypt via the Reed Sea to Sinai, on to Kadesh, and via Mount Hor to where they are now.]

[50]In the Moab steppes across the Jordan from Jericho, Yahweh spoke to Moses: [51]"Speak to the Israelites and say to them, 'When you are crossing the Jordan into Canaan, [52]you are to dispossess all the country's inhabitants from before you, destroy all their figures, destroy all their cast images, and demolish all their worship places. [53]You are to take possession of the country and live in it, because I have given the country to you to take possession of. [54]You are to share out the country by lot to your kin groups. To a large one make its share large and to a small one make its share small. Wherever the lot comes out for a group, that is where it will be, as you share it out according to your ancestral clans. [55]If you do not dispossess the country's inhabitants from before you, the ones among them whom you allow to remain will become barbs in your eyes and thorns in your sides. They will cause you trouble in the country where you are living, [56]and what I planned to do to them I will do to you.'"

[In Numbers 34 God lays out the boundaries of their country, moving anticlockwise from the Dead Sea through Kadesh to the Mediterranean, up the Mediterranean coast to the north of modern Beirut, east a hundred miles into Syria, then south and southwest to Lake Galilee, and south along the Jordan. Moses then notes that the allocation of this land does not need to take account of Gad, Reuben, and half of Manasseh. God also nominates the representatives of the clans who are to allocate the land.]

I have several friends in Beirut, including a former student who teaches the Bible in a Christian university (actually he is the guy who once threw me into the pool, as I mentioned in connection with Numbers 28–29). He has a hard time getting his students to focus on the Old Testament because it is difficult to disentangle the modern state of Israel from the ancient people of Israel, especially when the Old Testament speaks of God's preferential treatment of Israel and God's hostility to neighboring peoples. This is a problem for Christians in Palestine, all of whose bounds come within the bounds of the country God promises the Israelites. If my friend's students come to know that Numbers 34 envisages the Israelites possessing a country that includes most of modern Lebanon and a good chunk of Syria, including its capital, Damascus, I imagine they may blow more fuses.

One consideration that may help us in thinking about this issue is that whereas modern Israel is a powerful sovereign state (even though one that feels vulnerable to hordes of hostile states that surround it), ancient Israel was usually more like Kenya under British rule or the Philippines under U.S. rule or the Armenians, who mostly have no country of their own. The Israelites who read the **Torah** were usually people under the domination of a major power such as **Assyria**, **Babylon**, **Persia**, or **Greece**. Either they lived under their domination in **Canaan**, or they had been transported from Canaan to live in other parts of one of these empires. God's promise about their possessing land is designed to give them hope to hold onto. Reviewing the journey by giving the account of the route Israel has taken from **Egypt** to the edge of Canaan also has this effect: "Consider all the way God has brought you to get you here." We cannot locate many of the places that are mentioned, and neither would the Israelites be able to do so, but this does not take away from the effect; it may even add to it.

This is not to say God's promise has no practical implications, but those implications are worked out in relation to circumstances. This account of the dimensions of the country recognizes that. On one hand, it oddly extends Israel's territory to the far north, an area that is then ignored when the country is allocated to the clans. So why is land in Lebanon and Syria included? The bounds of Canaan as Numbers here describes them are the bounds of Canaan as a province of the Egyptian empire in Moses' time. In other words, detailing the bounds of the promised land thus is a way of concretely saying, "You will possess all Canaan," but what "Canaan" means is not fixed for all time. It is dependent on political circumstances in different periods. There would be a particular irony in promising Israel that it will take over the empire of the Egyptians in this part of the world, because the Israelites are thus reversing the relationship between Egypt and Israel that had obtained before the exodus. (The point will be taken further in Deuteronomy when it refers to the Israelites' land stretching as far as the Euphrates, which corresponds to Egyptian aims at some periods.) That piece of background meshes with the way God's description of the country omits the areas east of the Jordan that God has just granted to Gad, Reuben, and part of Manasseh. They have also become de facto part of the promised land because of some political events, the **Amorites**' stupidity in attacking the Israelites instead of letting them pass; but they are not part of the Egyptian province of Canaan.

Both the nature of God's promises and the fulfillment of God's promises interact with political realities. One implication is that the fulfillment of God's promises to the Jewish people today can be expected to take account of political realities. It is theologically appropriate for Jewish people to be free to live within the bounds of Canaan and politically necessary for them to have an independent state, but there is no theological necessity for it to include (for instance) the West Bank or Gaza, where it would be natural for there to be a Palestinian state.

There are also contextual features to God's instructions concerning the Israelites' occupation of the country. They include no commission to kill anyone. Like preceding instructions in the Torah, they speak only of dispossessing people. Numbers takes for granted the rationale for this. By their lives the peoples of the country have forfeited any right to live there. God kills two birds with one stone by throwing them out as a punishment and giving the country to Israel as a means toward fulfilling God's wider, more positive, and more far-reaching purpose for the nations. God also refers to the fact that the same principles will apply to the new inhabitants of the country: "What I planned to do to them I will do to you."

To avoid that, as well as chasing the Canaanites out of the country, the Israelites need to destroy their forms and places of worship. Their forms of worship will mislead the Israelites into thinking of God the same way as the Canaanites do; specifically, they will think that God can be represented by means of an image. That common human assumption does not work for the real God. It can only mislead. Deuteronomy 4 will expand on that logic.

They are also to destroy the Canaanites' places of worship, which are more literally their "high places." These were either natural elevated locations that were turned into places of worship or humanly constructed platforms for worship. In either case, they would be in the open air. Only here does the Torah refer to these, but they often feature in Israel's later story and in the Prophets, which yet again reminds us to put ourselves in the position of people hearing the Torah read. Recycling the Canaanites' worship places was a major way Israel let itself be misled into worshiping the Canaanites' gods, or worshiping **Yahweh** as if Yahweh were like those gods. It is in this metaphorical sense that they will be barbs and thorns to the Israelites and will cause them trouble. If only they really had destroyed those worship places. . . .

NUMBER 35:1–36:13

Ensuring Justice

¹In the Moab steppes across the Jordan from Jericho, Yahweh spoke to Moses: ²"Command the Israelites to give the Levites

cities to live in, out of the share they hold, and to give the Levites the surrounding pastureland belonging to the cities. ³The cities will be theirs to live in and their pasturelands will be for their cattle, their property, and all their animals. ⁴The city pasturelands that you are to give the Levites will be from the city wall outwards a thousand cubits around. ⁵Outside of the city, you are to measure on the east side two thousand cubits, on the south side two thousand cubits, on the west side two thousand cubits, on the north side two thousand cubits, with the city in the middle. This will be the city pasturelands for them.

⁶The cities you give the Levites will be the six asylum cities that you give to the person who has killed someone, a place to flee to, but you are to give [them] forty-two cities in addition to them. ⁷All the cities you give to the Levites will be forty-eight cities, them and their pasturelands. ⁸The cities you give from the Israelites' share: from a large one make it large and from a small one make it small. Each in proportion to the share it receives is to give some of its cities to the Levites.

[The rest of the chapter details the way the community is to utilize the asylum cities in dealing with cases of homicide.]

³⁶⁻¹The ancestral heads of the kin group of Gilead son of Machir son of Manasseh, one of the Josephite kin groups, came forward and spoke before Moses and the leaders, the ancestral heads of the Israelites. ²They said, "Yahweh commanded my lord to give the country to the Israelites as shares by lot, and my lord was commanded by Yahweh to give our kinsman Zelophehad's share to his daughters. ³If they become the wives of someone from the Israelite clans, their share will disappear from our ancestral share and add to the share of the clan to which they belong; it will disappear from our allotted share. ⁴If the Israelites have a jubilee, their share will add to the share of the clan to which they belong; from the share of our ancestral clan their share will disappear." ⁵So Moses commanded the Israelites at Yahweh's word: "The Josephite clan are speaking aright. ⁶This is what Yahweh has commanded concerning Zelophehad's daughters: 'They may become the wives of whoever is good in their eyes, but they are to become the wives of a kin group in their father's clan.'"

[The closing verses relate how they did so.]

A Florida lawyer commented this month that it is becoming more and more common to hear news accounts of people convicted of first-degree murder, sentenced to death, then released many years later after it is determined (usually through DNA testing) that actually they were innocent. Over a hundred people have been released from death row over the past thirty years (over a thousand have been executed). The lawyer described this statistic as horrifying, though one might also feel a certain relief. The execution of those released would be much more horrific; and there is no doubt that this has happened from time to time; last month Associated Press reported such a case in Texas. In Britain, several men were exonerated after their execution in the years immediately before the abolition of the death penalty in 1969.

Israel's institution of asylum cities relates to questions within Israel concerning certainty about people's guilt, though it functions within a different way of handling them. The administration of justice within Israel is radically localized rather than centralized. It is the responsibility of kin groups and local communities. There will be practical reasons for this; most Israelites live in villages, and it would not be practical to locate the administration of justice in cities or capitals. There are also advantages; the questions do not become the business of faceless professional lawyers. A disadvantage is that it will be easy for the administration of justice to give way to lynching.

The asylum cities provide some safeguard. A person responsible for someone's death or accused of being responsible can go to one of these cities and be secure there while tempers cool and investigations are undertaken. If at least two witnesses to the incident testify that the killing was deliberate, the murderer will be handed over to an executioner from within the kin group to which the victim belonged. Translations often call him the "avenger of blood," but the word is the one elsewhere translated "redeemer." His job is to **restore** the status quo, to close the circle for the community.

A person who killed someone by accident will stay in the asylum city until the death of the high priest, which is perhaps assumed in some way to cleanse the land of the stain caused by the homicide. Homicide is thus looked at in two ways. It is an offense against a family (hence the execution is the responsibility of a member of the kin group) and something that taints the land before God and imperils God's presence there. The ban on turning the penalty for homicide into a fine (a "ransom") would mean rich people cannot buy themselves out of the consequences of their deed in a way that was closed to ordinary people.

The asylum cities are six of the forty-eight cities where Levites live. Presumably the Levites are there to manage a local worship center, which is in itself a telling fact. Often the Old Testament is negative about local worship centers and assumes that Jerusalem is the only proper place of worship. Yet people will need local places of worship. If six of the Levitical cities are asylum cities, it implies that people involved in worship ministry are also involved in the administration of justice; they are to see that the asylum system works in a proper fashion so that people who go there really are under God's protection, but also that God is involved in resolving the case. Exodus 22 provides for people appearing before God when they cannot sort out a property dispute. The Levites would have the task of mediating this process in a way that distances it from the village where the incident happened and where feelings will run strong.

The Levites themselves have no land. They give themselves to their ministry and in return receive their food from the people, but they need somewhere to live, and it is assumed that they will have some animals, so they have grazing rights around these cities. The idea seems to be that these rights extend 1000 cubits beyond the city itself and thus 2000 cubits across (a cubit is half a yard or half a meter). This hints that the whole provision of this rule is rather theoretical, as it is hard to measure land in mountainous **Canaan** on that basis. Once again, the **Torah** is laying out an imaginative possibility. The community's task is to do something that embodies the kind of concerns that these imaginary rules express.

The book's last chapter returns to the five feisty women. Did the men need time to regroup in order to be able to reassert their authority? Or is this like a meeting where you make a decision and only afterwards does someone see a flaw in it? Or is this a question that arises in light of the material on distributing the land that has appeared since chapter 27? Like many decisions, the one concerning the women's case involves several principles that need to be safeguarded, and the men point to one that was not taken into account earlier. When the five marry, implementing the idea that they can inherit imperils the allocation of the country to the twelve clans. So they need to be required to marry within their clan. This would likely happen anyway; what chance does a Manassite girl have to meet a boy from Asher or Simeon?

DEUTERONOMY 1:1–45

Moses Begins His Last Sermon

¹These are the words Moses spoke to all Israel the other side of the Jordan, in the steppe near Suph, between Paran and Tophel, Laban, Hazeroth, and Di-zahab. (²It is eleven days from Horeb by way of Mount Seir to Kadesh-barnea.) ³In the fortieth year on the first day of the eleventh month Moses spoke to the Israelites in accordance with everything Yahweh commanded him for them, ⁴after he had struck down Sihon king of the Amorites who lived in Heshbon and Og king of Bashan who lived in Ashtaroth (in Edrei). ⁵The other side of the Jordan, in Moab, Moses undertook to expound this teaching: ⁶"Yahweh our God himself spoke to us at Horeb: 'You have been staying at this mountain for a long time. ⁷Set off, get yourselves on the move, go to the mountains of the Amorites and all their neighbors in the steppe, the mountain country, the slopes, the Negev, the sea coast (the country of the Canaanites), and the Lebanon, as far as the Great River, the river Euphrates. ⁸See, I have put the country in front of you. Go and take possession of the country Yahweh promised to your ancestors Abraham, Isaac, and Jacob to give to them and their offspring after them.'"

[The rest of the chapter reviews the story of Israel's journey from Horeb to Kadesh.]

This coming Saturday, I am taking part in a service in which the Episcopal Diocese of Los Angeles expresses its regret and contrition for the way we have treated African Americans. The church to which I belong was founded to provide a place where the white members of the big church in town could send their black servants. It is not the only church in the diocese that made clear in the early twentieth century that black people were encouraged to go somewhere else, to form their own congregation. Hardly anyone alive today was personally involved in those events, yet they are part of our history. I was not even in Los Angeles until a decade or so ago, but by becoming part of the diocese I become part of its history, and I have to come to terms with it, not least because it continues to have its effect on the present. So I shall join in expressing "my" contrition for what "we" did a century ago. In *Requiem for a Nun*, part novel, part play, William Faulkner has one of his characters say, "The past is never dead. It's not even past." Faulkner dealt with overlapping themes in an earlier novel, *Go Down, Moses*; significantly, this novel concerned race relations in the United States. In a speech during his presidential campaign, Barack Obama took up these themes and in effect urged the people of the United States to decide that the time had come to let the past be the past. In what the **Torah** presents as the last, greatest, and certainly longest speech of his life, Moses begins by urging Israel not to forget its past.

The story goes that Winston Churchill was once asked how long it took to prepare a speech. It depends on how long the speech is to be, he said. For a two-minute speech, he would like two days' notice. For a half-hour speech, he would like a half-hour's notice. For a two-hour speech, he is ready now. Moses here begins a final speech that would take rather more than two hours to deliver; you may think it unlikely that he actually delivered the speech in this form. It constitutes a systematic account of Israel's faith and life at this crucial moment in the story, when Israel stands on the edge of the promised land. It sums up what it is going to mean to be Israel. Like earlier sections of the Torah, it relates to questions that are not going to arise for a long time, such as choosing a king and distinguishing between true and false prophets. Sometimes it constitutes another run at issues the Torah has already covered, such as dealing with indentured servants and celebrating the annual pilgrimage festivals. Over the centuries the Holy Spirit guided the community into handling issues in changing ways as circumstances changed and in response to new questions that arose that were not issues in Moses' day. These constituted ways of understanding faith and life that were in keeping with Israel's life as it was at the beginning, in Moses' day. They are expressed as if Moses himself proclaimed them, but Deuteronomy pictures Moses speaking to people "the other side of the Jordan": in other words, the author lives "this side of the Jordan," in **Canaan**.

By the time Deuteronomy was written, Israel was part of the **Assyrian** empire, and its expression of Israel's faith and life makes use of a bit of experience from that time. The Assyrians had a set way of formulating treaty relationships between them and their underlings, and Deuteronomy formulates the **covenant** relationship between God and Israel as if it were one of those treaties. In due course the treaties go on to state the basic stance that the underling needs to take to the Assyrian king, and to lay down some concrete examples of what submission to him involves, and Deuteronomy will do this regarding God's expectations of Israel. Before that, the treaties give some account of relationships in the recent past between the Assyrian king and the underling, which provides background to what will follow. This is also where Deuteronomy begins, with a summary of the story since Sinai that forms background to the expectations laid out in subsequent chapters.

Deuteronomy refers to the content of Moses' address as "this teaching," using the word *torah*. Translations traditionally use the word *law*, but beginning with an account of what has been happening in the past indicates that the Torah includes more than that. One might have expected it to start with the distant past, with Abraham, Isaac, and Jacob, or with the exodus, and it will refer to them. Starting with the moment the people left Horeb (another name for Sinai) has particular significance for the people on the edge of Canaan and for people in later centuries who hear Deuteronomy read. The Torah expects them to live in light of what God did at Horeb/Sinai, but they were not present there. They did not hear God speak. Here Moses makes the link between them and the Sinai generation. It is as if "God said to *us* at Horeb" that it was time to leave there and make our journey to the promised land.

Deuteronomy 1 thus summarizes the story we read in Numbers, though it gives its own slant to it, as you do when you retell a story. It puts even more emphasis on the people's responsibility for what happened on that journey. In verses 11–18 Moses speaks of the pressure placed on him by the burden of leading them and commissions them to choose some further leaders (cf. Numbers 11; also Exodus 18). Verses 19–36 make it the people's idea to send the scouts to reconnoiter the country (cf. Numbers 13). Verse 37 makes explicit that it is the pressure they place on Moses that leads to his incurring God's anger and the declaration that like them he will not enter Canaan. The generation on the edge of Canaan (and each subsequent generation) is thus challenged to accept responsibility for its trust in God. It needs to be wary of thinking it can pass responsibility to its leaders. God makes the covenant with the community as a whole. Moses speaks to "all Israel" (verse 1).

When verse 8 says, "I have put the country in front of you," the "I" is apparently God, even though the next sentence refers to God in the third person. This alternating recurs in Deuteronomy; it is also common in the Prophets. Moses and the prophets speak for God and about God, and they can switch easily between the two ways of speaking.

DEUTERONOMY 1:46–3:29

No, But. . . .

⁴⁶[Moses continued] "When you had stayed at Kadesh for the long time that you did, ²:¹we set off and got on the move into the wilderness by way of the Reed Sea, as Yahweh spoke to me. We went around the mountain country of Seir for a long time. ²Then Yahweh said to me: ³'You have been going around this mountain country for a long time. Set off north.'"

[In chapters 2 and 3 Moses goes on to summarize the journey to the edge of Canaan and the victory over Sihon and Og.]

³:²¹"I commanded Joshua at that time, 'Your eyes see all Yahweh your God did to these two kings. So will Yahweh do to all the kingdoms into which you are crossing. ²²You will not fear them,

because Yahweh your God—he will do battle for you.' ²³I asked Yahweh for grace at that time: ²⁴'My Lord Yahweh, you yourself began to let your servant see your greatness and your strong hand. Who is the God in the heavens or on the earth who does things like your powerful deeds? ²⁵May I cross and see the good land across the Jordan, this good mountain country and the Lebanon?' ²⁶Yahweh got cross with me on account of you, because you did not listen to me. Yahweh said, 'That's plenty from you. Don't ever speak to me again about this matter. ²⁷Go up to the top of Pisgah, lift up your eyes west, north, south, and east. Look with your eyes, because you will not cross this Jordan. ²⁸Command Joshua, help him be strong and stand firm, because he is the one who will cross in front of this people and who will allocate to them the country you will see.' ²⁹So we stayed in the valley near Beth-peor."

I noted at the beginning of this commentary that my wife, Ann, died just before I started writing it. She had multiple sclerosis for forty-three years. The Sunday after her death, the set Scripture readings included Paul's account in 2 Corinthians 12 of begging God to take away a handicap he lived with (we don't know what it was). God wouldn't do so, but God promised, "My grace is enough for you. My power is made perfect in weakness." In the early years, the illness did not affect Ann too much, but later she gradually lost her physical capacities and her capacity for remembering things and so on, so that for most people in California she was a silent figure in a wheelchair. Three times and more we and other people begged God to remove this handicap, but God said the same thing to us. I know from things people said during her life and after her death that she ministered silently to hundreds of people. God declined to grant the prayers we prayed for her, as God did for Paul, but God did not simply do nothing.

Moses has this experience when he asks that he may go with the people into **Canaan**. God declines to grant that prayer, but Moses will still be glad he asked, because it leads to God's saying he can view the promised land from the height of the Pisgah mountain range nearby. His prayer does make a difference to what God had planned should happen; Moses would not have had this experience if he had not prayed. Perhaps God's

"No, but . . ." contributes to the way Deuteronomy can portray Moses as someone who came to terms with God's way of dealing with him. God's attitude does not leave him bitter or resentful. He focuses on his task, which is to ensure that the people get into Canaan and therefore to ensure that Joshua is well prepared to do the job that actually Moses wanted to do.

Moses had done his best to evade God's summons and continue leading a quiet life looking after sheep, but he had failed. He does not know that his leadership is monumentally important for the history of the entire world. It has given him little sense of fulfillment as far as we can tell; it has brought him lots of grief; and this is how it will end. Numbers has made clear that by his own action he has forfeited the possibility of entering Canaan. Once again Deuteronomy tweaks the story. It is also possible to say that it is because of the people that he has forfeited the possibility of entering Canaan. They drove him to the action that led to this end (see Numbers 20). They had already refused to heed his attempts to get them to believe God would get them into Canaan (Numbers 13–14). His fate is bound up with theirs. His job was to get them from **Egypt** to Canaan. If the exodus generation is not going into Canaan, how can their leader do so? God is tough with Moses, as God will be with Jesus and with people such as Peter and Paul. How extraordinary that Moses can ask for grace and not be granted it! God regularly makes decisions about what to do not merely on the basis of what individuals want but in light of a bigger picture to which they are subordinate. Leaders are not important. It is God and the people of God who matter.

Typically, the Old Testament makes that point by describing Moses not as a leader but as a servant—not the people's servant, but God's servant. That provides the framework for Moses' prayer. He prays as a servant to his master. This both makes his plea to God possible (masters have obligations to servants) and sets constraints for what he can expect (in the end, the master's agenda is what counts). God takes the edge off that toughness by not granting what Moses asks yet not granting nothing.

It is a recurrent feature of God's reaction to wrongdoing; it recalls God's making clothes for Adam and Eve and promising that Cain the murderer will be protected. It is also a recurrent feature of prayer in the Old Testament. God does not say either "Yes" or "No" or "Wait" (as is sometimes suggested); God declines to do what the prayer asks but does undertake to do something else. Prayer is almost a kind of negotiation, as it was when Abraham prayed for Sodom. It is also like an argument, and one in which God can get cross (Deuteronomy neatly uses similar words for Moses' plea to "cross" the Jordan and God's getting "cross" with his request). Prayer, after all, involves talking to your Father, and fathers sometimes get cross, but this does not stop wise children from asking them for things.

Whereas chapter 1 covers the journey from Egypt to Sinai and Kadesh, which led to the forty years of wandering, chapters 2–3 focus on the closing leg of the journey, from Kadesh to the Moab steppe, and especially on the Israelites' passage through the territory of their Edomite, Moabite, and Ammonite cousins, then on their victories over **Amorite** kings east of the Jordan. Despite their hostility, Israel is not to take over their cousins' land. Indeed, Moses notes how God was involved in the way Edom, Moab, and Ammon (and even the Philistines) gained their land. The activity of the God of Israel was not concerned solely with Israel. **Yahweh** is God of all the nations and is involved in their destiny. Israel would therefore have no right to steal their land.

In contrast, Deuteronomy portrays the victories over the Amorite kings as part of God's plan (in Numbers they come about purely because of the Amorites' hostility). The Amorites fell into God's trap by refusing the Israelites' offer of **peace**. It is as if God were tempting the Amorites to attack the Israelites, the idea expressed by speaking of God's stiffening their will or "hardening their hearts." It does not mean God forced them to do something they did not wish to do. They made their decision, but they responded to a temptation that they would have been wiser to resist. God's acting in this way was part of God's bringing judgment on them for their waywardness. The idea that God was thus judging the Amorites for their waywardness by commissioning the Israelites to defeat them goes back to the Abraham story (Genesis 15:16).

For later Israel listening to these chapters, a further point emerges. They are used to bad relations with Edom, Moab, and

Ammon, and the information that their ancestors were not to provoke them or fight them might raise some eyebrows. On the other hand, the information that they were to fight the Amorites has no contemporary significance; there are no Amorite or Canaanite powers in their day. Deuteronomy would thus not encourage the idea that Israel is to make war on other local peoples after entering Canaan.

DEUTERONOMY 4:1–49

The Attraction of Images

[1]"Now, Israel, listen to the rules and decisions I am teaching you to observe, so you may live, and may enter and take possession of the country that Yahweh the God of your ancestors is giving you. [2]You will not add to the word I am commanding you or take away from it, in keeping the commands of Yahweh your God that I am requiring of you. [3]Your eyes see what I did at [the city of] the Master of Peor, that Yahweh your God eliminated from among you every individual who went after the Master of Peor, [4]but you who stuck to Yahweh your God are all of you alive today. [5]See, I have taught you rules and decisions as Yahweh your God commanded me for you to observe in the country you are entering to take possession of. [6]Take care to observe them, because it will be your wisdom and discernment in the eyes of the peoples, who will listen to all these rules and say, 'This great nation really is a wise and discerning people.' [7]Because what great nation is there that has a God near it like Yahweh our God whenever we call to him? [8]What great nation is there that has rules and decisions as faithful as all this teaching that I am putting in front of you today? [9]Only take care for yourself and be very careful of yourself so you do not put out of mind the things your eyes have seen, and so they do not turn aside from your mind all the days of your life. Make them known to your children and your grandchildren."

[In verses 10–14 Moses continues to underline the point.]

[15]"Be very careful of yourselves, because you did not see any shape on the day Yahweh spoke to you at Horeb out of the midst of the fire, [16]so you do not become perverse and make yourselves a shaped sculpture (any figure, the form of a male or

103

female, ¹⁷the form of any animal on earth, the form of any winged bird that flies in the heavens, ¹⁸the form of anything that moves on the ground, the form of any fish in the waters below the earth), ¹⁹and so you do not raise your eyes and see the sun, the moon, and the stars, all the army in the heavens, and stray and bow down to them and serve them. Yahweh your God allocated them to all the peoples under all the heavens, ²⁰but Yahweh took you and brought you out of the iron furnace, out of Egypt, to be a people for him, his own, this very day."

[In verses 21–49 Moses underlines the point further, warns of the consequences of ignoring it, but also promises that people can always come back.]

Two or three weeks ago I went for a few days holiday and drove from Los Angeles up the coastal highway to Monterey. I had always heard it was a beautiful drive, and it is. The second night I stopped at a motel and noticed as I checked in that the manager had behind his desk a picture of Mother Teresa and alongside it a couple of pictures of gods, in partly human form but rather rotund and with lots of arms. Over breakfast next morning, the manager confirmed that he was a Hindu and treated me to quite a long sermon, covering much of the contents of the Sermon on the Mount. That stayed with me, but so did the pictures of the gods. The use of such images in worship is a regular feature of religions, and it was a regular feature of Israel's religion in practice, but not one the Old Testament itself approves.

Deuteronomy here turns from recollection of the events of the past forty years, recollection of how the relationship between God and Israel has been working, to a statement of expectations about how it is to work in the future. This in part builds on that recollection. One aspect is that Israel is to make no shapes, statues, figures, or forms. The multiplicity of the terms shows how comprehensive Deuteronomy wants to be, and the list of objects that people might seek to represent has the same effect. It is not concerned with banning artistic representation, though it might take the view that it is better to be safe than sorry, and many Jewish interpreters have thought it wiser to keep as far away as one can from possible wrongdoing rather than to look for ways of keeping the letter of the law but evading its spirit.

The spirit of the **Torah** is that worship needs to reflect the way God has appeared to us and acted among us. Israel did not see the shape of anything at Sinai—anything human or animal. They simply heard a voice speaking. God is quite capable of appearing in human form, as God did to Abraham and Jacob, and the Old Testament also sometimes uses animal images to describe God (God is a lion or a bull). Yet God did not appear in human form at Sinai, still less in animal form, and representing God in statue form as human or animal is bound to misrepresent God. The peoples among whom the Israelites will live did represent God in human and animal form. They also saw the planets and the stars as virtual gods, entities that determined what happened on earth. There was all the more temptation to try to discover what these gods intended to do and to stay on the right side of them. Deuteronomy bans this, too. The God who appeared at Sinai is the only God.

At least, this God is the only God for Israel. You could not blame the **Canaanites** for thinking it was okay to make statues to represent their gods, nor blame the **Babylonians** for thinking that the stars and planets govern what happens on earth. They were not there at Sinai. For the time being, God has left them with just those religious resources. Only as God uses Israel to enable them to see there are bigger things to be said about God can they be introduced to a bigger picture. Then (Moses points out) they will be in a position to marvel at the insight expressed in the Torah, the bigger picture of God and of God's relationship with us that it gives.

It is easy to think that having images makes God more accessible. It gives you something concrete to relate to. Deuteronomy sees things the other way around. The Torah gives you a bigger picture of God and also portrays this God as always accessible. You can talk to this God and get a response. God will do something when you need God to. It's not like talking to a statue. The rules about relating to God that God gives are not negative constraints but expressions of God's **faithfulness** because they make it possible for that relationship to work.

As Deuteronomy moves from recollection to exhortation, it introduces one of its characteristic motifs. It cannot make up its mind whether to address the community as a whole or as individuals. It speaks both of watching yourself and of watching yourselves. Both are important. The community is one entity; a church is the same. It has to attend to its attitudes as a body. These affect and influence each individual. The Israelites are also individual people, and so are Christians. They have to take responsibility for themselves. They cannot leave it to the Israelite or church body to do the right thing or make this body the excuse for their wrongdoing. A feedback loop operates between individual and community; the community shapes the individual; the individual shapes the community.

Moses sees obedience as the key to life. That has been misunderstood. In New Testament times, there were Christians who told people that unless you were prepared to obey the Torah, you could not really become a Christian; you could not be saved. This makes Paul blow a fuse (see Romans 10). As he points out, the Old Testament assumes it is God's grace and your response of trust that saves you, though he also assumes that once you are within the people of God, doing what God says is key to life. That is Deuteronomy's point. Because some of God's rules (such as the ban on images) may seem counterintuitive, it is important that Israel keeps reminding itself of them and makes sure they are passed on from one generation to the next.

DEUTERONOMY 5:1-15

Not with Our Parents

[1]Moses proclaimed to all Israel, "Listen, Israel, to the rules and decisions I am speaking in your hearing today. Learn them and be careful to observe them. [2]Yahweh our God sealed a covenant with us at Horeb. [3]It was not with our parents that Yahweh sealed this covenant but with us ourselves, these people here today, all of us who are alive. [4]Face to face Yahweh spoke with me on the mountain from the midst of the fire ([5]I was standing between Yahweh and you at that time to tell you Yahweh's message,

because you were afraid of the fire and you did not go up on the mountain): [6]'I am Yahweh your God who brought you out from Egypt, from the household of serfs. [7]For you there will be no other gods besides me. [8]You will not make yourself a statue of any form in the heavens above, on the earth beneath, or in the waters under the earth. [9]You will not bow down to them or serve them. Because I, Yahweh your God, am a passionate God, visiting the waywardness of parents on children and thirds and fourths for people who oppose me, [10]but keeping commitment to thousands for people who give themselves to me and keep my commands. [11]You will not lift up the name of Yahweh your God in respect of something empty, because Yahweh will not acquit someone who lifts up his name to something empty. [12]Guard the Sabbath day, sanctifying it as Yahweh your God has commanded you. [13]You can serve six days and do all your work, [14]but the seventh day belongs to Yahweh your God. You will not do any work, you, your son or daughter, your male or female servant, your ox, your donkey, any of your cattle, or the alien who lives in your settlement, so that your male and female servant may rest like you. [15]You are to keep in mind that you were a servant in Egypt but Yahweh your God brought you out from there with a strong hand and an extended arm. That is why Yahweh your God has commanded you to observe the Sabbath day.'"

This week I read an e-mail from a student now doing graduate work elsewhere: "I quit my job on Monday as I was averaging four hours of sleep a night and came down with two colds in the first two weeks of school. Best decision of the year." Last week in an introductory session about seminary life for our own new students, someone asked for advice about staying in good shape, in a broader sense than the physical. My answer was "Have a day off." For financial reasons, it's hard for students not to work 24/7, but then they get overtired, ill, and depressed. Admittedly, many others in the context of Western life are in the same position. I am not strict about keeping a twenty-four-hour Sabbath, but I am in a position to close the computer Saturday afternoon and go out to dinner and listen to some music, then give Sunday morning to church, then go to the beach for lunch and a nap. I am more strict about giving the beginning part of each day to a time consciously in God's presence and about stopping work at dinner time (admittedly because that is when my brain switches off) unless I have an evening class.

The **Torah** gives a number of different rationales for keeping Sabbath, but it commonly begins with the command to "sanctify" it. Maybe we should rather translate the verb as "let it be holy," because God personally sanctified it back at creation. God declared that Saturday was a special day because it marked the end of the process of creation. It was the day God "stopped" (the etymological meaning of "Sabbath"). God then claimed it. It belongs to God; people are therefore to hold back from it. Now, the idea of God making the world over a period of six days then having a day off is a metaphor, so transferring the stopping day to a different day or distributing your stopping in a different way might be fine. The point is to sanctify some stopping time, to surrender some time to God and thereby acknowledge that all time belongs to God. You could also say we keep Sabbath not because stopping is good for us but because we are called to be godlike. Stopping means looking back over what you have been doing and admiring it, as God did. Ignatian spirituality commends the idea of looking back over the day when bedtime comes, reflecting on what has happened and what we have done with the day. That may well lead to some confession, but this is not the heart of such reflection. Its heart is contentment and gratitude. You may do this at the end of each day; you may do it at the end of the week.

As I write, there have been reports of plans to ban the use of onboard computers in trucks while they are on the move. Like using cell phones, using computers while driving significantly increases the prospect of having an accident, and banning them might seem a no-brainer, but it does not seem so to the trucking industry. Banning onboard computers will make a significant difference to what truckers can achieve in a day. What matters is what we can get done, what we can earn. Stopping for a day is countercultural for the same reasons. In this connection, Deuteronomy emphasizes the responsibility of the people with power in the community, the heads of families who are thus also the heads of the family business. They must stop for a day, and they must make sure that their families who share in the family business and their employees (and animals!) stop for a day. That requires faith: supposing we miss the crucial opportunity for plowing or sewing or harvesting? Just do it, says God. Instead of pressuring them to work harder, pressure them to take time off.

The form of the Sabbath command thus hints at the way these ten commands are addressed to people with power in the community. It is their responsibility to make sure that **Yahweh** is the only object of the family's worship. This, too, requires some faith: suppose it looks as if the **Canaanites** can make a go of their farming because they seek the help of their Master? Just do it, says Yahweh. It is their responsibility to make sure that in worshiping Yahweh people resist the natural inclination to make an image of Yahweh; chapter 4 has suggested the rationale for that prohibition. Ignoring it will have horrendous consequences not just for the head of the household but for the two or three other generations who live together as a family. So just do it. It is not so immediately obvious what it means to avoid lifting up God's name in respect of something empty. People would lift up God's name when they made promises or delivered prophecies or made plans. Suppose they do not keep their promises, or suppose the prophecies come from inside themselves, or suppose the plans issue simply from their own minds. It is the attaching of God's name to such promises, prophecies, and plans that involves lifting up that name in respect of something empty (it has nothing to do with "profanity," which does not bother the Bible).

The ten commands already appeared in Exodus 20; the Sabbath command manifests the biggest difference between their two forms. Exodus expounds its rationale in God's activity in creation. Deuteronomy adds a rationale in God's activity in delivering Israel from **Egypt**. The reason the head of the family should be concerned for its members, and particularly its servants (Deuteronomy 15 will show how it is misleading to refer to them as slaves), is that Israel knows what it is like to be servants who are mistreated. Being the boss should never make someone forget what it's like to be a servant. God's rescuing Israel from Egypt is a more general rationale for the ten commands. Yahweh's self-identity is as the God who brought the people out from that position. God can therefore lay the law down to them. They owe him.

"I brought you out of Egypt." Not so. They were not alive then. "God sealed a **covenant** with us at Horeb." Not so. We

109

were not alive then. Yet God and Moses declare with outrageous explicitness that it was "you," "us." There is a song that asks, "Were you there when they crucified my Lord?" It invites people to say "Yes" even though in a superficial sense the answer is "No." While the song and the chapter invite people into an act of imagination, they imply more than that. If Jesus had not died back then, *we* would not be free. If God had not rescued Israel back then, later generations of Israel would not be free. If God had not sealed a covenant with Israel back then, later generations of Israel would not be in covenant relationship with God. In effect they were there in Egypt and at Sinai in their mothers' wombs. It was not (just) with that generation that God made the covenant. Therefore they are obliged to accept the challenge to keep God's rules and live by the decisions God has taken about what people should and should not do.

DEUTERONOMY 5:16–33

If Only. . . .

[16]"Honor your father and mother as Yahweh your God has commanded you, so you may live long and it may go well for you on the land Yahweh your God is giving you. [17]You will not murder. [18]You will not be adulterous. [19]You will not steal. [20]You will not give empty testimony against your neighbor. [21]You will not desire your neighbor's wife. You will not long for your neighbor's house or field, his male or female servant, his ox or donkey, or anything of your neighbor's.
[22]"These words Yahweh spoke to your whole congregation at the mountain from the midst of fire (the cloud and the deep darkness) in a loud voice, and did not add anything. He wrote them on two stone tablets and gave them to me. [23]When you listened to the voice from the midst of the darkness and the mountain was blazing with fire, you came near me, all your clan heads and elders, [24]and said, 'Now. Yahweh our God has shown us his honor and greatness, and we have listened to his voice from the midst of the fire. This day we have seen that God can speak with a human being and he can live. [25]So now, why should we die, because this great fire will consume us. If we continue to listen to Yahweh our God any more, we will die.

[26]Because who is there of all fleshly humanity that has listened to the living God's voice speaking from the midst of fire like us and lived? [27]You go near and listen to everything that Yahweh our God says, and you can speak to us everything Yahweh our God speaks to you, and we will listen and do it.' [28]Yahweh listened to the sound of your words as you spoke to me.

"Yahweh said to me, 'I have listened to the sound of this people's words that they have spoken to you. They have done well in everything they spoke. [29]Oh that this will be their mind, to revere me and keep all my commands for all time, so it may go well for them and their children forever. [30]Go, say to them, "Get yourselves back to your tents." [31]But you, stand here with me and I will speak to you every command, the rules and decisions you are to teach them so they will observe them in the country I am giving them to take possession of.' [32]You are to take care to do as Yahweh your God has commanded you. Do not turn right or left. [33]You are to walk on every way that Yahweh your God commanded you, so you may live and it may go well for you and you may live a long time in the country you are to take possession of."

Yesterday we had the service to which I referred in connection with Deuteronomy 1, when the Episcopal Church in Los Angeles expressed its contrition for the racism that has characterized it in encouraging segregation and condoning discrimination within the diocese since its founding in 1896. It also expressed regret for its broader identification with a denomination that accepted slavery and was conformed to the broader society rather than becoming an advocate for the oppressed and not profiting from their oppression. It now seems frightening that Christian churches could have been reading the Scriptures each Sunday and that individuals could have been reading those Scriptures privately day by day without seeing the clash between the scriptural message and the way the church and society worked. It is possible to listen but not hear, or to hear but not listen.

Moses, God, and the people talk a lot about listening in Deuteronomy 5. The people have listened to God speak, but they feel it is dangerous to listen any more. How right they are! Listening to God is almost as dangerous as not doing so. If God's voice can shatter eardrums, it is a symbol of the dangerous content to what God says. Let Moses do the listening, and they will listen to Moses. "If only," God says. Literally, God says, "Who will grant it that this will be their mind?" One might have thought that God is the only one who can grant that, yet God's words suggest that even God cannot force people to have the right attitude. You can make people hear by speaking loudly, but you cannot make people listen. God can be pleased with the reverence implied in their not wanting to be personally confronted by God's words and their willingness to listen via Moses and obey. But will it happen? There is listening, and there is merely hearing. Hebrew in fact uses the same word for hearing, listening, and obeying. They are three different actions, yet when humanity is working properly, they are three aspects of the same action. If only.

Yesterday's service emphasized how the church shared in the economic benefits of slavery and the continuing subjugation of African Americans. Yet every Sunday churches would have read out the Ten Commandments, with their devastating coup de grace, "You will not desire"—in the familiar version, "Thou shalt not covet." Coveting was the foundation of slavery, and it remains the foundation of our economy. If the nation stops coveting and seeking to fulfill its desires, its financial system cannot survive; it depends on people buying things, whether or not they have the money or the need. A recent news report highlighted the exponential growth of self-storage in the United States. There are enough square feet of self-storage in the country for the entire population to stand in self-storage. What are people storing? Often it is their previous generation of furniture, because there was nothing much wrong with it, so they don't want simply to throw it away. So why did they buy new? They yielded to the constant pressure to covet, coming from TV and elsewhere.

Translations' traditional use of the word *covet* and the command's association of wives with houses, fields, servants, and animals suggest that the command's warning about a man's wishing he had someone else's wife is concerned with more than her sexual desirability. A wife is an asset, a colleague in heading up the family farm. Proverbs 31 gives a wide-ranging job description for the ideal wife, and sex doesn't come into it (though Proverbs also critiques adultery). If you are the head of a family, you have to make the family business work. If only you had the wife of the man down the street who seems so much more competent. If only you had his house, which maybe has a less leaky roof or more room for the animals. If only you had his land, which seems to have better soil than yours. If only you had his servants, who seem to work harder than yours. If only you had his animals, who seem stronger than yours.

What is so wrong with wishing? The tenth command follows on four others and in doing so points to the answer. Wishing you had your neighbor's assets may not stop at wishing. It issues in killing, adultery, stealing, and swindling. Behind actions are attitudes, so we have to pay attention to attitudes if we are serious about living the right way. Specifically, learning to be content with what we have is a key to keeping in right relationships with other people and with life.

The command about parents may also link with the command about desire. Like the other commands, it will be addressed to the men who are responsible for the life of the family; it does not concern the obedience of little children (though Deuteronomy does expect small children to obey their parents). As parents grow older, they make a smaller contribution to the work the family needs to get done. They are useless, yet they are consumers of the results of that work. It would be tempting to neglect them. Once again, doing right by people overrides economic considerations. Or rather, paradoxically, such a commitment will in the end make economic sense. You have to trust that God is right about the long term. Deuteronomy does not say God will personally make things work out that way but rather implies that there is a moral structure about the way things work out.

The promise attached to this command points to another insight. Central to the role of parents in Deuteronomy is their teaching the faith to their children (again, grown-up children as much as small children). Honoring them means accepting that teaching and basing your life on it. Once again, this is a key to life working out well.

DEUTERONOMY 6:1–25

Listen, Israel

[1]"So this is the command (the rules and decisions) that Yahweh your God required to be taught to you, to be observed in the country to which you are crossing over to take possession of, [2]so that you may revere Yahweh your God by keeping all his rules and commands that I am requiring of you—you, your children, and your grandchildren—all the days of your life, and so that you may live long [3]and may listen, Israel, and take care to act so that it may go well for you and you may greatly increase as Yahweh the God of your ancestors spoke to you (a country flowing with milk and sweetness). [4]Listen, Israel: Yahweh our God Yahweh one. [5]You are to give yourself to Yahweh your God with your whole mind, your whole person, your whole might. [6]These words that I am commanding you today are to be on your mind. [7]Impress them on your children and speak of them when you stay at home and when you are going on a journey, when you lie down and when you get up. [8]Tie them as a sign on your hand. They are to be bands between your eyes [9]and you are to write them on the doorposts of your house and on your gates.

[10]"When Yahweh your God brings you into the country that I promised to your ancestors Abraham, Isaac, and Jacob to give you, great and fine cities that you did not build, [11]houses full of all fine things that you did not fill, wells dug that you did not dig, vineyards and olive groves that you did not plant, and you eat and are full, [12]take care for yourself that you do not put Yahweh out of mind, the one who brought you out from Egypt, the household of serfs. [13]You are to revere Yahweh your God, serve him, and make promises in his name. [14]You will not walk after other gods, the gods of the peoples that are around you, [15]because Yahweh your God in your midst is the passionate God, so that the anger of Yahweh your God does not flare up against you and destroy you from upon the face of the ground. [16]You will not test Yahweh your God as you tested him at [the place called] Testing."

[Verses 17–25 continue this exhortation.]

Many people in the West in the twenty-first century find it hard to believe there is one truth or one God; they find it easier to believe that there are lots of versions of the truth or angles on the truth. We all then choose a "truth" that makes sense to us or that we like. Life is like the supermarket. Yet at the same time, the United States (at least) is torn by virulent culture wars between right and left, liberal and conservative, atheists and believers. Asserting that my truth is as good as your truth does not imply the conviction that your truth is also as good as my truth.

The challenge "Listen, Israel: Yahweh our God Yahweh one" is a central expectation of Old Testament faith. In Judaism it is known by the word for *listen*: it is "the Shema" (the emphasis lies on the second syllable; the pronunciation is virtually "Shma"). It is the central affirmation of orthodox Jewish faith. As a sentence, "Yahweh our God Yahweh one" works in Hebrew, as it doesn't in English. Hebrew doesn't have a word for "is," and you can have a sentence of this kind without a verb. In this one, there are several places where you could put an "is" to produce a proper English sentence. Wherever you do so, it is clear where the emphasis lies. There is the repeating of the name **Yahweh**, then the declaration that this God is "our God," then the declaration in that closing word "one."

We could describe Israel's commitment to Yahweh as monotheistic, but this risks missing the point. The idea of monotheism has its background in a concern often debated in ancient Greek thinking, about whether there is a unity to all reality or behind all reality. Believing there is one God provides grounds for this conviction. When Jewish thinking and the Christian gospel came to be expressed in relation to such questions, Jewish and Christian monotheism were born. But Old Testament faith did not have this question in its background. For Israel, the question was not merely whether there is one God but who this God is and whether people acknowledge this God and repudiate others. Declaring that Yahweh is one does imply that there is only one God, but its more focal affirmation is that Yahweh is God and the god the **Canaanites** called the Master is not God. Such beings are gods but not God. The Old Testament does not dispute that there are many supernatural beings, but it knows that Yahweh belongs to a unique class of heavenly being, a class with only one member. Yahweh is the creator of all these other beings and the one with sovereignty over them all. They are Yahweh's underlings and **aides**, though often not very faithful ones.

Another important affirmation follows from this. Chapter 4 has noted that for the time being, God is content for other peoples to worship different gods, who are the real God's underlings and servants. For Israel that is impossible. Yahweh is the one. The first basic command in chapter 5 concerned taking Yahweh alone as God. Chapter 6 underscores that command. Both this command and the one in chapter 4 concerning images relate to temptations that will assail Israel over the centuries. By the end of Old Testament times Israel will have won the victory over these temptations, but it will take the best part of a thousand years after Moses' day.

In the traditional translation, the affirmation goes on to urge Israel to "love" Yahweh, but in English the word *love* suggests primarily emotions. The way Moses qualifies the word presupposes it has a wider significance. We are to "love" or dedicate ourselves or give ourselves to God with our whole mind, our whole person, and all our might. The word for "mind" is literally "heart," but once again in English *heart* suggests emotions. It does not usually do so in the Old Testament or in the New. The heart is the inner person as a whole, with particular reference to thinking things through, forming attitudes, and making decisions. The word for "person" is often translated "soul," but it does not denote the soul as opposed to the body but rather the whole person with all its life. The commitment Moses is looking for is a self-giving that involves all people's energy and focus. It is exclusive of any other loyalty.

There is yet another tricky word to note. Moses wants Israel to "revere" Yahweh. Translations often render this Hebrew word "fear"; it covers both the negative idea of being afraid and the positive idea of revering. Occasionally it denotes being afraid of God, and the end of the reading reminds people that their unfaithfulness to God will give them reason for such fear, but the Old Testament regards fear of God in that sense as generally unnecessary, while it sees a positive revering of God as important. As with love (and hate) it is then not merely a matter of feeling but of action. Revering motivates and implies obeying.

Two other important words here are ones usually translated "forget" and "remember." Once again these are words suggesting action, not just things going on inside our heads. Forgetting God's actions and words means ignoring them; remembering God's actions and words means living in light of them. Both words denote something deliberate, not accidental. Forgetting implies putting out of mind; remembering means consciously keeping in mind. Thus Deuteronomy encourages Israelites to have ways of encouraging themselves to remember. They are to talk about them a lot, at home and on a journey, morning and evening (in other words, all the time and whatever they are doing). Further, they have ways of encouraging this remembering. While the references to ties, bands, and door inscriptions might be metaphorical, Jewish people have assumed it was literal; the literal action has the potential to encourage memory and discourage people from putting things out of mind or letting them fall out of mind.

DEUTERONOMY 7:1–6

On Killing Enemies

[1]"When Yahweh your God brings you into the country that you are entering to take possession of, and puts down many nations before you (Hittites, Girgashites, Amorites, Canaanites, Perizzites, Hivites, and Jebusites, seven nations bigger and stronger than you), [2]and Yahweh your God gives them up before you and you strike them down, you will devote them totally. You will not seal a covenant with them. You will not show grace to them. [3]You will not intermarry with them. You will not give your daughters to their sons or take their daughters for your sons, because they will turn your sons from following me and they will serve other gods. Then the anger of Yahweh your God will flare up against you and he will quickly destroy you. [5]Rather, do this to them. Demolish their altars. Break up their pillars. Cut down their columns. Burn their statues with fire. [6]Because you are a people holy to Yahweh your God. It was you that Yahweh your God chose to become a special people for him from all the peoples on the face of the ground."

In the modern age, the way the Old Testament talks about the Israelites' destroying people troubles many Jews and Christians in the United States. It did not do so before the modern period, and it is not felt as so much of a problem in other countries. Whereas U.S. Christians often link their unease with Jesus' telling people to love their enemies, it seems unlikely that the origin of their troubled feelings lies simply there (Augustine comments that Jesus tells us to love our enemies; he does not tell us to love God's enemies). In the context of modernity people came to be troubled about the prevalence of warring between nations, with weaponry of developing sophistication, and came to generate the conviction that nations should be able to get together to eliminate war. Jesus' teaching and the rest of the Bible suggest that this is an implausible conviction ("there will be wars and rumors of wars"), and recent history confirms that. People in the United States may also be influenced by the fact that the United States is the great war-making nation; it has war deeply and recurrently part of its history.

Israelites listening to Deuteronomy 7 may also have been shocked or bewildered by these words of Moses, for different though overlapping reasons. There is nothing new about God's promising to strike down the **Canaanites**, and the background to the promise has been made clear. In part it is an ancient equivalent to eminent domain or compulsory purchase. God wants this country in order to give it to the Israelites, because God intends to bless the world by means of them. In the short term, therefore, these other peoples will have to lose out, but God is not simply being arbitrary. God has been giving them rope for centuries, and eventually they have hanged themselves. They have behaved in abominable ways (child sacrifice is one practice the **Torah** mentions), so they are to be banished from their country as Cain was once banished from his land.

In Deuteronomy 7 the difference is that God envisages the Israelites striking these peoples down; so far in the Torah, striking people down has been God's business. The exception that proves the rule is God's commissioning the Israelites to strike down the Midianites, not in order to occupy their land but because of wrong the Midianites had done. Israel was thus to act as God's agent. It was acting in the manner of the authorities Paul speaks of, acting as "God's minister, bringing punishment as an agent of wrath on the person who does wrong" (Romans 13:4).

This notion troubles many modern Jews and Christians for two reasons. One is that we prefer the idea of God's being loving and merciful to the idea of God's being tough with people. Yet Jesus doesn't regard having love as a defining characteristic as incompatible with sending trillions of people to hell.

The other is a fear that nations today may make it the excuse for making war, claiming they are only doing what the Torah told the Israelites to do. I am not aware of cases of nations that were peace loving and disinclined to make war but then decided to make a war because Deuteronomy said so. If Deuteronomy comes into consideration, it is when people use the book to provide an excuse for what they were going to do anyway. The way to undermine that claim is to point out that God's telling the Israelites to wage war in one or two circumstances doesn't imply that the command is transferable.

Jews and Christians sometimes argue that the Old Testament's attitude to war reflects its cultural context, which is of course true. It is also the case that our attitude to war reflects our cultural context. The Old and New Testament do not imply that the Torah was limited by the insights of its cultural context in what it told the Israelites, but neither does either Testament suggest that the Torah's commission applies in other contexts than the one in which Moses utters it.

The Torah goes on to speak of the Israelites "devoting" these peoples. Translations often use words such as "annihilated" or "destroyed," and that may be the implication, but it does not convey Moses' distinctive point. Devoting them means giving them over to God. This need not mean killing them. You could devote land, or an animal such as a donkey, and in effect Hannah will devote Samuel; the donkey or the human being then belongs to God and is committed to God's service. The Israelites did in effect devote many Canaanites to God's service in this way; they became people who chopped wood and drew water for the **altar**, its offerings, and the rites of the sanctuary. The Israelites have already devoted various peoples to God by killing them, though God never told them to do so. They were following a practice known from other peoples. Here God does tell them to do this.

In what sense does God mean it? After commanding Israel to devote the Canaanites, Moses goes on to a series of other commands. They are not to seal **covenants** with the Canaanites, show grace to them, or intermarry with them (because then they will end up serving their gods, as happened in connection with the Midianites), and they are to destroy their aids to worship and their places of worship. The talk of not showing grace again puts Israel in the position of people like the authorities in Romans 13. People such as judges and police often have to resist the temptation to show grace to wrongdoers. There are moments when it is necessary to be tough. This is such a moment.

What is odd about these other commands is that devoting the Canaanites will mean that questions such as intermarriage don't arise. So why mention them?

Jesus tells men who are inclined to fancy other women to gouge an eye out (Matthew 5:29). We assume he was absolutely serious but did not intend to be taken literally. It would make sense if Deuteronomy is absolutely serious about annihilating the Canaanites but does not intend to be taken literally. It would fit with this chapter's place in the exposition of basic attitudes that occupies Deuteronomy 4–11. These chapters are not laying down rules but seeking to form attitudes. It is vital that Israel totally repudiate Canaanite religion. As far as the Israelites are concerned, the Canaanites must no longer exist. They need to eliminate them from their lives. Or if Deuteronomy is laying down literal rules, it is in the imperatives that follow about intermarriage and the destruction of the Canaanites' aids to worship.

These imperatives also hint at another aspect of the significance of Deuteronomy for its readers. It forms the conclusion of the Torah and the introduction to the story from Joshua to Kings. One feature of that story is how Israel failed to do the kind of thing Deuteronomy said and ended up thrown out of the country like the Canaanites (only not permanently). It also indicated priorities the people need now to have. They need to take seriously these commands about intermarriage and destroying forms of worship. In a way Deuteronomy's message is "If only we had done these things, we would not be in so much trouble today." The people who read Deuteronomy also sometimes fought wars, as nations normally do. War is built into the notion of nationhood. But these people never assumed that they were supposed literally to eliminate peoples. It looks as if they knew how to read Deuteronomy, whereas modern people do not.

DEUTERONOMY 7:7–15

On Election

[7]"It was not because of your being bigger than all the peoples that Yahweh got attached to you and chose you, because you were smaller than all the peoples. [8]Because of Yahweh's giving himself to you and because of his keeping the promise he made to your ancestors, he brought you out with a strong hand, redeemed you from the household of serfs, from the hand of Pharaoh king of Egypt. So you are to acknowledge that Yahweh, your God, he is God, the God who is steadfast, keeping covenant and commitment to people who give themselves to him and keep his commands, to a thousand generations, [10]but who repays people who oppose him to his face by destruction. He is not slow with the person who opposes him to his face; he repays him. [11]So you are to take care to observe the command (the rules and the decisions) that I am requiring of you today. [12]As a result of your heeding these decisions and taking care to observe them, for you Yahweh your God will take care of the covenant and commitment he promised to your ancestors. [13]He will give himself to you, bless you, and multiply you. He will bless the fruit of your womb and the fruit of your land, your grain, wine, and oil, the offspring of your cattle and the young of your flock, on the land he promised to your ancestors to give you. [14]You will be blessed above all peoples. There will not be among you male or female who is infertile, or among your animals. [15]Yahweh will turn away from you every illness, and none of the terrible sicknesses of Egypt, which you know, will he bring on you, but will put them on the people who oppose you."

In a newsy e-mail, a former student included the following information (I have disguised the material, of course, as usual): "I have developed an embarrassingly silly crush on the postdoctoral fellow who teaches some of the Semitic languages here. He is gorgeous, shy, and a bit socially awkward. He has a PhD and is turning his dissertation into a book. He is very bright. Students tease me all the time about what a cute couple we would make. I do not know him well, as I do not do Hebrew and we do not have cause for interaction, so I do pathetic things like study in the student union when he has class so that we can 'spontaneously' run into each other. It's not working. Yes, I am pathetic. I know." What makes people fall for each other? It's a great mystery. Song of Songs 8:7 comments on how love can overpower a man but leave him unable to force the object of his love to reciprocate it; a man could give or offer all the wealth of his household for love and be laughed to scorn. Money can't buy me love.

What made God fall for Israel? In a class this week, a student asked me why God chose Israel when it wasn't a very impressive people. It looks as if this student hadn't noticed that the people God chooses are usually not very impressive. If God did not work that way, it would risk making people trust in the humanly impressive. When God works via ordinary people, it's clearer that God is the one who is at work.

God didn't choose Israel because it was bigger than the other peoples around. In our world, we could say God wouldn't have chosen Britain or the United States, who have fancied that they were God's chosen people. God would have chosen Ecuador or Cameroon. Israel was insignificant compared with the **Egyptians** or the **Canaanites**, let alone the **Assyrians** or the **Babylonians**. But God "got attached" to Israel. The word suggests falling for someone; Deuteronomy 21 will use it of a man's attraction for a woman. Consequently, God "gave himself" to Israel. This is the word chapter 6 used to describe Israel's relationship with God, the word often translated "love." Here it refers to God's attitude to Israel. It suggests love in a self-giving sense and an emotional sense. So why did God fall for Israel, love Israel? God only says what was *not* the reason. God never gives a positive reason. Maybe that hints at the mystery about love. What makes one person fall for another? It is often difficult to say. A person who is loved with enthusiasm may well be bemused by the fact. "What does she see in me that she should love me so much?"

122

What God makes clear is that you can never explain God's choice of a people or of individuals by their strengths, achievements, or potentials. The reasons come from inside God, and God is not telling. Maybe it's pure chance. Maybe God just tossed a coin.

For whatever reason, God "chose" Israel. The idea of God's choosing a people or choosing individuals can seem scandalous for more than one reason. Is it fair? No, fairness is not one of God's priorities. It's not fair that some people have more brains, beauty, or strength than other people or that some countries have more natural resources and a nicer climate. But being clever, strong, or beautiful isn't what makes you happy, nor is living in a nice climate (I know, because I live in a nice climate, and I meet many unhappy people here). God's concern is with what people do with their assets and their losses. Choosing a people or an individual may also seem scandalous insofar as it overrides human freedom. In a sense it does not do so; Israel has the opportunity to say "no" to God. But it's "Hobson's choice"; it seems like a free choice, but you have no real alternative. When the professor says, "Write this paper," you can choose whether to do so, but you know that if you decide not to bother, you fail the course.

The nearest God gets to explaining this love for Israel is that it fulfills a commitment God made long ago to Israel's ancestors. That only pushes the question one stage back; why did God choose Abraham and Sarah, a couple who couldn't have children, as the people to turn into a numerous nation? This shows that what happens does reflect God's power and not mere human potential. It also draws attention to Deuteronomy's wider context, in which God's choice of Israel was based on God's desire to bless the world by means of Israel. The technical term for this choice of Israel is "election," and election is designed to be inclusive, not exclusive. God really chooses one people and not another, but does so not in order to exclude the others but in order to include them. But Deuteronomy's own focus is on God's inexplicable love for Israel.

Election makes Israel a people holy to God. That doesn't mean they are now holy in the sense that they live righteous and committed lives (as Deuteronomy 9 will go on to remind them). When the Old Testament talks about holiness, it is referring to people's status or position, not their ethics or spirituality. God is the holy one, the one who is different from human beings—supernatural, transcendent, eternal. Israel becomes holy because God takes hold of this people and says, "They are mine; I claim them; henceforth they are in a different position from other peoples. They are not free; they belong to me in a special sense." They are special in the sense that God asserts these distinctive rights over them. As I write, I can look over my patio. It has a gate that opens onto the common area of our condo. Anyone can go there. But the patio is mine. Other people can come onto it only if I invite them. It is my special possession. That is the relationship with Israel that God asserts.

While God's election is not based on anything Israel has done, it needs to issue in things that Israel does. God's love is unconditional in the sense that it is not conditioned by anything we have done, but it makes absolute demands. While noting that Israel had not earned its special relationship with God through what it did, Deuteronomy adds that this relationship will work only if Israel responds to God's commitment with a commitment of its own.

DEUTERONOMY 7:16–9:3

Little by Little

[16]"You are to devour all the peoples Yahweh your God is giving over to you. Your eye will not pity them. You will not serve their gods, because it will be a snare to you. [17]When you say to yourself, 'These nations are more numerous than me—how will I be able to dispossess them?' [18]you will not be afraid of them. You are resolutely to keep in mind what Yahweh your God did to Pharaoh and all the Egyptians, [19]the great tests that your eyes saw, the signs and portents, the strong hand and extended arm by which Yahweh your God brought you out. Yahweh your God will do that to all the peoples of whom you are afraid. [20]Yahweh your God will also send off hornets against them until those who survive and are hiding from you perish. [21]You will not be in dread of them, because Yahweh your God is in your midst, a great and awesome God. [22]Yahweh your God will

clear away those nations from before you little by little. You will not be able to finish them off quickly, so that the animals of the wild do not multiply against you. ²³But Yahweh your God will give them over before you and throw them into a great confusion until their annihilation. ²⁴He will give their kings into your power and you will eliminate their name from under the heavens. No one will stand up before you until you have annihilated them. ²⁵The statues of their gods you are to burn with fire. You will not desire the silver and gold on them and take it for yourself, so that you do not ensnare yourself by it, because that would be an offense to Yahweh your God. ²⁶You will not bring something offensive into your house, or like it you will become something to be devoted. You will treat it as totally detestable, totally offensive, because it is something to be devoted."

[Chapter 8 underlines the exhortation to obedience and mindfulness and recalls how God led, tested, and provided for Israel through the journey from Egypt to Canaan.]

⁹:¹"Listen, Israel. You are now crossing over the Jordan to go and dispossess nations greater and stronger than you: great cities with walls to the heavens, ²a great and tall people, the Anakites whom you yourselves know and of whom you have heard it said, 'Who can stand up before the descendants of Anak?' ³You need to acknowledge now that Yahweh your God—he is crossing before you, a devouring fire. He is the one who will destroy them, the one who will put them down before you, and you will dispossess them and make them perish quickly, as Yahweh said to you."

In an agonized e-mail I received from a friend, she described herself as constantly frustrated by the fact that she is not as mature as she thinks she should be. "Why do I go back to fighting the same old battles in my spiritual life instead of newer ones? Why, after dying a million deaths to something, am I still not dead and done with it?" She had imagined that as a growing Christian, she would be done with a certain thing, such as anger or pride, and would face other, different types of things to fight and overcome. "I know that God's strength is manifest in my weaknesses," she continued, "that he is the mighty savior, my strong deliverer, one who works out my sanctification now and here, that I walk in daily fellowship with him, and that I become more than an overcomer by trusting Jesus to give me the victory." Her question was, Why was there such a gap between what she knew and what she experienced, even after walking this path for thirty years. "In my earlier years my hope had been that things were going to get better as I grew older," she said, "but at almost fifty, things have not gotten that much 'better.'"

The Israelites would often have felt like that about their position in **Canaan**. If the beginning of this chapter is bewildering for one reason, its last verses are bewildering for another, though putting them together helps make sense of both. There has been all that talk about God's expelling the Canaanites from the country and giving it to Israel, but in reality the Canaanites were alive and well for centuries after Moses' day. How were the Israelites to make sense of it? The close of chapter 7 offers one answer, picking up a declaration God already made at Sinai (Exodus 23:29–30). Making the Canaanites disappear only gradually is a strange kind of mercy. (We don't know what Deuteronomy means by the "hornet," but again it makes clear that the people's conquest of the country isn't simply a matter of their doing battle.)

There is then some tension between that mercy and the warnings about the temptation of the Canaanites' forms of worship. If the Israelites fall into the trap of worshiping this way, they will be like a bird caught in a net. Suppose God simply removed all our difficulties and temptations in one go. It would solve the problem. It would be like being back in the garden of Eden. Yet actually there were challenges to face in that garden: a world to subdue and a serpent to resist. People don't grow to maturity by sitting on the beach at Malibu. I know; I do it. We grow through facing things, wrestling with things. The Canaanites in the country that is destined to be Israel's fulfill a function like the serpent in the garden. They tempt and test Israel. Israel has to avoid falling into the trap, but that way, it can grow.

The chapter closes with an even more solemn warning. Whereas it opened by speaking of Israel's "devoting" the Canaanites, it closes by speaking of Israel itself becoming "something to be devoted." That indeed happened, when God let Jerusalem be destroyed and its people be taken into **exile** (Isaiah 43:28). There is a sense in which God is fair. While God feels free to bless some people more than others, because it will fit God's purpose, God does not feel bound to exempt from punishment the people who are thus blessed if they fail to respond to that blessing. Israel can be the agent of "devoting" people but also the victim of it.

One key to avoiding this fate is mindfulness, a favorite theme in Deuteronomy. First, Israel needs to be mindful of what God did in rescuing the people from **Egypt**: the tests God brought to Pharaoh by means of the signs and portents that came to the country (so don't fail the test, like Pharaoh!) and the power God showed in thus bringing Israel out of Egypt. When you fear God cannot bring you to your destiny, think about what God did in initiating you on the journey.

Then (chapter 8 says), be mindful of how God led you through the wilderness from Egypt to Canaan. God kept testing you, letting you get hungry, then feeding you, to show you that people do not live on bread alone (that is, in the context, on whether they can produce their own bread) but on whether God speaks the word that issues in bread to eat. Jesus picks up that affirmation when he is tested in the wilderness, as he picks up Deuteronomy 6:13 and 16 about revering and serving God and not testing God. All Jesus' responses to the tempter come from these chapters describing attitudes Israel is to have to God. God relates to Israel like a father disciplining his son or a trainer disciplining an athlete to bring the best out of him or her.

Third (chapter 8 goes on), continue being mindful of God's provision when you are enjoying the promised land and your stomachs are full. You may again be tempted to congratulate yourself on your houses, herds, flocks, and wealth, as if you manufactured it, and forget the expectations of the one who gave you the country. To put it another way, your life needs to be characterized by praise. The Hebrew word for praise in Deuteronomy 8 is the same as the word for bless in Deuteronomy 7. God blesses Israel with flocks, herds, and produce; Israel blesses/praises God in return. God can test Israel by withdrawing the blessing to see if Israel serves God merely for what it gets out of it; but giving Israel these blessings also tests Israel.

After the warning about God's taking time in dealing with the Canaanites, it is bewildering to find God again promising to do so quickly. This again reminds us not to take Moses too literally. The promise about speed is a promise assuring people of what God *can* do. Nothing and nobody can prevent God's will being fulfilled. The Canaanites will disappear as quickly as God decides they will. It's nice that the Hebrew verb for "put down" is very similar to the word *Canaan*. When God puts them down, they will become themselves. Further, for most Israelites reading Deuteronomy, the problem was not the Canaanites (who were long gone), but the **Assyrians**, **Babylonians**, or **Persians**; God can also dispose of them.

DEUTERONOMY 9:4–10:22

You Don't Deserve It

[4]"When Yahweh your God has expelled them from before you, you are not to say to yourself, 'It is because of my faithfulness that Yahweh brought me in to take possession of this country.' It is because of the faithlessness of these nations that Yahweh is dispossessing them from before you. [5]It is not because of your faithfulness and the uprightness of your mind that you are entering to take possession of their country. It is because of the faithlessness of these nations that Yahweh your God is dispossessing them from before you, and so as to establish the promise Yahweh made to your ancestors Abraham, Isaac, and Jacob. [6]You are to acknowledge that it is not because of your faithfulness that Yahweh your God is giving you this good land to take possession of, because you are a stiff-necked people. [7]Be mindful, do not put out of mind how you infuriated Yahweh your God in the wilderness. From the day you left Egypt until you came to this place you have been rebellious towards Yahweh."

[Moses goes on to tell the story of those forty years from this angle but focuses on the rebellion at Sinai itself.]

[10:12]"Now, Israel, what is Yahweh your God asking of you except that you revere Yahweh your God by walking in all his ways, give yourselves to him, and serve Yahweh your God with all your mind and with all your heart [13]by keeping Yahweh's commands and his rules that I am requiring of you today for your good? [14]There: to Yahweh your God belong the heavens, the highest heavens, the earth and everything in it. [15]Yet Yahweh got attached to your ancestors, giving himself to them and choosing their offspring after them, you, from all the peoples, this very day. [16]Circumcise the foreskin of your mind. You will not stiffen your neck any more. [17]Because Yahweh your God— he is God of gods, Lord of lords, the God great, mighty, and awesome, who does not show partiality or take a bribe. [18]He gives judgment for orphan and widow and gives himself to the alien by providing him with food and clothes. [19]So you are to give yourselves to the alien, because you were aliens in Egypt. [20]Yahweh your God: you are to revere him, serve him, hold fast to him, and swear by his name. [21]He will be your praise. He will be your God who did for you these great, awesome things that your eyes saw. [22]As seventy people your ancestors went down to Egypt, but now Yahweh your God has made you like the stars in the heavens in number."

I spotted an advertisement for a "You Deserve It!" event, "a quality day for women to relax, have fun, learn some new things, and spend time with other wonderful women." The last phrase is a giveaway. In inviting everyone to see themselves as wonderful, it presupposes that they probably do not always feel like that about themselves and might like to come to a day that will make them feel thus. Then I came across a travel agency called "You Deserve It"—you deserve that vacation, and I discovered a motivational speaker who markets a DVD with the secrets to a happy life called *You Deserve It!* The use of the phrase reminded me of McDonald's encouragement to "take a break—you deserve it!" The phrase "you deserve it" makes me uneasy. What are we doing to one another or what is life doing to us that we need that encouragement?

God took the opposite stance to Israel. Perhaps they thought they had deserved God's attachment to them. Not so much, says Moses. Under David and Solomon they might have been proud of being a powerful nation. When reduced to a little community no larger than a county or two, or in the **exil**e, they might have inferred that they deserved it, and they would not exactly be wrong. But God did not relate to them on the basis of merit. It was not their **faithfulness** that was key to God's giving them the land but the previous occupants' faithlessness. For *faithfulness* and *faithlessness* translations often have *righteous-ness* and *wickedness*, but Deuteronomy's words are more specific; they suggest doing the right thing by God or other people, or failing to do so. As Moses notes through much of these two chapters, Israel's story at Sinai and subsequently has not exactly been a model of faithfulness. To put it another way, they are stiff-necked. A farmer trying to get his ox to go in the right direction when they are plowing uses a goad to direct him, like a horse rider using spurs and reins, but sometimes the ox will not turn his head and go in the direction the farmer needs. He is stiff-necked. Israel's stiff-neckedness is a fourth reality for Israel to "be mindful" of, adding to the three we considered in connection with Deuteronomy 7:16–9:3.

Moses goes on to note that Israel has been more a model of faithlessness. The Hebrew word is not related to the word for faithfulness in the way *faithfulness* and *faithlessness* are related, but in substance it does denote the opposite of faithfulness. It speaks of the way people are unrighteous in their relationships with one another and with God, the way they do wrong by one another. We have noted one horrific way the **Canaanites** were faithless, their practice of sacrificing children to their gods (Deuteronomy 12:31 will refer to that). The Prophets will also attack Israel for its faithlessness, and specifically for following this practice. The Canaanites had no special divine revelation forbidding a practice such as sacrificing children, but the Old Testament assumes you don't need a special revelation to know such acts are wrong. We are hardwired to know the basics about right and wrong.

The Canaanites' faithlessness gives God reason to throw them out of the country and God's promises to Israel's ancestors gives God another reason, but there is something paradoxical about God's making those promises. God possesses everything in all the heavens, even the highest and farthest heavens (we know much more about how impressive a fact that is). God also possesses everything on earth (we know more about how impressive that is, too). Yet God got attached to Israel's ancestors; Moses again uses that word for an emotional or romantic attachment. There's no explanation for this, but it happened. It led God to make those promises, and God's own faithfulness compels fulfillment of them.

Israel did not deserve any of this, but God does deserve a response. One way of describing the appropriate response is to speak of revering God and giving themselves to God. Concerning the words used here, often translated "fear" and "love," see the comments on 6:1–25. Whereas there is a kind of fear that love drives out (1 John 4:18), there is another kind that is quite compatible with love. To revere God and to give oneself to God are entirely compatible.

Another way to describe the appropriate response is to talk (somewhat bizarrely) about circumcising your mind. Circumcision involves cutting off an unnecessary elongation; it symbolizes the disciplining of a man's sexuality. Circumcising the mind suggests an analogous disciplining of our thinking and decision making, a broader disciplining. Moses gives a concrete example. It is natural to want to look after ourselves. Follow God's example instead, Moses says. Look after the vulnerable people in your community, the widows, the orphans, and in particular the aliens. You know what it is like to be aliens; you have heard your parents talk about it. You ought to sympathize with aliens. You know God does so, because God acted to rescue you from that position. Circumcise your minds so that you act the same. Give yourself to them as you give yourself to God. If you become the "giving oneself" kind of person, you will be like that in both directions. And hold fast, cling or cleave, to God: the word suggests an appropriate response to God's "getting attached" to them because it also denotes the way a man clings or cleaves to a woman.

DEUTERONOMY 11:1–32

It Never Rains in Southern California

[1]"So give yourselves to Yahweh your God and keep his charge, his rules, his decisions, and his commands always. [2]Recognize today that it was not your children, who did not know or see the discipline of Yahweh your God, his greatness, his strong hand and his extended arm, [3]the signs and the deeds he did.

[*Verses 3b–6 summarize the story from Egypt to where the people now are.*]

131

⁷But it was your eyes that saw all the great deeds Yahweh did. ⁸So you are to keep all the commands that I am giving you today, so you may be strong and may enter to take possession of the country that you are crossing over to take possession of, ⁹and so you may live long on the soil Yahweh promised to your ancestors to give them and their offspring, a country flowing with milk and sweetness. ¹⁰Because the country you are entering to take possession of is not like Egypt, which you left, where you would sow your seed and water it by foot, like a vegetable garden. ¹¹The country you are crossing over to take possession of is one with mountains and valleys, that drinks water from the heavens' rain, ¹²a country Yahweh your God looks after. The eyes of Yahweh your God are on it continually from the year's beginning to the year's end."

[Verses 13–25 urge the importance of obedience to Yahweh if this is to work out.]

²⁶"Look, I am putting before you today blessing and belittling: ²⁷blessing because you obey the commands of Yahweh your God that I am giving you today, ²⁸and belittling if you do not obey the commands of Yahweh your God but turn aside from the way that I am commanding you today, to go after other gods that you have not acknowledged. ²⁹When Yahweh your God brings you into the country that you are entering to take possession of, you are to put the blessing on Mount Gerizim and the belittling on Mount Ebal. ³⁰There they are, the other side of the Jordan, beyond the westward road in the country of the Canaanites who live in the steppe near Gilgal, by the oaks at Moreh. ³¹Because you are going to cross the Jordan to enter to take possession of the country that Yahweh your God is giving you to take possession of. You will dwell in it. ³²You are to take care to keep all the rules and decisions that I am putting before you today."

"It never rains in southern California," the song says, though it goes on to comment that they don't warn you how it pours. It's raining this morning. It is several months since it rained, and that is no problem to me as a British person who has seen plenty of rain, but I know we need rain. We are in the midst of a long-term drought. We are banned from irrigating our gardens most days of the week, and we are urged to take short showers, which are trivial deprivations, but they herald a bigger problem.

The governor is threatening to veto seven hundred bills unless the legislature agrees on a deal to repair the state's water ecosystem and increase water conservation. This morning I also received an e-mail from friends in the Philippines who have been on the receiving end of a typhoon (actually our rains are apparently related to those rains the other side of the Pacific) that has caused serious flooding in different parts of the country. It seems quite likely that both excess of rain in some places and shortage of rain elsewhere result from humanly induced climate change. If so, we are experiencing the consequences of our own wrong actions in the way we have treated the world.

The Old Testament assumes a link between the way Israel lives and the way its life works out. Elsewhere it can speak of the "natural" link between our actions and their positive or negative consequences; here it emphasizes the way God is involved in this process. People listening to Deuteronomy being read know they sometimes do experience drought and failure of the harvest, and they have listened to prophets telling them this is not mere chance; God withholds the rain to try to bring them to their senses. They also know that there is no one-to-one correspondence between faithfulness and blessing, or between faithlessness and trouble. Sometimes a drought is just a drought; the rain falls and the sun shines on the faithful and the faithless. But when drought comes, it is always worth asking whether it results from human action.

The importance of rain makes it a fitting symbol of blessing. Blessing and belittling refer both to words and to experiences. God speaks words that promise and commission blessing for people and also speaks words that warn them of trouble or bring trouble about. "Belittling" suggests cutting them down to size in words and thus in reality. When Abraham arrived in **Canaan**, God appeared to him by the oak at Moreh near the city of Shechem (modern Nablus) in the center of the country and for the first time promised to give him this country (Genesis 12:6–7). When the Israelites enter the land, they will go straight to Shechem as they symbolically enter into possession of the country in fulfillment of that promise. The city stands between two mountains, which Israel is to turn into places symbolizing the alternatives standing before it. Blessing suggests fertility.

Belittling suggests the opposite, being cut down to much less than you are and hope to be. Israel chooses its destiny. In setting Abraham on his journey to Shechem, God promised that he would be blessed but also that anyone who tried to belittle him would be belittled. Israel is again reminded that the same principles apply to it as apply to other peoples. It does not get away with things just because it is God's special people.

Rain can become a sign because of the geography of Canaan. In **Egypt**, it doesn't matter whether it rains. The Nile is people's water source, and the Nile keeps flowing. The Egyptians looked down on a country like Canaan that had to make do with a kind of substitute for the Nile in the form of rain. Deuteronomy turns this argument on its head. In Egypt you have to put in effort to irrigate the land (the reference to feet maybe denotes having to walk with buckets of water). In Canaan the rain falls more conveniently onto the land itself. Deuteronomy again speaks to its audience as if it personally experienced life in Egypt and experienced God's rescue, even though the generation Moses is notionally speaking to was not alive then, and neither was Deuteronomy's later audience. But their parents or earlier ancestors were there, and they have told the later generation about it, so it is as if they were there themselves, and they must live as if they had been.

DEUTERONOMY 12:1–32

On Not Following Your Instincts

[1]"These are the rules and decisions you should take care to keep in the country Yahweh the God of your ancestors has given you to take possession of, as long as you live on the land. [2]You are totally to wipe out all the places where the nations you are going to dispossess have served their gods, on high mountains and hills and under any flourishing tree. [3]You are to tear down their altars, break up their columns, burn their pillars in fire, cut down the statues of their gods, and wipe out their name from that place. [4]You will not serve Yahweh your God in this way, [5]but you are to have recourse to the place Yahweh your God chooses among all your clans to put his name, as his dwelling, and to go there. [6]You are to bring there your whole offer-

ings and sacrifices, your tithes and the offering of your hands, your vows and voluntary offerings, and the firstlings of your cattle and flock. [7]You are to eat there before Yahweh your God and rejoice in all the undertaking of your hand (you and your households) in which Yahweh your God has blessed you."

[Verses 8–23 add that people may slaughter animals for eating without bringing them to the sanctuary, as long as they do not treat this as a sacrificial meal and as long as they drain the blood out of them.]

Tomorrow morning I shall go to seminary chapel. Except that it isn't a chapel. It's an auditorium. On other occasions, I have lectured there, sung the blues in a concert there, listened to jazz concerts there, and taken part in faculty meetings there. We do sometimes have services in a big nineteenth-century church on the edge of the campus, but mainly we do so when we need a building that holds many hundreds of people. It feels churchy, which is fine by me but is alien to many students. On other days of the week, there are other meetings for worship and prayer that follow the patterns of different denominations and traditions, and there is no seminary control over them. In the past, at least, there have been happenings there that people from other traditions would disapprove of (for instance, things that were a bit too Pentecostal or a bit too Catholic). There are advantages and disadvantages in having a special building, as well as advantages and disadvantages in leaving people free to worship in the way they feel led.

The instincts of Israelites and **Canaanites** were different from ours, and they were more like each other's than ours, but they raised issues that overlap with ours. In connection with Numbers 33:52 we noted the way the Old Testament talks about the Canaanites' "worship places," literally their "high places," and about the way the Israelites were supposed to "demolish" them. The Old Testament never said the Israelites did so, and if they did, they evidently then rebuilt them, because it refers frequently to their worshiping at these places. It does not invariably express disapproval of this practice. If the "high place" was at the top of the hill where a city or village was located, it would continue to be the natural place for worship, like Christian churches built at the height of a village, sometimes on pre-Christian worship sites. Here, indeed, Deuteronomy refers to worship sites on mountains and hills and also to worship under flourishing trees, which were perhaps symbols of fertility. Evidently worship was an open air activity. It takes place out in the world, like baptism in the New Testament, not as something separated from the world.

Genesis relates how Israel's ancestors also worshiped near well-known and flourishing trees; indeed, Deuteronomy 11 referred to "the oaks at Moreh." With the high places and such holy trees, everything would depend on whether the pagan site was properly "converted." That would involve destroying the Canaanites' aids to worship. In many cases this would be necessary because something about them was incompatible with the **Torah**. That would be true of having statues of a divinity, on which Deuteronomy 4 has spoken at length. It would probably be true of the "pillars," since the Hebrew word is suspiciously similar to the name of a goddess, Asherah, whom Israelites sometimes worshiped as **Yahweh**'s consort. The "columns," too, were probably stylized images. On the other hand, many Canaanite **altar**s, like other aspects of Canaanite worship, were not so different from ones the Torah approves, so destroying them more reflects the conviction that this is a necessary aspect of "wiping out the name" of the Canaanite gods. When you worship, you call on God's name—on Yahweh, or on Jesus. If you eliminate the name, you eliminate the worship.

Deuteronomy emphasizes the importance of worshiping at a site God chooses. The importance of God's choice (the theological term is *election*) runs through Deuteronomy. Our natural human instinct is to worship according to our natural human instinct, which means worshiping in light of the culture to which we belong. Deuteronomy is aware that following this instinct results in assimilation to the culture. The real truth about God and thus the real nature of worship get lost. It knows people have to keep going back to the special revelation they have been given in the way God has acted, and to keep checking their worship by that revelation. Exodus and Leviticus emphasize in detail how the sanctuary and its worship must follow God's prescription; Deuteronomy puts the emphasis on the place where people worship.

Deuteronomy does not make explicit that there can be only one such site, though it likely assumes this. In practice, Israel always had one central sanctuary, the place where the moveable dwelling with the **covenant** chest was. It was located in various places for the first two or three centuries, then David moved it to Jerusalem. The theoretical advantage of having a central sanctuary is that priests and prophets who know what the Torah says can make sure that its worship sticks by the Torah. On the other hand, priests and prophets were often not inclined to stick by the Torah, so the worship of the central sanctuary became something detestable and offensive. Further, confining worship to one sanctuary that was days or weeks away from where most people lived would cut people off from worship except for the one or two times a year they might make pilgrimage there. So local worship places were a practical necessity, and having a number of places would not be incompatible with the requirement that people follow Yahweh's choice.

Deuteronomy perhaps assumes that while the location might change, the central sanctuary would always be the sole sanctuary, the only place where sacrifices could be offered. Deuteronomy 12:15–25 then has a solution for one aspect of this difficulty. For Western people, eating meat is a regular activity, and we do not think of it as involving God except in the sense that we may say grace before a meal. In Israel (as in many other traditional cultures), eating meat is a much more special event, something you associate with a party, and you invite God to this party—or rather, God invites you to bring your party to God's house. In other words, the party is also a sacrifice. You eat much of the animal you bring, but you also give some to God; God joins in the party.

For most of the Israelite clans the dynamics of this practice cannot work if the only place you can party is the one central sanctuary, so it allows people to party in their own villages as long as they do not turn the meal into a sacrifice. The downside is that people lose the reality of combining partying with worshiping. The upside is that it removes the necessity to go to the local high place for the party, which brings the possibility of sacrificing in a way that reflects Canaanite assumptions about the kind of person God is and the kind of worship appropriate to God. The one condition the villagers have to accept is the basic kosher rule that you must let an animal's blood pour out before roasting it. You mustn't consume the blood. Blood is a sign of life; when we lose blood, we die. In letting the blood pour out, you are recognizing that this was a creature with God's life in it, and you are respecting that fact.

Permitting the slaughter and eating of animals where people live applies only to what would otherwise be fellowship sacrifices, which God and the people share. Other sacrifices and offerings have to come to the site God chooses.

DEUTERONOMY 13:1–18

False Prophets

[1]"If a prophet or someone who has a dream arises in your midst, and gives you a sign or portent [2](and the sign or portent of which he told you comes about), saying, 'Let's follow other gods (which you have not acknowledged) and serve them': [3]you will not listen to the words of this prophet or dreamer, because Yahweh your God is testing you so as to know whether you do give yourselves to Yahweh your God with all your mind and heart. [4]Yahweh your God is the one you will follow and he is the one you will revere. His commands you will keep and to his voice you will listen. He is the one you will serve and to him you will hold fast. [5]That prophet or dreamer: he is to be put to death, because he spoke of turning against Yahweh your God (who brought you out of Egypt and redeemed you from a household of serfs) to push you off the way Yahweh your God commanded you to follow. So you will consume away the evil from your midst.

[6]"If your brother, your mother's son, or your son or daughter, or the wife you hold in your arms or your closest friend entices you secretly, saying, 'Let's go and serve other gods' (which you yourself and your ancestors have not acknowledged, [7]from the gods of the peoples that are around you, near to you or far away from you, from one end of the country to the other end), [8]you will not agree with them or listen to them. Your eye will not pity them. You will not spare them or shield them [9]but simply slay them. Your own hand will be the first in putting them to death; the hand of the entire people will be after. [10]Stone them

to death, because they sought to push you away from Yahweh your God who brought you out of Egypt, out of a household of serfs. [11]Thus all Israel will hear and be afraid and will not again do such an evil thing in your midst."

[Verses 12–18 apply the same principle to a whole city that has yielded to such enticement.]

I received an e-mail this morning from a friend troubled by the evil in the world, as we often are, and wondering why God bothered to create it "if he is all-knowing and so on, and knew that there would be evil, genocide, starvation, dictatorships, etc. Surely it would be better that the world was never created than have all the suffering we see around us. It seems a cynical act." She had talked to a pastor about this who, she said, "reckons God didn't know that this would happen, but I can't go along with that." In my reply I said some of the things I usually say: I suspect God created the world because creating is simply built into existing, for God as for us; I think the "problem" of how much goodness and beauty there is in the world is at least as big as the problem of evil; and for Israel and for Christians, God's activity in the world in events such as the exodus and the coming of Christ is a large part of what makes it inevitable that we keep believing in God's goodness. But it was interesting that the pastor had wondered whether God knew how wrong things would go, and that my friend "couldn't go along with" the idea that God didn't know.

Deuteronomy here assumes God doesn't know whether Israel will be faithful in the way Moses has been urging Israel, yet Deuteronomy 31 will later speak of God's knowing Israel will not be faithful. Which is the real truth? People sometimes say the Old Testament is being anthropomorphic when it speaks of God's testing people in order to discover something. The same idea arose in a different context in connection with Numbers 28. The Old Testament portrays God as "human-shaped"—as like a human being. The real truth then lies in the Deuteronomy 31 angle. It is of course right that the Bible portrays God as human-shaped; that is the other side of the coin to our being made in God's image. Because we are made in the image of God, who is a person, we love, we think, we plan, we act, we get angry, we rejoice, we grieve. If we say Deuteronomy is being anthropomorphic about God's not knowing, what would be the basis for rejecting its anthropomorphic picture of God as loving, thinking, planning, and doing those other acts?

Both Deuteronomy's angles are telling us something. I can say that I know a certain student will get an A (or will fail), but it doesn't mean I abandon the test that proves this. As a result of the test, I "know" in a new sense. Deuteronomy presupposes that God lives with Israel in that kind of relationship. God knows Israel will be unfaithful (indeed, in light of the story so far you don't need divine insight to work this out), but until it happens, the knowledge is theoretical. When it happens, that gives God a different kind of knowledge. Thus God sets the test in order to find out, giving Israel opportunity to do what God expects—or not to do so.

Sometimes God takes a direct initiative when setting a test, as happened with Abraham in Genesis 22. Sometimes God works via human agents (or via a snake, as in Genesis 3). In Deuteronomy 13, prophets and dreamers are means of God's testing the people without their realizing what they are doing. They are not being manipulated by God into doing something they do not wish to do, but God is making use of what they do wish to do. When we think of "prophets" we usually think of good guys such as Elijah and Jeremiah, but most prophets the Old Testament mentions are bad guys, people who just support the establishment or offer people reassuring messages and avoid delivering bad news, or act like the prophets Deuteronomy 13 describes. The time just before Jeremiah and the time during which Jeremiah lived is when this issue is most pressing for Israel, and Deuteronomy likely has this context in mind.

Why would prophets suggest praying to other gods? One hint lies in the reference to dreamers. Dreams can be a means of discovering the future. Like anyone else, Israelites will want to know what the future holds in order to take appropriate action, and if the future is threatening, to evade the threat. Other Middle Eastern peoples had ways of doing this; prophets and dreamers would be directing people toward the resources of other people's religions to this end.

Deuteronomy presupposes that bad guys can do miracles, as good guys can; Jesus also assumes this (Matthew 7:22–23). Jesus says such people will get excluded from the kingdom of heaven; Deuteronomy says they are to be executed. Like other rules about capital punishment, Israel does not seem to have taken this literally. Its point is more to underline how serious an offense it is. Encouraging people to turn from **Yahweh** and follow other gods is an evil that must be removed from the people's midst. The point is underscored by the requirement concerning family members who behave like those prophets. Again, as far as we know Israel did not take this literally, any more than Jesus' requirement about cutting off your hand was usually taken literally by his followers. Both statements are to be taken absolutely seriously, though not literally. (If Israel had literally obeyed the last part of the chapter about "devoting" cities that followed other gods, there would be no cities left in Israel!) The point is underscored further by the method of execution. Killing someone by throwing rocks is not aseptic and distanced from the community. It involves the whole community. Just to imagine starting the process of stoning a family member should be enough to make anyone think twice about turning to another god.

DEUTERONOMY 14:1–29

You Are What You Eat

[1]"You are the children of Yahweh your God. You will not cut yourselves or make a bald space between your eyes for a dead person, [2]because you are a people holy to Yahweh your God. Yahweh chose you to be his, a special people, from all the peoples on the face of the ground.
[3]"You are not to eat anything offensive. [4]These are the animals you may eat: ox, sheep, goat, [5]deer, gazelle, roebuck, wild goat, ibex, antelope, mountain sheep, [6]any animal that has a divided hoof (has a cleft in its hoofs) and brings up its cud: you may eat it. [7]On the other hand, these you will not eat: ones that bring up their cud or have a divided hoof (have a cleft in their hoof): camel, hare, and rock badger, because they bring up their cud

but do not have a divided hoof—they are taboo for you; [8]pig, because it has a divided hoof but does not bring up its cud—it is taboo for you. You are not to eat their flesh or touch their carcasses."

[Verses 9–21 lay down similar rules about sea creatures (people may eat only ones that have both fins and scales), birds (people may not eat birds such as eagle, vulture, ostrich, and bat), certain other winged creatures, and anything that has died a natural death. In addition, they may not cook a kid goat in its mother's milk.]

[22]"Each year you are to tithe carefully all the yield from your seed, which your fields produce. [23]Before Yahweh your God at the place Yahweh chooses to have his name dwell there, you are to eat the tithe of your grain, wine, and oil, and the firstlings of your cattle and sheep, so you may learn to revere Yahweh your God always. [24]If the journey is too great for you, because you cannot carry it (if the place where Yahweh chooses to put his name is too far for you because Yahweh blesses you), [25]you may turn it into silver, tie up the silver in your hand, go to the place Yahweh your God chooses, [26]and turn the silver into anything your appetite wishes: cattle, sheep, wine, liquor, anything your appetite desires. You will eat there before Yahweh your God and rejoice, you and your household. [27]And do not neglect the Levite in your settlement, because he has no allocation of his own with you. [28]At the end of three years you will bring out the entire tithe of your yield that year, but leave it in your settlement. [29]The Levite, who has no allocation of his own with you, and the alien, orphan, and widow in your settlement, will come and eat their fill, so Yahweh your God may bless you in all the work of your hand that you undertake."

Three nights ago I got very sick just for a little while after eating out; what I ate was salad, halibut, rice, and vegetables. I should doubtless have complained to the restaurant or reported the matter to the city, but I was too busy being ill to manage that (and anyway, it might have been caused by the flu shot I had that morning). Last night at a rehearsal dinner in connection with a wedding tomorrow I ate a magnificent pork barbecue. I had three helpings and some strawberry shortcake and cream, and drank several glasses of iced tea, and didn't sleep too well, though I nevertheless invited the groom to get married once a month so we could repeat the event. It was as well that the company was Christian; a Jew would not have been able to take part (though there were also some veggie burgers). Why?

Deuteronomy's rules about what Israelites may or may not eat are more or less the same as the ones in Leviticus 11; two versions of the rules as they were taught in different contexts in Israel are brought together in the **Torah**. Although you can get sick through eating pork, most people get sick through eating other things (like me, if it was the food that did it). Staying healthy isn't the main point about these rules, though it may be one point about them. Economics may be another; keeping pigs doesn't make sense in the mountain country that forms Israel's heartland. Staying distinctive from the religion and life of Israel's neighbors will be another point about them; the **Canaanites** did eat pork. God's original strategy for reaching out to the world via Israel involved keeping Israel distinctive. Eventually God changed this strategy and told Jews who had come to believe in Jesus to give up being different in this way in order to be able more easily to mix with Gentiles and tell them about Jesus (see Acts 10).

Deuteronomy does mention the principle of being different from the peoples around, but it does so in relation to the chapter's opening rules about cutting and shaving in connection with mourning. These were religious practices among the Canaanites, though it is a matter of guesswork what exactly they signified. Deuteronomy's specific rationale for the rules about food is that Israel should eat only creatures that belong to "proper" categories. Animals that have split hoofs or that chew the cud but don't have both characteristics are neither one thing nor the other. The same applies to sea creatures with fins or scales but not both.

The fuller explanation in Leviticus points more explicitly to the idea that such a commitment with regard to food is Israel's way of living with the orderliness of creation; in creating the world, God fitted things into categories, and by its practice Israel witnesses to this (though of course the creatures that don't fit into categories were also created by God). There is then

143

a link with the rule about not cooking a goat in its mother's milk. Cooking in milk would make the meat tasty, but a family would not have a huge number of goats, and it would quite likely be a baby goat's own mother's milk that a family used. There is something inhumane about the means of life thus being associated with the death of the mother's offspring. All this might make us think about the way we relate to the animals we eat; factory farming seems a contradiction of the idea that we try to fit into the way God created the world.

The rules about tithes and firstlings relate food to God in some other ways. They give expression to the fact that your food comes from God; you give some back to God in recognition of this fact. It helps you "revere" God as the great giver. You give some to God, but you also join in eating them. Eating in God's presence brings home the link between God and food. You cannot take your food for granted or let it be a part of your life that has nothing to do with God. While this eating is thus tied up with revering, it is also a celebration, a feast, an occasion of rejoicing; you eat whatever and as much as you like. Deuteronomy is full of rules but does not assume that these are a burden that makes life solemn; it uses the word "rejoice" as frequently as almost any book in the Old Testament.

A common grace before meals asks God to make us mindful of the needs of others. I always feel like suggesting that thinking about the people who don't have anything to eat will surely stop us from enjoying our meal. Deuteronomy's example avoids this problem because it assumes we invite the needy to eat with us. The people who don't possess land and cannot provide for themselves thus take part in the family's celebration.

As happened with the rule about sacrificing only at the central sanctuary, Deuteronomy tries to think through the practicalities of these rules. Would it be feasible to transport all that stuff there, given the magnitude of the way God will bless you with an abundant harvest? Okay, turn it into cash and then turn it back into food when you get there. What about the needs of the Levites, widows, and orphans for the rest of the year? Okay, one year in three let's give the tithes directly to them. Your giving is then bookended by blessing: because you are blessed, you give; because you give, you are blessed. We might wonder what

144

these people would eat during the other two years. Maybe the rule presupposes that families would not all count the years in the same way, so there would always be families for whom this was year three, and things would even out. Or maybe the practicalities of the rules are illusory. This is not the only example of a rule that would raise problems in its implementation. It reminds us once again that the "rules" are more like imaginative ideas than a code of laws. They indicate what is important and give people ideas about how to implement them. The people have to work out the practicalities.

DEUTERONOMY 15:1–18

Helping People Get Back on Their Feet

[1]"At the end of seven years you are to practice release. [2]This is the nature of the release: every creditor is to release what he lends to his neighbor. He is not to press his neighbor, his kin, for it, because Yahweh's release has been proclaimed. [3]You may press a foreigner, but what is yours from your kin you are to release. [4]Nevertheless there will not be needy among you, because Yahweh will really bless you in the land Yahweh your God is giving you as your own to take possession of, [5]if only you really listen to the voice of Yahweh your God, taking care to keep this entire command that I am requiring of you today. [6]Because Yahweh your God will have blessed you as he declared to you. You will lend to many nations but you yourselves will not borrow. You will rule over many nations but over you they will not rule.

[7]"If there is a needy person among you, one of your kin, in one of your settlements in the country Yahweh your God is giving you, you will not harden your attitude or close your hand against your kin who is needy. [8]Rather, you are to open your hand wide to him and freely lend sufficient for the lack he has. [9]Take care with regard to yourself that the worthless thought does not come into your mind, 'The seventh year, the release year, is drawing near,' so that the way you look at your needy kin becomes mean and you do not give anything to him. He may then cry to Yahweh against you, so it becomes an offense. [10]Give generously to him. Your attitude must not be mean when you give to him, [11]because the needy will not cease from the

country. Therefore I am commanding you, 'Open your hand wide to your weak and needy kin in your country.'

[12]"If someone from your kin, a Hebrew man or woman, sells himself to you, he may serve you for six years. In the seventh year you are to send him off from you as a free person. [13]When you send him off from you as a free person, you will not send him off empty-handed. [14]Supply him liberally from your flock, your threshing floor, and your winepress, that with which Yahweh has blessed you. [15]Bear in mind that you were a serf in Egypt and Yahweh your God redeemed you. Therefore I am commanding this thing today. [16]If he says to you, 'I will not go out from you,' because he has been giving himself to you and your household, because it is good for him with you, [17]you will take an awl and put it through his ear and through the door, and he will be your servant forever. You will also do this for your female servant. [18]When you send him off from you as a free person, it should not be hard in your eyes, because he has served you for six years for the equivalent of the wages of an employee. And Yahweh will bless you in all you do."

According to a legal record from July 6, 1773, James Best, a laborer, "doth voluntarily put himself Servant to Captain Stephen Jones Master of the Snow Sally" (a snow was a kind of sailing ship). Jones would take Best from London to Philadelphia, and Best would work there for three years for someone who bought Best; he would provide Best with food, drink, clothing, lodging and whatever else he needed for the three years. Then Best would be freed. Alternatively, if Best was in a position to pay fifteen pounds on his arrival in America, he could be freed then. A subsequent legal record in Philadelphia records how Best was duly "redeemed by" (that is, sold to) one David Rittenhouse in Philadelphia (presumably this was David Rittenhouse the famous astronomer and public servant), who paid Jones the fifteen pounds and took on the obligation to supply Best's needs in return for the three years' service. Best's story is in outline a typical one; maybe the majority of people who came from Europe in the seventeenth and eighteenth centuries came as indentured servants in this way. It would be nice to hope that Rittenhouse treated him well, though many such servants were ill-treated on the voyage and after their arrival in America.

Modern translations have Deuteronomy 15 speaking of "slaves," but this is misleading. The lifelong chattel slavery in which Britain and America cooperated after Best's day is largely a European phenomenon; it was unknown in the Middle East. The King James Bible more appropriately has "bondservants," something similar to the institution that was of key importance to giving people from Europe a new start in America. Deuteronomy presupposes a situation in which a family was unable to make ends meet because it could not grow enough to survive. It incorporates a promise that this situation need not arise, but it knows that people are free (for instance) to be inefficient or lazy as farmers and not just unlucky, and it also incorporates the realistic acknowledgment that there will always be needy people in the community. Either way, in the first instance it would be the responsibility of someone else in the village to lend them what they need for the next year. The loan thus need not have a seven-year term, but if the person could not pay it back by the seventh year, the loan would be cancelled. Lending in the **Torah** is thus not a way of making money but a way of helping needy people. You are not to begrudge a loan because the imminence of the seventh year increases the chances of your not getting it back.

One feature Deuteronomy typically adds is that its rules apply to women as well as men. It adds some incentives to you to do the right thing. You will find that doing the right thing in light of the way God has blessed you is the route to further blessing. Conversely, a person to whom you decline to be generous may then cry out to God about it, and your neglect will become a problem between you and God. You are to remember how you were serfs in Egypt and that God redeemed you (Deuteronomy thus speaks as if God were a boss buying a servant, like Rittenhouse); you are called to be godlike. You are to remember that the needy people are your kinfolk, your brothers and sisters. They are fellow members of Israel, and Israel is your family. So treat them the way you would treat members of your family in need, which is different from the way you treat other people. As Paul puts it, you do good especially to people who belong to the household of faith (Galatians 6:10). But the reference to foreigners may suggest something more like commercial loans rather than loans to someone in need, since a foreigner could not own land and therefore could not get into the position Deuteronomy is presupposing. This has been the Jewish understanding of the passage, which freed Jews to become financiers and businesspeople in Europe when the church did not allow lending at interest, and encouraged the development of the Western lending system. You could say we made the mistake of failing to distinguish like Deuteronomy between lending as a means of encouraging development and creativity and lending as a means of helping the needy, and our use of loans in relation to needy individuals and needy countries becomes a means of adding to their oppression.

Suppose you get into a real mess on the farm and a mere loan is not enough. In these circumstances you can then let members of your family and yourself become the servants of another farmer, who may be able to make a go of your farm as you could not. You thus no longer carry responsibility, and the other farmer is supposed to look after you. Once again this arrangement holds for a maximum of seven years, though it may work so well that you never wish to go back to "freedom" even if your boss provides you with the means of making a good fresh start. The incentive to your boss to take you on is that he gets better service from servants who are like members of the family, with the obligations that follow from this position and whom you simply have to provide with their keep, than he does from someone who just works eight hours a day, six days a week, and is then "outta here."

Like the rest of the Torah, Deuteronomy thus does not take for granted that the basis for work is that some people pay other people for their labor, one of the foundations of our Western system. It assumes that selling your labor is a rather odd thing to do. The natural basis for work is a family working together at a project that is the basis for their common livelihood, and even someone who wants to stay a servant works within the context of that system. The system has the potential to work much better than the system of work and employment (not to say unemployment and poverty) that we use in the West.

DEUTERONOMY 15:19–16:17

The Rhythm of Pilgrimage

[Deuteronomy 15:19–23 gives some rules about offering firstlings.]

[16:1]"Keep the month of Aviv and observe the Passover of Yahweh your God, because in Aviv Yahweh your God brought you out of Egypt, by night. [2]You will sacrifice as the Passover of Yahweh your God from the flock and the herd at the place Yahweh will choose to have his name dwell there. [3]You will not eat anything yeasted with it. For seven days you will eat flat bread with it, bread of affliction, because it was in haste that you came out of Egypt, so that you may be mindful of the day you came out of Egypt all the days of your life. [4]Yeast will not appear among you, in any of your territory, for seven days, and none of the meat you sacrifice on the evening of the first day will stay until morning. [5]You will not be able to sacrifice the Passover in one of your settlements that Yahweh your God is giving you, [6]but at the place Yahweh your God chooses to have his name dwell there you will sacrifice the Passover, in the evening, at sundown, the time you came out of Egypt. [7]You will cook and eat at the place Yahweh your God chooses, and turn round in the morning and go to your tents. [8]For six days you will eat flat bread and on the seventh day there will be an assembly for Yahweh your God; you will not do any work.

[9]"You will count seven weeks for yourselves; from when you begin [to put] the sickle to the standing grain you will begin to count the seven weeks. [10]You will observe the Weeks Festival for Yahweh your God as an appropriate voluntary offering from your hand, which you will give according as Yahweh your God blesses you. [11]You will rejoice before Yahweh your God, you, your son and your daughter, your male and female servant, the Levite in your settlement, and the alien, the orphan, and the widow in your midst, at the place Yahweh your God chooses to have his name dwell there. [12]Keep in mind that you were a serf in Egypt and take care to keep these rules.

[13]"The Shelters Festival you will keep for yourself for seven days when you have gathered in [the produce of] your threshing floor and your winepress. [14]You will rejoice at your festival, you, your son and daughter, your male and female servant, the

149

Levite, the alien, the orphan, and the widow in your settlement. [15]For seven days you will hold a festival for Yahweh your God at the place Yahweh chooses, because Yahweh your God will bless you in all your produce and all the work of your hands. You will be simply rejoicing."

[Verses 16–17 form a summary.]

Five or six miles from where I live is an Episcopal church whose leadership and congregation recently decided to withdraw from its identification with the Episcopal Church in the United States, while staying Anglican in a broader sense. It thus became a missionary parish under the oversight of a bishop in another part of the world, one of a number of parishes in Los Angeles that have taken this action. While the denomination's stance on same-sex marriage has been one factor in this development, these congregations have a broader conviction that the denomination plays fast and loose with Christian doctrine. If a congregation does believe that the church at the center has gone off the rails and that it can no longer associate with it, it is wise to submit itself to some other oversight rather than to assume it will be fine on its own. (I am not concerned to comment on the rights and wrongs of these congregations' action; I am still in the Episcopal Church myself.) In contrast, sometimes the center may stay on the rails, and its job is to take action if the church locally falls off them. The Episcopal bishops recently declined to ordain as bishop a priest who said he was a Buddhist as well as a Christian.

Deuteronomy wants Israel to stay on the rails, and this concern underlies its distinctive instructions concerning the three annual festivals, Passover and Flat Bread in the spring, Weeks or Pentecost in early summer, and Shelters or Tabernacles or Booths in the fall. It is the **Torah**'s fourth set of instructions about this (compare Exodus 23, Exodus 34, and Leviticus 23). The three festivals combine two themes. One is a celebration of the stages of the harvest, which is more explicit here in connection with Weeks and Shelters. The other is a celebration of the acts whereby God brought Israel into existence as a people, which is more explicit here in connection with Passover. The two themes are related. Bringing Israel out of **Egypt** had as its goal taking the people into the country where they will grow their crops. Growing their crops issued from God's bringing them out of Egypt and giving them land. Their everyday or every-year lives and the great acts whereby God delivered them and fulfilled promises to them were two aspects of God's activity.

This is the fourth time God has given the Israelites a set of instructions like this. Again the Torah is bringing together sets of rules God gave Israel at different points in its history, and/or in different social contexts, and/or through people with different backgrounds (for instance, Leviticus 23 reflects more the interests of priests, whereas Deuteronomy may reflect the priorities of the great prophets). One might compare the very different ways in which the church has worshiped in different centuries and in different parts of the world. Different situations suggested different ways of tweaking the rules, all of them working out the implications of what Moses would have said if he had been faced with the different contexts.

Elsewhere in the Torah, Passover and the Flat Bread festival come close together in time but are semi-independent because Passover is celebrated at home whereas Flat Bread is celebrated at a sanctuary. When there are many sanctuaries, there need be no tension between this, as our celebration of Christmas can involve both a family meal and a church service. But Deuteronomy expects Israel to destroy all these local sanctuaries and thus to celebrate both Passover and Flat Bread at the central sanctuary, and 2 Kings 23:21–23 refers to the celebration in King Josiah's day as the first of this kind in the entire period of the monarchy. This would be more feasible in his period because the community in his day only comprises **Judah**, and Judah is much reduced in size. Its size is more like that of a mere county in the United States or Britain. The assumption that Passover will be a big central festival will explain the provision for the sacrifice of cattle and not merely lambs (which would be quite enough for an extended family celebration).

The context in Josiah's story helps explicate the logic of centralizing the observance of Passover and other sacrifices. For decades before Josiah's day, worship in Jerusalem and in the local sanctuaries had been influenced by the way Baal was worshiped, and/or it explicitly involved the worship of Baal. In light of the discovery of a "**covenant** scroll" in the temple, Josiah made it his business to desecrate the local sanctuaries and thus attempt to stop worship there once and for all, and also to clean up the worship in the temple itself. The parallels between what he did and what Deuteronomy enjoins make it plausible that the covenant scroll was Deuteronomy, or something like it. Centralizing festivals and sacrifices in Jerusalem would make it possible to ensure they were celebrated and offered in a way that truly honored God. Of course this would work only when someone like Josiah was king and someone like Hilkiah was priest, and in the decades after Josiah things in Jerusalem deteriorated again. But if you do have faithful leadership at the center, it can exercise oversight of the worship.

DEUTERONOMY 16:18–17:13

Justice and Only Justice (Absolute Faithfulness)

[18]"Appoint for yourself officials with authority in all the settlements that Yahweh your God is giving you for your clans. They are to make decisions for the people in a faithful fashion. [19]You are not to twist decision making. You are not to pay attention to [someone's] person. You are not to accept gifts, because gifts blind the eyes of the experts and twist the words of the faithful. [20]You are to pursue absolute faithfulness so that you may live and take possession of the country Yahweh your God is giving you."

[Deuteronomy 16:21–17:3 reverts to some prohibitions with regard to worship and then to the accusation that someone has worshiped other gods.]

[17:4]"If it is reported to you or you hear of it, you are to investigate well. If it is indeed true, the thing is established, this offense was committed in Israel, [5]you are to take that man or woman who did this evil thing out to the gates of the city and stone them to death. [6]At the word of two or three witnesses is a person to be put to death. He may not be put to death at the word of one witness. [7]The hand of the witnesses is to be the first against him to put him to death and the hand of the entire people afterwards, and you will consume away the evil from your midst.

[8]"If a matter is too hard for you to decide, concerning blood-shed or a dispute or assault (matters of conflict in your settle-ment), you are to set off and go up to the place Yahweh your God chooses [9]and come to the Levitical priests, to the authority who is there at that time, and inquire. They will tell you the word of decision, [10]and you are to act in accordance with the word they tell you from that place Yahweh chooses. You are to be careful to act in accordance with everything they teach you."

[Verses 11–13 summarize the instructions.]

The last time I took a student group to Israel, among the speak-ers we had in the evenings was a Christian Palestinian Israeli called Naim Ateek; his son was subsequently a student at our seminary. Dr. Ateek was born in Palestine during the British Mandate, and his family lived in one of the areas that were taken over by Israel in 1947–1948. He was eventually one of the pastors at the Episcopal Cathedral in Jerusalem and lived in East Jerusalem; it gave me food for thought that he was a bit concerned about walking around the Old City of Jerusalem late at night (I did so without thinking). In his doctoral dissertation he sought to think about the theological position of the Pales-tinian people and published the work as a book called *Justice, and Only Justice: A Palestinian Theology of Liberation.* His title came from this passage in Deuteronomy; it was shrewd to take up a passage from Deuteronomy in arguing the rights of the Palestinian people.

His phrase "justice and only justice" is the NRSV's transla-tion of the phrase I have rendered as "absolute faithfulness." **Faithfulness** (*sedeq*) denotes doing the right thing by people in your community. In Spike Lee's movie *Do the Right Thing* the question of doing right concerns race relations, so the context is not so different from that of relations between Palestinian and Jewish Israelis. (The movie even ends with two contrasting quotations. Martin Luther King declares, "Violence as a way of achieving racial justice is both impractical and immoral." Malcolm X declares, "I am not against using violence in self-defense. I don't even call it violence when it's self-defense; I call it intelligence.") Jews and Christians (and Muslims) all belong to Abraham's family. Shouldn't they do the right thing by one another, the absolutely faithful thing, pursuing justice and only justice for the other person?

Deuteronomy is especially concerned with doing the right thing within the community. In the villages where most people lived, the elders would be the people who dealt with disputes and conflicts, including homicide, and thus had responsibility for doing the right thing. A village would hardly need "officials," but as cities developed in Israel, the system that worked in villages might not work as well, and 2 Chronicles 19:5 describes King Jehoshaphat as appointing "authorities" in all the big cities. Deuteronomy gives them some principles that are obvious and basic but that can never be taken for granted (as the Prophets show, and as our own experience does). That will perhaps be more so in the cities, where everything is less personal and where economic differences grow. The authorities are to make legal decisions in a way absolutely faithful to the community rather than twisting their decision making. They are to take no notice of the importance of the person involved in a dispute. They are not to accept gifts from people. This obviously applies to accepting gifts from people in the midst of a dispute, but Deuteronomy does not limit itself to that. A judge might be expert and faithful, but having accepted someone's offer of two weeks' holiday at his or her condo on the Mediterranean does not make it easy to be objective when a case involving that person comes up in the future.

Deuteronomy goes on to concern itself with another aspect of doing justice: ensuring that the wrong person doesn't get executed. The asylum cities described in Numbers 35 deal with this in connection with homicide; Deuteronomy is concerned with the accusation that someone has worshiped other gods, which is also a capital offense (though we have noted that Israel does not seem to treat it as a "law" for literal implementation). Once again at least two witnesses are required for conviction. Of course if you can hire one, you can probably hire two, as King Ahaz found (1 Kings 21). But the witnesses need to be pretty audacious as well as unprincipled to take the leading action in the execution that Deuteronomy here describes.

Deuteronomy finally provides for the equivalent of a higher court when local officials cannot resolve a case; or rather, it reformulates the rule in Exodus 21. In keeping with its regular policy, it requires that coming before God means coming to the central sanctuary, rather than allowing for the possibility that people might resort to one of the sanctuaries that go back to **Canaanite** times. Second Chronicles 19 also describes Jehoshaphat as setting up a higher court of this kind and appointing some Levites and elders to serve in this capacity.

DEUTERONOMY 17:14–18:22

Kings, Priests, Levites, Prophets

[14]"When you enter the country Yahweh your God is giving you to take possession of and you are living in it, and you say, 'I intend to set a king over me, like all the nations around me,' [15]you may indeed set over you a king whom Yahweh your God chooses. From the midst of his brothers you may set a king over you. You cannot put over you a man who is a foreigner, who is not your brother. [16]Moreover, he may not multiply horses for himself and he may not get the people to return to Egypt so he may multiply horses, given that Yahweh said to you, 'You may never again return that way.' [17]He may not multiply wives for himself, so that they do not turn his mind astray. Nor may he greatly multiply silver and gold for himself. [18]When he sits on his royal throne, he will write for himself a copy of this teaching on a scroll in front of the Levitical priests. [19]It will be with him and he will read out of it all the days of his life so that he may learn to revere Yahweh his God by observing every word of this teaching and these rules, by doing them, [20]so that his mind does not rise above his brothers and he does not turn aside from the command right or left, in order that he may stay long over his kingdom, he and his sons, in the midst of Israel."

[Deuteronomy 18:1–17 covers the support of priests through the people's offerings, the right of Levites to go and live at the central sanctuary and share in what is brought there, and the importance of the people's seeking guidance only from Yahweh and not by other religious means—which leads into talking about prophets.]

[18:18]"'I will produce a prophet for them from among their brothers like you. I will put my words in his mouth and he will speak all that I command him. [19]The person who does not listen to the words he speaks in my name—I myself will take it up with him. ²⁰Moreover, the prophet who presumes to speak a message in my name that I did not command him to speak or who speaks in the name of other gods: that prophet will die. ²¹If you say to yourself, "How will we recognize the message that Yahweh has not spoken?": ²²what the prophet speaks in Yahweh's name but the message does not come about or come true, that is the message Yahweh did not speak. The prophet spoke it presumptuously. You will not be in dread of him.'"

In the seminary where I taught in England, from time to time we would have someone delivering a prophetic message in the context of worship. Generally these messages were reassuring and general, promising people God's love, protection, and provision. One of my colleagues once commented that two-thirds were trivial, but that one out of three ain't bad. On a couple of occasions I was given promises for myself that were more concrete and that God indeed honored. On the other hand, for a couple of years in the seminary we had a student who would rather regularly come out with tough (but vague) messages of judgment, and it was a puzzle how to evaluate these. It was complicated by the fact that the "prophet" was a rather angry and bitter person, and it was tempting to infer that he was working out his own issues. Yet God works through personalities, so that would be a dangerous basis on which to ignore him.

In what it says about prophets, Deuteronomy both offers encouragement and recognizes this dilemma. The background of the encouragement is the natural human desire to know what the future holds, which makes people have recourse to diviners and soothsayers and seek contact with dead family members on the assumption that dead people ought to have special knowledge. Elsewhere the Old Testament refers to consulting the stars. It's understandable that other peoples do that, Deuteronomy says, but God has rescued you from it by sending you prophets. They are your means of knowing what God wants you to know about the future (and you must learn to live in trust with not knowing what God does not want you to know).

Yet how do we know if a prophet is really prompted by God? Raising the question again reflects how the Holy Spirit is enabling people in a later century to work out what Moses would say if he were here now. It is especially an issue in the time of Jeremiah, the same period as the one when Josiah is centralizing **Judah**'s worship (see the comments on Deuteronomy 16) and the time when "false prophets" are a big problem in Judah. They are a particular problem for Jeremiah, who is practically a minority of one in declaring that God is going to bring calamity on Judah. Other prophets are declaring that God is a God of love and will always be faithful to the people. "Let's see how things turn out, then," says Jeremiah. "Events will establish who is the true prophet"; so they did. This is the test in Deuteronomy 18. It doesn't say a false prophet's word will never come true; Deuteronomy 13 has acknowledged that it may. It does say that when a prophet's word doesn't come true, you needn't worry about this prophet. As Jeremiah acknowledges, this principle is only of limited help (Deuteronomy 13 offered another test, also of limited help). There are no knockdown tests. But it is of some help.

It is from "your brothers" that God will produce a prophet (perhaps I should translate "from your siblings," as the first prophet after Deuteronomy 18 is Deborah, and in connection with Josiah's reform Huldah plays a key role as prophet). It is one of Deuteronomy's favorite words, and it plays a key role in connection with the ruling about kings that opens the section of Scripture we are considering. There it has a couple of significances, which perhaps apply to prophets, too. One is that the king is to be appointed from within Israel; he is not to be a foreigner. Within God's providence and under God's sovereignty Israel has the resources within itself for leadership and guidance; it does not need to look outside, and it will be dangerous to do so. Another is that the king has to keep reminding himself that he is only one of the band of brothers; he must not fall into the trap of thinking he is more important than they are. It is virtually impossible for leaders to avoid that trap, partly because the people themselves put their leaders on pedestals. Deuteronomy also reminds them that prophets, too, are just brothers through whom God speaks.

In prescribing what people should do when they wish to have a king, yet again Deuteronomy handles something that will not become an issue for centuries after Moses' day. When the question does arise, in the time of Samuel, the Old Testament shows itself aware of the ambiguity of the idea of kingship. Having kings is suspect because God is supposed to be Israel's king. Yet when Israel has no human kings, "people do what is right in their own eyes," resulting in moral and social chaos. Deuteronomy's angle offers another take on coping with this ambiguity. Israel can have a king, but God will choose him, and he needs to avoid being tempted into the self-indulgence that regularly characterizes people in leadership, who have bigger houses and better health plans than the people they lead. Further, he needs to have ways of making sure he avoids becoming a law unto himself. So he is to make himself a copy of *the* law, the teaching in this very scroll, and live and rule by it, so that (for instance) he does not let himself be led astray through his political marriages. Some irony attaches to such hopes, as Solomon's story has shown by the time Deuteronomy was written.

Both king and prophet became ways of picturing the redeemer God will eventually send Israel, as the Messiah and *the* prophet. There is no direct suggestion here that Israel will ever need a redeemer king, but the failure of kings to live by Deuteronomy's prescription is one background to Israel's coming to hope for one who will. Likewise, Deuteronomy's talk of "a prophet like Moses" does not refer to a single prophet, but in due course it provided another image for a redeemer figure that God will eventually send (see, for example, Acts 7:37).

DEUTERONOMY 19:1–20:20

How to Make War (or How to Make War Impractical)

[Deuteronomy 19:1–13 restates the rules about asylum cities in Numbers 35.]

[19:14]"You will not move your neighbor's boundary marker, which previous generations laid down in the property you receive in the country Yahweh your God is giving you to take possession of.

[15]"One witness will not stand up against a person in connection with any waywardness or offense, with regard to an

offense he commits. At the word of two or three witnesses the statement will stand. [16]If a criminal witness stands against a person to testify lies against him, [17]the two people who have the dispute will appear before Yahweh, before the priestly authorities who are there at that time. [18]The authorities will investigate well, and if the false witness has testified falsehood against his brother, [19]you will do to him as he intended to do against his brother and consume away the evil from your midst, [20]while the rest will hear and be afraid, and people will not ever again act in this evil way in your midst. [21]Your eye will not pity: life for life, eye for eye, tooth for tooth, hand for hand, foot for foot.

[20:1]"When you go out to battle against your enemies and you see horses and chariots, a people bigger than you, you will not be afraid of them, because Yahweh your God, who brought you out from Egypt, will be with you. [2]When you are drawing near the battle, the priest will come forward and speak to the people, [3]and say to them, 'Listen, Israel. You are drawing near to battle with your enemies today. You will not be fainthearted. Do not be afraid, do not panic, do not be in dread of them, [4]because Yahweh your God is going to be with you to battle with your enemies for you, to deliver you.' [5]Then the officials will speak to the people: 'Who is the person who has built a new house and not dedicated it? He is to go and return to his home so that he does not die in battle and another person dedicate it. [6]Who is the person who has planted a vineyard and not initiated it? He is to go and return to his home so that he does not die in battle and another person initiate it. [7]Who is the person who has betrothed a woman and not married her? He is to go and return to his home so that he does not die in battle and another person marry her.' [8]The officials will speak further to the people and say, 'Who is the person who is afraid and fainthearted? He is to go and return to his home so that he does not make his brothers' heart weaken like his.' [9]When the officials have finished speaking to the people, they are to appoint army commanders at the head of the people. [10]When you draw near a city to do battle against it, you are to proclaim peace to it."

[Verses 11–20 describe what is to happen if the city surrenders and if it does not, distinguishes the treatment of the local peoples in Canaan, and forbids the destruction of fruit trees in a siege.]

Last night at dinner, a friend of mine was hopping mad about a meeting she had attended the previous night, when an ex-marine who had become a pacifist was lamenting the wrongness of the war in Afghanistan on the basis (she said) of a confused understanding of recent history and of U.S. policy and self-understanding. "Not that I am simply for our being at war in Afghanistan," she said. "The situation and the background and the policies just require a lot more understanding than this guy showed." One of my colleagues has a sticker on her door that reads, "I guess when Jesus said we are to love our enemies, he probably meant we aren't to kill them." There is a place for such straightforward, no-nonsense statements and simple commitments that make a witness to the rest of us as well as a role for people who let themselves be killed for these statements and commitments. But these differing perspectives need to be combined with insight into complexities and ambiguities.

Numbers 20–21 and Deuteronomy 7 have already shown how the **Torah** recognizes that war is a complicated business. Deuteronomy 20 adds another angle, nearer to just war than to the other theological and ethical approaches to war that we noted in connection with Numbers 21, though very distinctive. Like the rest of the Bible, it takes war for granted as a facet of the way the world is and the way nations relate to one another. It is through war that nations such as Britain and the United States are what they are. Deuteronomy's aim is to constrain war. With some subtlety it does that in revolutionary ways.

It is the people as a whole (or at least, the menfolk) who make war; they do not commission people who like fighting or have no jobs or prospects in life to fight on their behalf so that they can carry on with their ordinary lives, essentially unaffected. Further, the people in charge of war making are not the generals but the priests and the community leaders. Indeed, the community leaders appoint the generals. When battle is imminent, the priests come and give the army a pep talk; then the community leaders come and give all sorts of people the opportunity to excuse themselves and go home. Home building, the development of the farm, and marriage have priority over war. Anybody who is scared can go home too! On the other hand, the basis on which you decide whether you can undertake war is not whether you think you can win. It's the fact that you know God is with you. You know this is what will make the difference, not your rational assessment of your weaponry and that of your enemies. When the army is about to attack a city, it first proclaims **peace** to it. You could say it is taking a peacemaking stance and operating in love toward its enemies, though admittedly "peace" is a euphemism for "surrender." But while such surrender will mean the city's people will lose their independence, they will not lose their lives. If the city refuses to surrender and the Israelites lay siege to it, there are limits to the way they can do so. War regularly ravages the country where it is waged; you can eat the fruit of the trees but you can't destroy the trees, Deuteronomy says. Such a list of constraints would be the despair of any general.

As many modern people are offended at the Torah's talk of war, so we are offended by its talk of an eye for an eye. That formula appears in three different contexts. Here it is again taking up its concern with perjury. First Kings 21 tells a chilling story about a man executed on the basis of false testimony. Suppose like those false witnesses you are made an offer you can't refuse, in order to get you to offer false testimony, or suppose the family next door has better land than you and you are tempted to lie in order to defraud them of it. The warning about not moving your neighbor's boundary marker in order to appropriate some of his land makes one think of a situation of this kind.

Deuteronomy attaches a chilling sanction to such action. It speaks poetically, as Jesus will when he speaks of cutting off your own hand, and we have no indication that anyone ever understood the formula with prosaic literalness. The story in 1 Kings 21 illustrates the point in its own way: the couple who commission the false testimony that costs Naboth his life are not brought to court and executed, but God does see that they lose their lives. What the rule indicates is that whenever you are inclined to try to swindle a person of something, you risk losing an equivalent to whatever you were hoping to gain. As the Naboth story also suggests, you are unwise to think that your power or resources can give you ways of distancing yourself from the act you commission and/or of evading the penalty for the act. Everyone is to be treated the same way. You are not to think of sparing someone because of who they are.

DEUTERONOMY 21:1–23

Murder Desecrates the Land

[1]"If a slain person shows up on the soil Yahweh your God is giving you to take possession of, falling in the open country, and it is not known who struck him down, [2]your elders or authorities will go out and take measurements to the cities around the slain person. [3]The city nearest the slain person—the elders of that city will get a heifer that has not been worked, not pulled in a yoke. [4]The elders of that city will bring the heifer to a wash that is flowing and that is not worked or sown, and they will break the heifer's neck there, in the wash. [5]The Levitical priests will come forward, because Yahweh your God chose them to minister to him and to bless in Yahweh's name, and every dispute or assault rests on their word. [6]All the elders of that city that is nearest to the slain person will cleanse their hands over the heifer whose neck has been broken in the wash. [7]They will declare, 'Our hands did not shed this blood; our eyes did not see. [8]Make expiation for your people Israel whom you redeemed, Yahweh. Do not put the blood of an innocent person in the midst of your people Israel.' And the blood will be expiated for them. [9]You yourself will consume away the blood of the innocent person from your midst, because you will be doing what is right in Yahweh's eyes.

[10]"When you go out to battle against your enemies, Yahweh your God gives them into your power and you take them captive, [11]and you see among the captives a beautiful woman, get attached to her, and take her as wife [12]and you bring her into your house, and she shaves her head, trims her nails, [13]puts away her clothes as a captive, lives in your house, and grieves for her father and mother for a month, and after this you have sex with her and become her husband and she becomes your wife: [14]if you then do not want her, you are to send her off wherever she wishes. You will certainly not sell her for money. You will not do whatever you like with her, because you humbled her."

[The chapter goes on to cover three further matters relating to polygamy, family life, and execution.]

Last night I watched the second episode of an enchanting TV series called *The No. 1 Ladies' Detective Agency*. At one level it's just another detective series of the "Miss Marple" genre, but it has a winsomeness deriving from its setting in Botswana. The community's life straddles traditional and modern society, and the former of these elements stands closer to the Old Testament than Western life does; an incident in the first episode involves a meeting of the village elders to decide a dispute over a missing goat. The scene compares with the kind of procedure the **Torah** prescribes. Last night's episode involved a missing person. The lady detective proved he had been eaten by a crocodile. His wife was not as saddened as one might have expected, but he was a womanizer (she said).

The concern in Deuteronomy 21 with an unsolved death begins with a dead body rather than a missing person, and it has a different starting point from the rules about asylum cities (Numbers 35 and Deuteronomy 19). Those passages start from an awareness that a homicide causes trouble within the community, and they look for a fair way of resolving that trouble. In Deuteronomy 21 no one knows whose body it is, who the killer was, or whose family the person belonged to (or if there are answers to these questions, the rule is not concerned about them). Maybe it is someone from far away who has suffered the fate that nearly fell on Joseph at the hands of his brothers. All that's irrelevant. The point is that murder stains the community and the land. Elsewhere the Torah speaks of it as an assault on God because humanity is made in God's image, or it speaks of the victim's blood crying out from the ground. So the stain needs to be cleansed, and the community has to take responsibility for this. They cannot say, "It was nothing to do with us." Or rather, they must say, "It was nothing to do with us" in that we as a community were not responsible for the killing, but "it is our business" in the sense that we will take on responsibility for dealing with the matter.

The procedure is a means of gaining **expiation**, of removing the stain that has come on the land and the people because of the murder. That cannot be done by convicting the murderer, but the case cannot be simply filed under "unsolved homicides." The stain lies on the land and the people. The death of the animal counterbalances that. It is not exactly a sacrifice; the animal is not killed at the sanctuary and not killed in such a way that its blood flows, as it would at a sacrifice. The animal is in its newborn, unsullied, pure state, and so is the canyon where the rite takes place. The elders as the community's representatives do not put their hands on the animal in a way that suggests that they identify with it or that it takes their place, but they do wash their hands over it, so that the stain on their hands moves to the animal.

Why the ritual should have the desired effect is not clear, and Deuteronomy's not offering a rationale for it may suggest no one knew. The rule resembles ones known from other Middle Eastern peoples, so it looks like another example of a practice God takes over and makes the means of achieving something. Here it is God's means of providing expiation for the land. As there is no exactly logical reason for God's accepting a sacrifice as making up for wrongdoing, so there is no exactly logical reason for God's accepting this heifer's death as a means of cleansing. But God does so. The idea of God's making expiation underlines the grace involved. By its nature, making expiation, doing something to put things right when they are wrong, is the business of the people responsible for the wrong. It is usually human beings who make expiation. Here God makes expiation. The community can relax about the possible aftermath of this horrible event in its midst; if it does what God says, things will be okay.

The rule about the treatment of a woman captive starts realistically from another aspect of how things are and seeks to limit their negative consequences. It takes for granted the way fighters end up marrying women from the people they fought against and seeks to protect the women from the worst consequences of this fact. When a man marries such a woman, he may be inclined to treat her as less than a real wife. The rule requires that this shall not happen. If he decides he made a mistake, he cannot just treat her as if she is a foreign slave that he bought. She has the same right to a proper divorce as any other woman. Of course (Deuteronomy would assume) ideally you shouldn't be divorcing, but such things happen, and in these circumstances, the person without any power in the situation needs protecting.

164

A subsequent rule about how you treat your sons also circumscribes the rights of husbands. Like the preceding rule it is not concerned with theoretical questions about whether polygamy ought to happen. Polygamy happens. It wants to deal with one of its possible consequences. A man cannot decide to treat his second son as his firstborn (with the status and privileges and responsibilities that go with this) just because he likes his mother more. A rule like this seeks to preserve proper order in the community. The following rule about the rebellious son is also in part concerned with order in the community. It concerns an adult son, not a child. An adult is capable of profligacy and drunkenness, which are likely to involve other people. They affect the community and are thus the entire community's business. It is therefore his parents' responsibility to bring him before the community court. Their concern will also be that his action will imperil the entire family (and thus ultimately the community, which will have to deal with there being an impoverished family in its midst). The parents cannot let him simply use up its resources. He is himself protected by their not being able to take action against him on their own, maybe because of a grudge against him. The sanction of stoning shows how important the matter is.

The last rule in the chapter pairs with the first. A man who has been executed may be exposed, to shame him, as happened to Saul. But the exposed body itself defiles the land; as murder defiles the land, so does capital punishment. There is an ambiguity about this act. One act of defilement must not be followed by another.

DEUTERONOMY 22:1–12

On Keeping Things Separate

[1]"You will not see your brother's ox or sheep straying and ignore them. You will return them to your brother. [2]If your brother is not nearby to you or you do not know him, take it into your house. It will be with you until your brother is looking for it and you return it to him. [3]You will do this in respect of his donkey or cloak or anything lost by your brother, which gets lost from

him and which you find. You will not ignore it. ⁴You will not see your brother's donkey or ox falling on the road and ignore it. Do lift it up with him. ⁵A man's things will not be on a woman and a man will not wear a woman's garment, because anyone who does this is offensive to Yahweh your God. ⁶When a bird's nest happens to be in front of you on the road, in some tree or on the ground, with young ones or eggs and the mother sitting on the young or on the eggs, you will not take the mother along with the offspring. ⁷You absolutely must let the mother go, but you may take the offspring for yourself, so that things may go well with you and you may live a long life. ⁸When you build a new house, you will make a wall for your roof so that you do not bring bloodguilt on your household if someone should fall from it. ⁹You will not sow your vineyard with two kinds of seed, or else the whole crop from the seed you sow and the yield of the vineyard become holy. ¹⁰You will not plow with an ox and a donkey together. ¹¹You will not wear a mixture of wool and linen together. ¹²You will make yourself tassels on the four corners of the garment with which you cover yourself."

A house where we once lived in England had a small back garden with a nice rose patch but no room for growing vegetables (the previous occupant was a big gardener but had an allotment elsewhere for growing huge amounts of things to eat, so the back garden was dominated by lawn and flowers). So I used to grow green onions or radishes or lettuce underneath the roses. This always seemed a slightly odd thing to do as it involved mixing things that didn't belong together, but I liked the roses, and I liked growing green onions and lettuce.

Maybe the instinct to feel uneasy about mixing things that don't really belong together helps me understand one of the instincts lying behind some of these verses. Israelites were not to mix things that didn't belong together. This would have some humane benefits; putting an ox and a donkey together could be uncomfortable, at least for the donkey. This consideration might also underlie the ban on taking a mother bird (for sacrifice?) and also her chicks and eggs. Yet this consideration does not explain the prohibitions as a set. As was the case in Deuteronomy 14, a possible overarching principle is that people should live in light of the way God created the world. God made things different from one another and fitted them into categories, as Genesis 1 emphasizes. Ignoring that may mean forfeiting your crop (that is, it may become holy and untouchable).

In turn, these differences become another reminder of the difference between Israel and surrounding peoples. Israel does not have to avoid contact with other peoples, but it does have to maintain a distinctive lifestyle to remind it of its different place in God's purpose. Not wearing the opposite sex's clothes or "things" (for instance, weapons or tools) similarly preserve the distinction between the sexes, to the same end. If you are a woman who likes wearing pants or a man who has to wear a dress in church, like me, it's okay. These rules are among the ones God eventually had a change of mind about, like the rules about what you can eat (see the comments on Deuteronomy 14). The tassels may come in here because they form an exception to this rule about not mixing things (see the comment on Numbers 15:37–41).

One could see the opening instructions (and the rule about having a parapet around your flat roof in verse 8) as concrete illustrations of what loving your neighbor means. The context of that command in Leviticus 19 makes clear that it has in mind the way your neighbor can be your enemy. The same would likely apply here. You hardly need to be told to care about your neighbor's animals if the two families get along fine. But if you are fed up with your neighbor's son's practicing his drums when you've gone to bed, when his animal is in trouble you may well be inclined to look the other way. The same applies if you simply don't know whose animals they are. Why should you not just mind your own business? To hold you back from those reactions, Deuteronomy typically describes this person not merely as your neighbor but as your brother. Other people in the village are members of your family, the family of Israel; treat them that way.

DEUTERONOMY 22:13–30

Sex in the City

¹³"If a man marries a woman and has sex with her, then repudiates her ¹⁴and lays accusations against her and gives her a bad name, saying, 'This woman: I married her and had sex with her

167

and I didn't find in her evidence of virginity,' ¹⁵the girl's father and mother will get the evidence of the girl's virginity and produce it to the elders of the city at the gate. ¹⁶The girl's father will say to the elders, 'My daughter: I gave her to this man as wife and he repudiated her. ¹⁷Now. He himself has laid accusations, saying, "I did not find the evidence of virginity in your daughter." This is the evidence of my daughter's virginity.' So they will lay out the cloth in front of the elders of the city, ¹⁸and that city's elders will get the man, chastise him, ¹⁹charge him a hundred silver [shekels], and give it to the girl's father, because he gave a bad name to an Israelite virgin. And she will be his wife; he will not be able to divorce her as long as he lives. ²⁰But if this thing is true, if the evidence of virginity was not found for the girl, ²¹they will produce the girl at the entrance of her father's house and the men of her city will stone her to death, because she has done something outrageous in Israel by being immoral in her father's household. You will consume the evil from your midst."

[Verses 22–30 go on to impose the death penalty for adultery and for a couple who have sex when the woman is betrothed to someone else and it is reasonable to reckon that she did not resist the man's advances; if she may well have resisted, the death penalty applies only to the man. If a man forces himself on an unengaged girl, he pays compensation to her father and must be prepared to marry her without right of divorce. A man may not marry his father's wife.]

I've been reading a book that interweaves the story of three iconic 1960s singer-songwriters—Carole King, Carly Simon, and Joni Mitchell. The key to Joni Mitchell's life story and music is something that happened when she was a teenager and that has haunted her ever since. She got pregnant, and in the social and cultural context of the Canada of her youth, it was absolutely essential and inescapable that her parents should find a way of her having the baby in secret and then surrender it for adoption. "Ever since then," a friend has said, "she's never really been able to live with herself." She wrote a song about the baby that virtually no one was able to interpret when she finally recorded it, long after she wrote it. Eventually, after more than thirty years, she found her daughter.

In Britain or North America in the third millennium it may be hard to imagine living in the context of the sexual and family mores of the early 1960s. Understanding Deuteronomy's rules about sexual relationships involves a similar effort of the imagination. Implicit in many of the rules is the importance of the kin group or extended family within the context of the villages where most Israelites lived. The average village might comprise three kin groups, each perhaps of fifty people. The kin group would be spread over a number of households. The head of the kin group would be responsible for ensuring that a girl from his kin group made a good marriage with someone in one of the other kin groups. A good marriage will mean one that enhances relationships between the groups as well as being good for the girl and the man, though many Old Testament stories indicate that this does not mean the young people have no say in the matter. It will be important to keep those community relationships on even keel, otherwise village life as a whole may implode. The ban on a man's marrying one of his father's wives (not his own mother) after his father's death will link with such considerations. Such a marriage would be designed to enhance the man's position; he is claiming to take his father's place. The rule makes particularly clear a different cultural assumption about marriage from the one that obtains in the West, where marriage is all about a close, romantic personal relationship.

The advantages and disadvantages of this set of attitudes and style of life and of ours in the West mirror each other. Where the **Torah** was implemented, it would mean everyone had a place in the community, "no child got left behind," no one was short of something to eat when other people had plenty, but individuals had much less independence than we are used to in the West.

Admittedly, we always have to remind ourselves that we cannot infer from the rules in the Torah how Israelite life actually was. We would get a weird picture of life in the United States from reading state legal codes. Law focuses on marginal situations, on coping when things go wrong. Deuteronomy is certainly doing that (we will note a comment of Jesus about that in connection with Deuteronomy 24). We cannot infer from the rules in the Torah what regular life was like for ordinary people; stories in Genesis or later narrative may give a better impression of that.

The nature of village life is the background of Deuteronomy's rules relating to when sex goes wrong. As is the case in many societies, virginity matters, so if a man regrets the marriage he has undertaken and wants an excuse to get rid of his wife, then he might think of accusing her of not having been a virgin. Deuteronomy 22 protects her. He cannot simply accuse her and throw her out. He has to prove it, a tough challenge. Even if he was right, it would not be difficult to cast doubt on his claim by producing an alleged bed sheet from her wedding night spotted with blood, suggesting that it was the first time she had had sex. The chances that the girl could ever be convicted and thus subject to the stated sanction are virtually nil.

The subsequent rules about sex also offer a woman some protection and a man some deterrence. There is no double standard about adultery: the same sanction applies to the man as to the woman. (This rule is a good illustration of how one cannot infer from the rules how life actually was; the Old Testament records no instances of adulterers being executed.) If a girl has sex with someone when she is betrothed and thus "legally" married, like Mary when she gets pregnant, she is viewed as having committed adultery, but the sanction for adultery is not applied when there is reason to think she may have been a victim rather than a willing partner. The importance attached to virginity means that a girl who has been raped might have a hard time finding a man to marry her and/or that a man who did agree to marry her would not expect to produce as impressive a marriage gift ("bride price" would be a misleading term; the Torah does not think of a wife as someone whom a man "buys" and thus "owns"). That's not fair to the woman, but Deuteronomy is again starting from how things actually are. So the rapist makes some compensation to the girl's family and has to be prepared to marry her (the rule will again not imply she is obliged to marry him, only that he is obliged to be willing to marry her).

DEUTERONOMY 23:1–25

Attitudes to Egyptians (and Others)

[1]"No one whose testicles are crushed or whose penis is cut off will enter Yahweh's congregation. [2]No one misbegotten will enter Yahweh's congregation; even his tenth generation will not enter Yahweh's congregation. [3]No Ammonite or Moabite will enter Yahweh's congregation; even their tenth generation will not enter Yahweh's congregation ever, [4]because they did not meet you with food and water on the way when you came from Egypt and because [Balak] hired against you Balaam son of Beor from Pethor in Aram Naharaim, to belittle you [5](but Yahweh your God would not listen to Balaam, and for you Yahweh your God turned the belittling into blessing, because Yahweh your God gives himself to you). [6]You are not to seek their welfare or benefit ever, as long as you live. [7]You will not reject an Edomite, because he is your brother; you will not reject an Egyptian, because you were an alien in his country. [8]Children born to them, their third generation, may enter Yahweh's congregation."

[Verses 9–14 deal with the need to provide the camp with a procedure for dealing with nocturnal emissions and for defecation that avoids unseemliness.]

[15]"You will not hand over to his master a servant who escapes to you from his master. [16]He will live with you, in your midst in the place he chooses in one of your settlements, as he pleases. You will not ill-treat him. [17]No Israelite woman will become a hierodule; neither will any Israelite man. [18]The gift of an immoral woman and the fee of a dog will not come into the house of Yahweh your God for any vow, because both of them would be an offense to Yahweh your God. [19]You will not exact interest from your brother, interest on money, food, or anything that can be the subject of interest. [20]Of a foreigner you may exact interest, but of your brother you will not, so that Yahweh your God may bless you in every venture of your hand in the country you are entering to take possession of."

[Verses 21–25 urge people to keep their promises to God and permit them to sample grapes or ears of grain from their neighbor's land, but only to sample them.]

I have recently been to two concerts where the band included musicians from British towns within an hour or two of my own hometown—singer Graham Nash and guitarist Slash. Both have lived in Los Angeles for decades, and I don't know whether they are now U.S. citizens, but if not, they live with the oddities of being resident aliens here, as I do. We have certain rights but also certain insecurities; we can never take our residence for granted. Even as citizens, at one time if any of us had been women we would not have had the right to vote. If any of us were black, then at one time we too would not have had that right. In Britain, Roman Catholics and Jews long had no right to vote, and in both cases, votes for women came much later.

Deuteronomy here deals with the status of foreigners in the Israelite community. Like the rules about creatures you may or may not eat, the rules about who may enter **Yahweh**'s congregation combine several concerns. A recurring one is suggested by the use of the word for "congregation." There would always be people from neighboring countries in a village or in a capital city such as Jerusalem. One bit of background is the subsequent rule about not surrendering an escaped servant to his master (other Middle Eastern societies expected the opposite). Some of these foreigners would be refugees; others would be merchants. Suppose you have **Egyptians** living in your city. What rights do they have? What is their status?

Deuteronomy 15 has already noted that in the village or the city there is a difference between members of the family and people who don't belong to the family. You don't charge interest on loans within the family, because lending is not a way of making money as it is in the modern world; it is a way of caring for the needy and helping them get back on their feet. Foreigners are outside the family, not because the family won't admit them (families embrace foreigners as resident aliens) but because they don't identify with the community and its families and therefore choose to be resident aliens; perhaps they are merchants who are there only temporarily. So if they want a loan to develop their business, you can charge them interest.

Read in isolation from the rest of the Old Testament, Deuteronomy 23 could seem to marginalize foreigners totally, but elsewhere the **Torah** makes clear that foreigners can become part of the **covenant** with Abraham and join in Passover if the men are circumcised. Deuteronomy is not simply being ethnically exclusivist. One of its concerns will be religious. Foreigners who come to believe in Yahweh are one thing; foreigners who stick with their own religion are another. There may be a link with the exclusion of people who have allowed themselves to be genitally mutilated, as this ritual was part of religious practice among some peoples. But it is an example of a rule that may combine several concerns, since such people would seem to have gone against God's creative purpose and God's concern that Israel should be procreative. (We do not know what is being condemned by the word "misbegotten"; it might be people with one Israelite parent and one foreign parent, whose loyalty to Yahweh would therefore be uncertain; or it might be someone born as a result of one of the unions forbidden in passages such as Deuteronomy 22:30.) Banning people until the tenth generation is in effect banning them forever, though if they come to commit themselves to Yahweh, this would change the situation.

There may also be a link with the ban on "hierodules." The Hebrew word is the ordinary word for a holy person (and etymologically a hierodule is a temple slave), but in passages such as this it denotes a person involved in a religious observance that Israel saw as immoral. We don't know what this activity entailed, though referring to such people as sacred prostitutes is misleading. They may simply be people who have functioned as ministers in other religions; for Israelites to be so involved implies unfaithfulness to Yahweh and thus something analogous to sexual immorality.

Foreigners who stick by their own religion can hardly be accepted as members of the Israelite *congregation*. But in Israel, church and state are interwoven (to use our terms); Israel is more like nineteenth-century England than the United States. That interweaving makes it hard to draw the line between religious questions and political questions. The congregation is also the *assembly*. So foreigners who don't want to identify with Israel's faith also can't take part in Israel's politics. Forbidding people to seek these other nations' welfare or benefit sounds unethical, but the expressions have political connotations (TNIV translates "do not seek a treaty of friendship with them"). It suggests a mutual commitment between peoples, which again inter-weaves the religious and the political; a treaty would involve a religious ritual. The Old Testament commonly disapproves of Israel's making alliances with other peoples, because that stands in tension with reliance on God, and in this respect the nations mentioned, being Israel's actual immediate neighbors, stand for any peoples they might make alliances with.

At the same time, Deuteronomy knows there is bad blood between people such as Ammon or Moab and Israel. It does not expect Israel to behave as if their acts of enmity should simply be ignored and as if these peoples can be trusted. It is another reason to trust God rather than trusting alliances with them, an argument buttressed by the reminder about the way God looked after Israel when it was subject to their hostility. Surprisingly, Deuteronomy then takes a softer stance to Edom and Egypt. The prophets often see Edom as the object of God's judgment because of its acts against Israel; Deuteronomy reminds Israel that Edom is its brother (see Numbers 20:14–21 and the commentary on that passage). Egypt turned Israel into serfs; Deuteronomy looks behind that to the time Egypt gave hospitality to Jacob's hungry family. In other words, Deuteronomy affirms both the principle that wrongdoing is subject to punishment and the principle that Israel should love its enemies. In different contexts, one or the other may have priority.

DEUTERONOMY 24:1–22

On Sacred Inefficiency

[1]"If a man marries someone and becomes her husband, and she does not find favor in his eyes because he finds something objectionable in her, and he writes her a divorce document, hands it to her, and sends her off from his household, [2]and she leaves his household and comes to belong to another man, [3]but the other man repudiates her, writes her a divorce document, hands it to her, and sends her off from his household, or if the other man who married her dies, [4]her first husband who sent her off will not be able to marry her again after she has been made taboo, because this would be an offense before Yahweh. You will not pollute the country Yahweh your God is giving you

as your own. [5]When a man takes a bride he will not go out with the army, nor will he transfer to it for anything. For a year he will be free for his household to bring happiness to his wife whom he has married."

[Verses 6–18 go on to ban kidnapping people in order to force them into servitude and to give a reminder about dealing with the kind of skin disease that afflicted Miriam (see Numbers 12), but it gives most space to declaring various requirements concerning attitudes to needy people. You may not take away their millstones as security for loans; you may not go into someone's house to seize his pledge; if he gives his blanket as pledge, you must return it at night; you must not ill-treat a laborer; you must pay him on the day he does his work; and you must not take a widow's garment as security.]

[19]"When you reap your harvest in your fields and overlook a sheaf in the fields, you will not go back to get it. It will belong to the alien, the orphan, and the widow, so that Yahweh your God may bless you in all the work of your hands. [20]When you beat your olive tree, you will not go over it again. It will belong to the alien, the orphan, and the widow. [21]When you cut the grapes from your vineyard, you will not pick it over again. It will belong to the alien, the orphan, and the widow. [22]You are to keep in mind that you were a servant in Egypt. That is why I am commanding you to do this."

Just once in my life I had to give someone the sack because we needed to economize in the seminary and we saw a post we could terminate without too much loss to the enterprise's efficiency. The person had worked for the seminary for many years and was a good friend of it, but terminating this position seemed necessary. A catchphrase emerged from the 1992 U.S. presidential campaign: "It's the economy, stupid." In other words, you can get (say) foreign policy right, but it will get you nowhere with the people of the United States unless you get the economy right—that is, unless people have a sense that they are doing well, that they can make ends meet, and that they are doing a bit better than they were a decade ago or than their parents did. It's an exaggeration to say that this is the only thing that matters to people, but it's not much of an exaggeration.

Analogously, every company has to make the "bottom line" its priority. It always has to look for "economies" that will enable it to make more money.

Deuteronomy is blithely unconcerned about the bottom line. It has twice spoken about not charging interest on loans because you are going to treat all the members of your community as your brothers and sisters. This is no way to make money. Here it tells farmers to make a point of not being too efficient in the way they go about their harvest. This is crazy. Suppose the family needs every bit of grain, olive oil, and grapes over the next year? In effect, Deuteronomy has a different understanding of the word *economics*. In origin the word means something like "household management," and Deuteronomy takes a broad view of what this means. It often sees people such as aliens, orphans, and widows as part of a household, but it evidently recognizes that they will not always be in this position, as the story of Naomi and Ruth shows. In that situation, a family (with its farm) cannot simply ignore their needs but deliberately avoids being too efficient in order to leave them something. That is more important than making sure it has every sheaf of grain in store in case things are tough over the next year.

The middle part of the chapter makes analogous assumptions, pushing a bit further the principle that lending is an act of mercy, not a way of making money. It means you continue to be merciful and considerate in the way you relate to the person to whom you might make a loan. You don't treat this person as someone over whom you have rights so that you could walk into his house without being invited. You don't take as surety necessities of life such as the millstones needed to bake bread or a widow's garment. You don't hold onto necessities of life such as the coat that doubles as a person's blanket. If people have to work for you as employees, you pay them that day because they need the money (remember that working for money is an odd situation; only people who have become needy sell their labor). Underlying all these rules is your knowing what servitude is like, which is also a reason you would not dream of kidnapping someone for selling into servitude.

The precise point of the opening rule about divorce and remarriage is to ban a man remarrying a woman he divorced.

Maybe it is designed to guard against too-easy recourse to divorce (you need to remember you will not be able to remarry her), though it is unclear why Deuteronomy needs to make a rule to cover such an unusual situation. It nevertheless makes some telling points, and maybe this is why it appears in the **Torah**. Whereas an attractive, idealistic strand of thinking runs through those exhortations about generosity, this rule starts from the real world in which marriages break down. In this connection it gets taken up in Mark 9 in a discussion between Jesus and some other Jews. The question is, what is the Torah's attitude to divorce? The Pharisees allow divorce in light of this passage. Jesus points out that it presupposes a different attitude from one implicit in Genesis 1–2 that suggests lifelong marriage as God's vision. Deuteronomy 24 makes allowance for the hardness of human hearts. Marriages will break down, and God does not then leave people on their own to live with the consequences; the Torah incorporates a rule to help people manage this situation.

Specifically, Deuteronomy presupposes a world in which a man has the power to decide to divorce his wife. The reference to "something objectionable" is vague, and we have no basis for seeking to tie it down. Once more, the point about the rule is to be realistic. Men sometimes want to divorce their wives. Deuteronomy is not saying they should have that power; it knows this is just how things are in a patriarchal world. When a husband initiates a divorce, it leaves the woman in an ambiguous position. Her rights need protecting. The assumption that her husband provides her with divorce papers making clear her status is one way the Torah seeks to offer that protection. There is no reason to reckon that a woman would have no right to divorce her husband, though she would likely put up with a bad situation in her marriage (as women used to in the West more often than they do now) unless she could see a way of coping if she did walk out.

The rule about a man's being excused military service for a year after marrying "in order to make his wife happy" makes for a neat visionary companion to the divorce rule. The two belong in different worlds. Deuteronomy is concerned for both worlds.

DEUTERONOMY 25:1–19

Maintaining the Family Name

[1]"When there is a dispute between people and they come for a decision, and a decision is made for them and one is declared to be in the right and the other in the wrong, [2]if the one in the wrong is to be beaten, the one who makes the decision will have him fall down and beaten in his presence with the number that accords with his wrongdoing. [3]He may have him beaten forty times but he will not do more, so that he does not do more beating on top of this (a huge beating) and your brother is belittled in your eyes.

[4]"You will not muzzle the ox when it is threshing.

[5]"When brothers live together and one of them dies and has no son, the dead man's wife will not go outside, to a man who is a stranger. Her brother-in-law will have sex with her; he will marry her and act as brother-in-law to her. [6]The first son she bears will stand in the name of his dead brother so his name is not erased from Israel. [7]If the man does not want to marry his sister-in-law, his sister-in-law will go up to the gate, to the elders, and say, 'I do not have a brother-in-law to establish a name in Israel for his brother. He is not willing to act as brother-in-law to me.' [8]The elders of his city will summon him and speak to him. If he maintains his stance and says, 'I do not want to marry her,' [9]his sister-in-law will come to him in the sight of the elders, pull his shoe from his foot, spit in his face, and declare, 'This is what happens to the man who does not build up his brother's household.' [10]He will be named in Israel, 'Household of the man who had his sandal pulled off.'

[11]"If men fight each other and the wife of one comes to rescue her husband from his attacker's grip, and puts out her hand and seizes him by his private parts, [12]you will cut off her hand. Your eye will not pity."

[Verses 13–19 outline rules regarding honest measures and the obligation to punish the Amalekites for attacking the Israelites when they were exhausted on the way out of Egypt.]

I have just read about a court in Britain sending a woman to prison for killing someone in a car crash that happened while she was texting. The victim's mother and the prosecution are appealing for a stiffer sentence. The newspaper comments that texting while driving has become a practice that is widespread and socially acceptable, but the court has treated this death as not a tragic accident and "just one of those things" but a heinous crime. It is often tricky to negotiate between personal responsibility, personal freedom, and social obligation, and tricky to discern what counts as punishment that properly recognizes the "heinousness" of a crime and acts as a deterrent to other people yet does not excessively humiliate the person about whom many other people would have to acknowledge, "It could have been me."

Two of these rules raise related issues. The first presupposes a dispute between two people over a matter such as the ownership of an animal or responsibility for some damage. The ideal is for disputes to be settled between individuals or families, but when this does not work, the two parties come to the community authorities to decide who is in the right. They come to the equivalent of a court, which decides who is in the right and who is lying and committing perjury (not to say blaspheming, because the process would involve swearing in God's name that one was telling the truth) and imposes physical punishment on the person who was lying. The rule's particular concern is to make sure that the person is properly punished but also that the punishment is not excessive. It became customary to limit the beating to thirty-nine lashes to stay on the safe side (cf. 2 Corinthians 11:24).

The rule about brother-in-law marriage once again shows how Old Testament rules often don't function as laws but more as social and moral obligations. It places a strong obligation on a man, and he can be brought before the elders (in effect, taken to court) for failing to keep it, but they cannot actually *do* anything about it. He simply has to put up with being shamed. It is often said that Middle Eastern societies were shame-based in a way that Western society is not, but the point can be overstated. Shame is a big issue in Western societies; teenagers and Old Testament professors do not want to be discovered acting or thinking too differently from their peers. Conversely, shame is not the ultimate deterrent in Israel. Perhaps the man on whom the brother-in-law obligation rests sees it is not in his economic interests to fulfill this obligation and decides he will put up with the shame.

Leviticus 18 and 20 forbid a man's marrying his sister-in-law. Possibly these are rules that belong to different contexts from Deuteronomy 25, or possibly this rule is an exception to the Leviticus rule. Either way, each rule is concerned to maintain a particular principle, and it is often the case that one has to cope with the fact that different principles point toward different rules. There is a tension between the principle of personal freedom and a law that requires drivers to wear seat belts. It is a judgment call in different situations which principle gets priority. The principle behind the brother-in-law rule is the importance of maintaining the traditional allocation of the land among Israel's families rather than having a particular stretch of land come to belong to someone outside the family. The rule presupposes that the widow is keen for her brother-in-law to do his duty; one need not suppose that a widow *has* to marry him if she does not wish to do so, though this might also involve her risking shame in the community.

The context suggests that the point of verses 11–12 is to make a parallel point about women's obligation to men. A woman is not to imperil a man's capacity to beget children. While once again one should likely not take the sanction too literally, here ignoring the rule carries a quasi-legal consequence and not just a shaming. It is more like a legal issue than a moral and social one.

The humane rule about the ox is then succeeded by a purely moral and social rule about honest weights. Alongside the **Canaanites**, the Amalekites are the one nation whose wrongdoing Israel is not to forget, not merely because it was done against Israel but because it indicated that they had no reverence for God. Israel is supposed to be the means of God's punishing these two nations for their wrongdoing, though in neither case will Israel be very good at doing so; leniency with the Amalekites is one reason Saul gets rejected as king by God.

DEUTERONOMY 26:1–19

A Wandering Aramean Has Become a Great Nation

[1]"When you enter the country Yahweh your God is giving you as your own, and take possession of it and live in it, [2]you will

take some of the first of all the fruit of the soil, which you produce from the country Yahweh your God is giving you, put it in a basket and go to the place Yahweh your God chooses to settle his name there. ³You will go to the priest who is there at that time and say to him, 'I declare today to Yahweh my God that I have entered the country Yahweh promised our ancestors to give them.' ⁴The priest will take the basket from your hand and set it before the altar of Yahweh your God. ⁵You will testify before Yahweh your God, 'My father was an Aramean refugee and went down to Egypt and stayed there, few in number, but there became a great, strong, numerous nation. ⁶The Egyptians caused us trouble, oppressed us, and put harsh servitude upon us. ⁷We cried to Yahweh the God of our ancestors, and he listened to our voice and saw our affliction, our hardship, and our oppression. ⁸Yahweh brought us out from Egypt with a strong hand and an extended arm, with great awesomeness, signs, and portents. ⁹He brought us to this place and gave us this country, a country flowing with milk and sweetness. ¹⁰So now, here, I have brought the first of the fruit of the soil that you, Yahweh, have given me.' You will set it before Yahweh your God and bow low before Yahweh your God, ¹¹and rejoice in all the good that Yahweh your God has given you and your household, you, the Levite, and the alien in your midst.

¹²"When you finish setting aside the entire tenth of your yield in the third year, the tithe year, and give to the Levite, the alien, the orphan, and the widow, and they eat in your settlement and are full, ¹³you will say before Yahweh your God, 'I have cleared out what was holy from the house. Further, I have given it to the Levite, the alien, the orphan, and the widow in complete accordance with the command you required of me. I have not transgressed any of your commands, or put them out of mind. ¹⁴I have not eaten of it while mourning, I have not cleared out any of it while taboo, I have not given any of it to a dead person. I have listened to the voice of Yahweh my God. I have acted in accordance with all you commanded me. ¹⁵Look down from your holy abode, from heaven, and bless your people Israel and the soil you have given us as you promised our ancestors, a country flowing with milk and sweetness.'"

[Verses 16–19 issue a command concerning obedience, to close off chapters 4–26.]

Last Friday we had our harvest celebration at the seminary, and a great occasion it was. There was a wide range of food cooked by people of different ethnic backgrounds; there were games for children; there were rides in a hay wagon pulled by a genuine horse (looking a little incongruous on our palm-lined streets)—all designed to provide an alternative to Halloween. Later there was energetic dancing for the slightly less young. It didn't really have much to do with harvest, but you could say it was an imaginative cultural adaptation of the harvest celebration idea.

Israel's harvest celebration does something analogous. Peoples in general bring samples of their harvest before their gods as an expression of gratitude. One special feature of Israel's version of this practice arises from its awareness that its origins do not lie in this country whose produce it brings. It comes before God with a sense of astonishment as a people descended from a mere Aramean refugee, a person with his origins "back east" who had lived with his family as aliens in **Canaan**. Then they couldn't even stay there because of a famine, and they ended up in **Egypt**. Though they became an impressive people there, they found themselves reduced to serfdom, but God brought them out, and here they are in possession of this rich country with its hills for sheep and its fruit trees (milk and sweetness). For Moses, these words are anticipatory; Deuteronomy pictures him encouraging Israelites to imagine themselves inside the country they are still on the edge of, not only in possession of it but having already done a year's farming and able to thank God for the results and not for merely being in the country. Deuteronomy invites its readers to imagine what it would have been like to have that insecure background and then to be in a position to bring God the fruits of this land that has indeed become theirs.

The other feature of Israel's cultural adaptation of the harvest is the way Deuteronomy turns it into something celebrated not just for God's sake and for the family's sake but for the sake of Levites, aliens, orphans, and widows. Such people will never be in a position to fill their baskets with the fruit of their land, because for varying reasons they have no land. At Thanksgiving Israelites are not given permission to shut their doors and enjoy a family celebration. Or rather, they are given permission to do so but only on the basis of having extended the embrace of the family so that it incorporates these other people.

Their commitment to people outside the family is expressed in another way in the institution of the triennial tithe, which was either a different way of using the tithe in the third year or was additional to the regular annual tithe. The years are divided into seven, with two regular years, then a third year with this distinctive provision, then two more regular years, then another year with the distinctive provision, then the Sabbath year, after which the sequence starts again. In the triennial tithe year, the regular tithe or the additional tithe was given to those needy groups. Like the earlier account in Deuteronomy 14, the idea raises practical questions. If the needy groups received this tithe only every three years, how did they live in the other years? Or did different families have a different starting point in operating the seven-year system? Perhaps this is another example of the way the rules are more visions or imaginative ideas than literal proposals; Israelites then had to work out a sensible arrangement to embody their implicit principles. If so, that puts them in the same position as it puts us; as we read the rules, we have to think through imaginatively how in our social context we might embody the principles underlying the rules.

To underline the obligation to give to the needy in this way, Deuteronomy treats this tithe as something holy. It is just like an offering due to God. Eating of this produce that is due to the needy would be like eating something due to God. It would be as bad as diverting some of your produce into rites designed to facilitate contact with dead family members and with the deities associated with death whom other peoples acknowledged.

DEUTERONOMY 27:1–28:68

Curses and Blessings and Curses

¹Moses and the Israelite elders commanded the people, "Keep the entire command I am requiring of you today. ²As soon as you cross the Jordan into the country Yahweh your God is giving you, you will set up large stones. Coat them with plaster ³and write on them all the words in this teaching, when you

cross so you may enter the country Yahweh your God is giving you, a country flowing with milk and sweetness, as Yahweh the God of your ancestors told you. ⁴When you cross the Jordan you will set up these stones that I am commanding you today on Mount Ebal and coat them with plaster, ⁵and build an altar there for Yahweh your God, an altar of stones. You will not wield iron on it; ⁶you will build the altar of Yahweh your God from whole stones. You will offer on it whole offerings for Yahweh your God, ⁷and sacrifice fellowship offerings and eat there and rejoice before Yahweh your God, ⁸and write on the stones all the words in this teaching. Make it good and plain."

⁹Moses and the Levitical priests spoke to all Israel: "Be quiet and listen, Israel. This day you have become a people belonging to Yahweh your God. ¹⁰You will listen to the voice of Yahweh your God and keep his commands and his rules, which I am commanding you today." ¹¹Moses commanded the people that day: ¹²"These will stand to bless the people on Mount Gerizim when you have crossed the Jordan: Simeon, Levi, Judah, Issachar, Joseph, and Benjamin. ¹³These will stand for the belittling on Mount Ebal: Reuben, Gad, Asher, Zebulun, Dan, and Naphtali."

[The rest of chapters 27–28 describes the curses and blessings and then many more curses that will follow according to whether Israel obeys or disobeys.]

Last night I had a lovely dinner with some students. I accepted a second helping of pasta and a second glass of wine, and ate a magnificent brownie dessert with strawberries and ice cream. When it came to coffee, I declined because I feared this addition would overwhelm my digestive system. Then the smell of newly ground coffee made by the host, who is also a part-time barista, wafted across from the kitchen, and I was overcome. Through the night I proved myself right (again): it was all too much for my digestive system. In the end, I didn't take enough account of the predictable consequences of my action, and a small curse overwhelmed me. I could give one or two examples of a more serious kind of my failing to consider the likely consequences of my actions for myself (let alone for other people), but I am ashamed of them, so you will have to use your imagination or reflect on your own life and the curses you have brought on yourself.

We noted at the beginning of Deuteronomy that the way it expresses the **covenant** relationship between God and Israel overlaps with the way the **Assyrians** made treaties with their underlings. The amount of space Deuteronomy gave to detailed rules in chapters 12–26 took us some distance from the characteristic nature of those treaties, but as the book draws near its close, it comes back to something like them. Loyalty will mean blessing; disloyalty will mean trouble. If the underling dares to be disloyal to the superpower, trouble will follow. If it stays loyal, the superpower will look after it.

Deuteronomy looks forward to Israel's entering **Canaan** and proceeding straight to a natural center of the country, Shechem, the first place Abraham stopped when he came to the land. It is nowadays the center of the northern half of the West Bank. Here a main west-east route from the Mediterranean to the Jordan crosses the north-south route along the mountain ridge running through **Ephraim** and **Judah**. On either side of the city are the mountains of Gerizim and Ebal. There at the center of the country the terms of the covenant relationship will be put on display. Moses also envisages half the clans standing on one mountain and half standing on the other—one half will declaim the blessings; the other, the curses. There's no significance in who stands on which mountain or which side stands for blessing and which for curse. The whole people needs to associate itself with the whole proclamation.

The first set of curses, in Deuteronomy 27, include reference to people who make images, move their neighbor's landmark, and mislead a blind person, as well as people who get involved in various sorts of forbidden sexual relationships or act in a way that harms someone else. A thread running through many of these wrongs is their being the kind of thing no one else might know about. The curses warn Israelites not to think that they will get away with things just because they do them in secret. Saying, "Cursed is [such and such a person]" might have several implications. One is that consequences are built into the way life works, to the way God created the world. The kind of action the curses describe has an effect on the community; it brings trouble on the people who do them as well as on their victims. Another is that the passive participle "cursed" implies an agent, and the agent is God. God sees that these acts rebound on their perpetrator. Yet another emerges from the fact that "Cursed is [such and such a person]" implies "Cursed *be* such and such a person." In pronouncing these words, we are cursing ourselves. You need to be a cool person to do that. Indeed, your willingness to utter them is tantamount to giving an assurance that you will not act in this way.

The blessings in the first part of Deuteronomy 28 simply describe the good things that will come to the person who lives God's way. Whereas the curses relate to the acts of individuals, the blessings relate to the experience of the community. Things will go well in city and country, in the home and on the farm, in setting off and in arriving, in protecting you when attacked, in providing the rain you need, and in granting you prosperity. Conversely, the curses in the latter part of Deuteronomy warn of the opposite. Things will go badly in city and country, in the home and on the farm, in setting off and arriving, in assailing you with epidemic, in withholding the rain you need, in enabling your foes to defeat you. The chapter goes into horrific concrete detail about how this will work out, stressing the horrible consequences of defeat and **exile**. A Jewish commentator notes that people were hesitant to read the curses when they came up in the synagogue lectionary. The preponderance of the curses again compares with the Middle Eastern documents whose form Deuteronomy is following. No wonder King Josiah tore his clothes in grief when he read the teaching scroll discovered in the temple in his day (2 Kings 22), which seems to have been some form of Deuteronomy. And when his reforms failed to bring about a long-term change in the life of Judah, something like these curses overwhelmed the community; the book of Lamentations grieves over it.

Life does not always work out as neatly as Deuteronomy 27–28 describe it. As 2 Kings tells his story, Josiah provides an example; he dies an early death despite his brave and faithful life. Deuteronomy believes that this should not make us lose track of the way blessings often follow faithfulness, or lose faith in God to make them do so, or fail to maintain a proper solemn recognition of the way bad decisions often have bad consequences.

DEUTERONOMY 29:1–30:20

The Mystery of Obedience and Disobedience

¹These are the words of the covenant that Yahweh commanded Moses to seal with the Israelites in Moab, in addition to the covenant he sealed with them at Horeb. ²Moses summoned all Israel and said to them, "You have seen all that Yahweh did before your eyes in Egypt to Pharaoh, all his servants and his whole country, ³the great tests that your eyes saw, those great signs and portents. ⁴But Yahweh has not given you a mind to acknowledge or eyes to see or ears to listen, to this day."

[Verses 5–28 recall God's leading and protection on the journey from Sinai, challenge the people to enter into their covenant commitment to God, and warn them once more about the consequences of unfaithfulness.]

²⁹"The things that are hidden belong to Yahweh our God, but the things that are revealed belong to us and our children forever, to observe all the words of this teaching. ³⁰:¹But when all these things come upon you (the blessing and the curse that I have set before you) and you call them to mind among all the nations where Yahweh your God has driven you, ²and turn to Yahweh your God and listen to his voice in accordance with everything I am commanding you today, you and your children, with all your mind and heart, ³Yahweh your God will restore your fortunes and have compassion on you and gather you again from all the peoples where Yahweh your God has scattered you. ⁴If your scattered people are at the end of the world, from there Yahweh your God will gather you, from there he will get you. ⁵Yahweh your God will bring you to the country your ancestors took possession of and you will take possession of it. He will enable you to do better and be more numerous than your ancestors. ⁶And Yahweh your God will circumcise your mind and the mind of your offspring to give yourselves to Yahweh your God with all your mind and all your heart, so that you may live. ⁷Yahweh your God will put all these curses on your enemies, on your opponents, who have pursued you. ⁸You yourselves will again listen to the voice of Yahweh and observe all his commands that I am requiring of you today. ⁹Yahweh your God will make you exceed in all the work of your hand, in the fruitfulness of your womb, of your cattle, and of your soil,

so that you do well, because Yahweh will again rejoice over you so that you do well, as he rejoiced over your ancestors, [10]when you listen to the voice of Yahweh your God so as to keep his commands and rules written in this book of teaching, when you turn to Yahweh your God with all your mind and heart. [11]Because this command that I am requiring of you today is not too overwhelming for you, nor beyond reach. [12]It is not in the heavens, to make you say, 'Who will go up to the heavens for us and get it for us and enable us to hear it so we may observe it?' [13]It is not across the sea, to make you say, 'Who will go across the sea for us and get it for us and enable us to hear it so we may observe it?' [14]Because the thing is very near you, in your mouth and in your mind, to observe it. [15]See, today I have put before you life and well-being, death and trouble."

[So choose life, verses 16–20 urge, by doing what Yahweh says.]

My wife and I often used to go for lunch on a Saturday or Sunday to a restaurant hanging over the ocean where you can watch the surf (I have simple tastes), but we would leave in the early afternoon before the place became a "madhouse" (as a server once called it). One Monday I read about a film star and director having gone on a bender at the restaurant after the time we would have left. He then drove up the coastal highway, was pulled over by the police, and got into a lot of trouble with the media for apparently making anti-Semitic remarks. The media were pardonably gloating because he is well-known as a Christian yet is someone who has had a lot of trouble with drinking; one aspect of the occasion's sadness was that he was not supposed to be drinking at all. How stupid can you get? The answer with respect to all of us is that we can get pretty stupid. You can know the sensible and right thing to do, and be committed to it, yet go and do the opposite.

Deuteronomy knows that Israel's life is characterized by such a tension. Boldly, it here starts from the fact that "God has not given you a mind to acknowledge or eyes to see or ears to listen." We know that is true from the story so far in the **Torah**. From the perspective of people reading Deuteronomy seven centuries after Moses' day, it is even more self-evident. Chapter 30 presupposes a time when both the blessings and the curses have become reality in Israel's experience. The people have gained possession of **Canaan** but have then behaved like the Canaanites and been thrown out of the country as the Canaanites were. *Now* will they listen to Moses? Because **exile** need not be the end. God is prepared to bring them back from their scattering in **Babylon**, Moab, **Egypt**, and elsewhere. But first, they have to pay heed to the teaching.

Then Deuteronomy becomes a bit paradoxical, because it promises that to this end God will circumcise their minds and hearts so that they do so. Literal circumcision involves some cutting down to size and suggests some disciplining of sexual activity. This metaphorical circumcision has parallel implications on a broader front. Literal circumcision is undertaken by human beings; God has to circumcise the mind and heart. God will at last give people a mind to acknowledge, eyes to see, and ears to hear. So does God do this after restoring the people to their country? The order of events in the chapter seems to imply so. How, then, can they be expected to heed Moses' teaching, which is apparently a condition of God's restoring them?

Anyway, is obedience so difficult? There are indeed many things hidden from us (What *is* the solution to the problem of evil? How does economics work? In what circumstances is abortion justifiable?). But many things *are* revealed to us, and 99 percent of the time our problem is not whether we know enough to go and do what we should do, but whether we are prepared to do it. God's expectations are not rarified or obscure. You don't need a PhD to understand them. They are there in your mouth, in your mind. You can think about them and talk about them, and you do so if you follow what Deuteronomy has urged.

Well, yes, obedience is difficult. Israel and the church know what they are supposed to do and are not very good at doing it. There is a mystery about obedience and disobedience, an aspect of the mystery of any relationship as it develops. One person makes a tiny move and consciously or unconsciously waits to see what response it provokes. A positive response encourages another move. Gradually mutual commitment develops. It may be hard subsequently to analyze stage by stage how this happened. Trust and obedience between Israel and God develop like that.

In the event, God did not wait until Israel became more obedient before taking the scattered people back to their country. As far as one can tell, they gained no insight through being in exile. God took them back anyway. It would be no good if God waited for us to learn obedience before acting; God would wait forever. There is again a parallel with other relationships. Someone else's acting in love and generosity may not win you into mutual commitment, but it has more chance of doing so than their doing nothing and waiting for you to make a move. Somehow, after the exile, Israel did become a people whose mind and heart were much more circumcised than they had been before the exile. They did start living more the kind of life Deuteronomy urged. They did pretty much give up serving other gods, making images, misusing God's name, and breaking the Sabbath. It is a mystery how that came about. But it somehow involved some interaction between an extraordinary openhandedness on God's part and an eventual responsiveness. How our part and God's part interweave—that remains a mystery. Deuteronomy leaves us with two facts: God is compassionate and gracious. We are challenged to respond; for all that God does for us, we have to do that.

DEUTERONOMY 31:1–32:47

Moses' Last Song

[In 31:1–8 Moses reminds Israel and Joshua that Joshua is the one who will lead Israel into the promised land.]

⁹Moses wrote this teaching and gave it to the priests, the descendants of Levi, who carried Yahweh's covenant chest, and to all the Israelite elders. ¹⁰Moses commanded them, "After the end of [each] seven years, at the time set for the release year, at the feast of Shelters, ¹¹when all Israel comes to appear before Yahweh your God at the place he chooses, you are to read this teaching before all Israel, in their hearing. ¹²Gather the people—the men and the women, the young people and the aliens in your settlements—so they may listen, and so they may learn to revere Yahweh your God and take care to observe all the words in this teaching, ¹³along with their children who have not known it: they are to listen and learn to revere Yahweh your

God all the days you live on the soil that you are crossing the Jordan to enter into possession of."

[In 31:14–30 Moses speaks of the way they will actually break the covenant and follow after other gods, and pay the price for doing so, so that the teaching deposited in the covenant chest will serve as a witness against them. He then introduces this "song."]

^{32:1} "Give ear, heavens, and I will speak;
    the earth is to hear the words of my mouth.
² May my instruction fall like rain,
    my speech drop like dew
like showers on grass,
    like a downpour on shoots,
³ because I proclaim the name of Yahweh:
    ascribe greatness to our God!
⁴ The crag: his action is perfect,
    because all his ways are decisive.
A truthful God with whom there is no wrongdoing;
    he is faithful and upright.
⁵ In their shame they have acted corruptly with him,
    not [as] his children, a perverse and crooked generation.
⁶ Is this the way you repay Yahweh,
    a people that is stupid, not wise?
Isn't he your Father who brought you into being?—
    he is the one who made you and established you.
⁷ Be mindful of the days of old,
    consider the years of generations long past.
Ask your father, and he will explain to you,
    your elders, and they will tell you.
⁸ When the Most High allocated the nations,
    divided up humanity,
He set the boundaries of the peoples,
    according to the number of the divine beings,
⁹ Because his people is Yahweh's allotment,
    his designated allocation is Jacob."

[Verses 10–47 expand on that summary of Israel's history, describing at length God's provision to Israel, Israel's faithlessness, and God's chastisement of the people.]

In commenting on Deuteronomy 1, I referred to a service of contrition in our Episcopal diocese concerning the way we had treated African Americans. In the early decades of the twentieth century, in different parts of greater Los Angeles there were three Episcopal churches where it was made clear that "we" would prefer it if African Americans would form new congregations not far away from the existent white congregations (though in one of these white churches, African Americans were allowed to sit in the balcony). I noted how this is part of "our" history that "we" have to own ("we" being white people, and not least white clergy, like me). The end of Deuteronomy reminds us of an astounding companion fact. Solemnly, God remains mindful of such events from the past (and rejoices at our act of contrition, though I suspect is also wondering what we are going to do about it). Indeed, God was mindful of our wrongdoing before we undertook it. God and Moses knew what Israel's wayward future would look like; one might infer that God knew what the church's wayward future would look like. Yet with Israel and with us, God did not therefore abandon the project but remained committed to bringing it to a successful completion, a completion that glorifies God.

Admittedly there is some paradox about Deuteronomy's account of this. We have noted points when Deuteronomy is not addressing issues of Moses' day but issues that will arise in future centuries, questions relating to the appointment of kings or to discernment between true and false prophets. At other points Deuteronomy is taking another run at matters Exodus and/or Leviticus handle, such as the celebration of the three annual festivals or the practice of indentured servitude. These are again issues that would not arise once on the way to the promised land, let alone three times. While we do not know how the **Torah** came into being, in principle it is clear that this involved combining several versions of God's guidance of the community over the centuries as it faced questions raised by different social contexts.

When Deuteronomy pictures Moses writing down the teaching in this book, it speaks metaphorically. It is affirming that this really expresses a lifestyle that works out the implications of Moses' leadership for a later century. When Deuteronomy pictures Moses speaking of the way the future will work out, it speaks metaphorically. It is a way of affirming that the waywardness of God's people does not catch God off guard. The church's failures may embarrass us; they aren't something God is unprepared for. God can be disappointed and frustrated, but not defeated, crushed, or caused to give up on us.

Not only so. In the context of reminding Israel of its waywardness, Moses' song reminds Israel about the nature of its God, as a decisive, truthful, **faithful**, and upright Father, as someone with the reliability of a crag or cliff onto which you can climb and find certain safety. Our waywardness is the more horrible and astonishing in light of who God is, but the facts about God are also our encouragement when we come to own our waywardness. God continues to be that kind of God.

Deuteronomy makes the point another way by recalling who Israel is. God was the one who spread all the nations around the world and gave them their territories. Having a special relationship with Israel does not mean God declines to be involved with other peoples. Choosing Israel does not mean rejecting other peoples. Not being the chosen doesn't mean being neglected or damned. What about the "gods" these various nations worshiped? The Old Testament does not deny they exist but sees them as underlings of the real God, exercising responsibility for these nations on God's behalf. In contrast, God in person looks after Israel. The broader context of the Torah makes explicit that this is because Israel is God's means of bringing blessing to the world as a whole. Deuteronomy itself, however, focuses on God's commitment to Israel, in order to encourage Israel itself. As the song goes on to note, how astonishing and horrible it is, then, that Israel starts serving these other so-called gods! Yet how reassuring that God does not go back on the determination to be Israel's God. It's really hard to get God to give up. How stubborn God is.

DEUTERONOMY 32:48–34:12

On Dying outside the Promised Land

[Deuteronomy 32:48–33:29 repeats Yahweh's bidding from Numbers 27:12–13, then introduces Moses' dying blessing on each of the clans.]

³⁴:¹So Moses went up from the Moab steppes to Mount Nebo, to the top of Pisgah, which is opposite Jericho, and Yahweh showed him the whole country, Gilead to Dan, ²all Naphtali, the country of Ephraim and Manasseh, the whole country of Judah to the Western Sea, ³the Negev and the Plain (the vale of Jericho, the city of palms) to Zoar. ⁴Yahweh said to him, "This is the country I promised Abraham, Isaac, and Jacob, 'To your offspring I intend to give it.' I have let you see it with your own eyes, but you will not cross there." ⁵So Moses, Yahweh's servant, died there in Moab at Yahweh's word, ⁶and he buried him in a valley in Moab near Beth Peor, but no one knows his grave until this day. ⁷Moses was a hundred and twenty years old when he died. His eye was not weak and his strength had not gone. ⁸The Israelites wept for Moses in the Moab steppes for thirty days, then the days of grieved weeping for Moses came to an end.

⁹Now Joshua son of Nun was full of a wise spirit because Moses had put his hands on him, so the Israelites listened to him and did as Yahweh commanded Moses. ¹⁰There did not again arise in Israel a prophet like Moses, whom Yahweh acknowledged face to face, ¹¹for all the signs and portents that Yahweh sent him to do in Egypt for Pharaoh and all his servants and all his country, ¹²and for all the mighty power and great awesomeness that Moses showed before the eyes of all Israel.

I just read the obituary of a fine trumpet player and singer and even lovelier flugelhorn player, Stacy Rowles, who died after a car accident. My personal memory is of the way she once came to give a CD to my wife, Ann, in her wheelchair, and subsequently would regularly come to hug Ann when we went to hear Stacy play. The obituary described Stacy as "perpetually underdiscovered," better known in Europe than in the United States and better known on the West Coast than in New York. And now it's too late for her to be properly discovered. Her early death brings out something you might say is true of many deaths. We die before our work is done, or before we could achieve all we wish we could achieve. It's sometimes said that actually we die only after our work is done, but I am not clear on what basis we can believe this is so. There is such a thing as early death; and while God knows about it, that does not mean we have done all that God might have wanted us to do.

Once again God tells Moses he is going to die on the mountain heights east of the Jordan; he will not lead Israel into the promised land. Yet there is a sense in which his work is done. The point is implicit in the opening to his final blessing on the twelve clans, paralleling Jacob's blessing (Genesis 49). It first describes God's awesome appearance to the people, bringing "the teaching Moses commanded us, the possession of the congregation of Jacob" (33:4). Usually it is Israel that is God's distinctive and valued possession; here the teaching is Israel's distinctive and valued possession. It expresses the way God "became king over Jeshurun when the heads of the people assembled, the clans of Israel together" (33:5). Laying down the teaching marks God as Israel's king and Israel as God's people (Jeshurun is another term for Israel). The really important thing about Moses is his mediating God's teaching. Even if Moses accompanies Israel into Canaan, eventually he will die. What matters is that his teaching will endure.

With a prophet's foresight and authority he goes on to say something about each clan's destiny. Like Jacob, he notes the puzzling way the descendants of Jacob's oldest son, Reuben, end up as one of the smallest clans. He refers to **Judah**'s reversals, perhaps suggesting the time most of the clans separate off and form the much bigger nation of **Ephraim**. He emphasizes Levi's role as the teaching clan. He presupposes Benjamin's status as Jacob's beloved youngest son. Alongside Levi he gives most space to the Joseph clans, Ephraim and Manasseh, marveling at the fine land they will occupy. He speaks of Zebulun and Issachar to the far northwest with access to the riches of the sea, Gad with its fertile land east of the Jordan, Dan in connection with its move to the far northeast, Naphtali with its expansion around Lake Galilee, and Asher with its territory that is both rich and vulnerable to attack. At different points over future centuries as the clans read Moses' blessing, they can see how their advantages and vulnerabilities, their blessings and troubles, have been within God's purview.

The Moses project is complete. Moses dies when he has lived a full life, three whole generations. My rector used to say, "Moses spent forty years learning to be somebody, forty years learning to be nobody, and forty years showing what God could do with someone who had learned to be nobody." If that is right, it suggests another sense in which God is done with Moses. Yet Moses dies unnaturally, without setting foot in the promised land. Deuteronomy doesn't seem to fret about that on Moses' behalf. God invites Moses to savor the sight of the length of the land from where he is on its east side, up the Jordan Valley to its northern extremity, across the heartland of Ephraim, Manasseh, and Judah to the Mediterranean on the west, down to the Negev and back to the Rift Valley where Moses now stands. Deuteronomy rather implies that being able simply to view the whole land is enough.

God has an excuse for not allowing Moses to enter the land, but God's instinct to be merciful would surely make it natural to overlook the rebellion that sealed Moses' and Aaron's fate. Moses' fate ironically parallels that of the **Canaanites** themselves. Although they were an immoral society and cannot claim they do not deserve judgment, they were no more immoral than (say) the people of California in the twenty-first century; but the Canaanites were in the wrong place at the wrong time. Moses has been a faithful servant who has made one mistake, and God could have overlooked it but does not do so.

Maybe something else is going on. Moses belongs to the age that is passing; there is an appropriateness about having a new leader to take Israel into the land itself. Either way, God is prepared to be tough. When God commissioned Moses, it was not for Moses' benefit, and when God decommissions Moses, it is not essentially for reasons to do with Moses but with God's purpose and Israel's destiny. The point is summed up in the title Deuteronomy gives to Moses. He is not a leader but a servant—not a servant of the people but a servant of God.

It is easy to attach too much importance to a leader such as Moses, and God wants Israel to attach importance to Moses in the right way. On one hand, the mystery about Moses' death is that he simply disappears. He climbs the mountain and never comes back. His disappearance recalls that of Enoch, who one day just disappeared, and Elijah, whom God visibly took. But Moses did die; and they could never find his body. Apparently God buried him. That meant they could never turn his grave into a pilgrimage site. The location of his body was not what mattered. The way to remember Moses was not to put flowers on his grave but to follow his teaching.

GLOSSARY

aide

A supernatural agent through whom God appears and works in the world. English translations call them "angels," but this suggests ethereal figures with wings, wearing diaphanous white dresses. Aides are humanlike figures; hence it is possible to give them hospitality without realizing that this is who they are (Hebrews 13). They have no wings, hence their need of a stairway or ramp between heaven and earth (Genesis 28). They appear in order to act or speak on God's behalf and represent God so fully that they can speak as if they are God (Exodus 3). They thus bring the reality of God's presence, action, and voice, without bringing such a real presence that it would electrocute mere mortals or shatter their hearing. That can be a reassurance when Israel is rebellious and God's presence might indeed be a threat (Exodus 32–33), but they can themselves be means of implementing God's punishment as well as God's blessing (Exodus 12).

altar

A structure for offering a sacrifice (the word comes from the word for sacrifice), made of earth or stone. An altar might be relatively small, like a table, and the person making the offering would stand in front of it. Or it might be higher and larger, like a platform, and the person making the offering would climb onto it.

Amorites

The term is used in several ways. It can denote one of the original ethnic groups in **Canaan**, especially east of the Jordan. It can denote the people of Canaan as a whole. Outside the Old Testament it denotes a people living over a wider area of Mesopotamia. "Amorites" is thus a little like the word "America," which commonly refers to the United States but can denote a much broader area of the continent of which the United States is part.

Apocrypha

The contents of the main Christian Old Testament are the same as those of the Jewish Scriptures, though there they come in a different order, as the Torah, the Prophets, and the Writings. Their precise bounds as Scripture came to be accepted some time in the years before or after Christ. For centuries, most Christian churches used a broader collection of Jewish writings, including books such as Maccabees and Ecclesiasticus, which for Jews were not part of the Bible. These other books came to be called the "Apocrypha," the books that were "hidden away"—which came to imply "spurious." They are now often known as the "deuterocanonical writings," which is more cumbersome but less pejorative; it simply indicates that these books have less authority than the Torah, the Prophets, and the Writings. The precise list of them varies between different churches.

Assyria, Assyrians

The first great Middle Eastern superpower, the Assyrians spread their empire westwards into Syria-Palestine in the eighth century, the time of Amos and Isaiah, and first made **Ephraim** part of their empire. When Ephraim kept trying to assert independence, they invaded, in 722 destroyed Ephraim's capital at Samaria, transported many of its people, and settled people from other parts of their empire in their place. They also invaded **Judah** and devastated much of the country, but did not take Jerusalem. Prophets such as Amos and Isaiah describe how God was thus using Assyria as a means of disciplining Israel.

Babylon, Babylonians

A minor power in the context of Israel's early history, in Jeremiah's time they succeeded Assyria as a superpower and remained that for nearly a century until conquered by **Persia**. Prophets such as Jeremiah describe how God was using them as a means of disciplining **Judah**. They took Jerusalem and transported many of its people in 587. Their creation stories, law codes, and more philosophical writings help us understand aspects of the Old Testament's equivalent writings, while their astrological religion forms background to aspects of polemic in the Prophets.

Canaan, Canaanites

As the biblical terms for the country of Israel as a whole and for its indigenous peoples, "Canaanites" is not so much the name for a particular ethnic group as a shorthand term for all the peoples native to the country. See also **Amorites**.

covenant

Contracts and treaties assume a quasi-legal system for resolving disputes and administering justice that can be appealed to if people do not keep a commitment. In contrast, a covenantal relationship does not work within a legal framework, and someone who fails to keep a commitment cannot be taken to court, so a covenant involves some formal procedure confirming the seriousness of the solemn commitment one party makes to another. In covenants between God and humanity, in Genesis the emphasis lies on God's commitment to human beings, and to Abraham in particular. On the basis of God's having begun to fulfill that covenant, the rest of the **Torah** also puts some stress on Israel's responsive commitment at Sinai and in Moab on the edge of the promised land.

Egypt, Egyptians

Egypt was the major regional power to the south of Canaan and the country where Jacob's family had found refuge, where they ended up as serfs, and from which the Israelites then needed to escape. In Moses' time Egypt controlled Canaan; in subsequent centuries it was sometimes a threat to Israel, sometimes a potential ally.

Ephraim, Ephraimites

After David and Solomon's reigns, the nation of Israel split into two. Most of the twelve Israelite clans set up a state in the north separate from **Judah** and Jerusalem and from the line of David. Because it was the bigger of the two states, politically it kept the name **Israel**, which is confusing because Israel is still the name of the people as a whole as the people of God. So the name "Israel" can be used in both these connections. The northern state can, however, also be referred to by the name of Ephraim, one of its central clans, so I use this term to refer to that northern state, to try to reduce the confusion.

exile

When **Babylon** became the major power in **Judah**'s world at the end of the seventh century but Judah was inclined to resist its authority, as part of a successful campaign to get Judah to submit to it the Babylonians transported many people from Jerusalem to Babylon in 597 and in 587 BC, particularly people in leadership positions such as members of the royal family and the court, priests, and prophets. These people were compelled to live in Babylonia for the next fifty years or so. Through this period, people back in Judah were also under Babylonian authority, so they were not physically in exile but were also living in the exile as a period of time.

expiation

A key concern in the **Torah** is keeping the sanctuary pure. While God may be able to tolerate a small amount of impurity there (as we can tolerate a small amount of dirt), if the place people have made as a home for God becomes too affected by things that are alien to God, then God can hardly carry on living there. So it is important to deal with impurity that comes on the sanctuary through the infringement of **taboos**. While one way of conceiving this is to think in terms of atonement (at-one-ment), which suggests the healing of a relationship, and another is to speak of propitiation, which suggests the mollifying of someone who was angry, expiation relates to the thing that has caused the problem rather than to the person. It suggests the removal or wiping away of a stain. The removal of the stain means that the threat to the relationship is gone and it is now possible for God to be in easy relationship with the people; in this sense expiation and at-one-ment are closely related. On the other hand, "propitiation" is a more questionable idea in connection with the Torah; while the Torah implies that God is offended by people and unwilling to associate with them, it does not speak of sacrifices as a way of dealing with God's anger.

faithful, faithfulness

In English Bibles the Hebrew words *sedaqah* or *sedeq* are often translated "righteousness," but they denote a particular slant on righteousness. They suggest doing the right thing by the people with whom one is in a relationship, with the members of one's community, and with God. Thus they are closer to "faithfulness" or even "salvation" than "righteousness." In later Hebrew *sedaqah* can refer to almsgiving. It suggests something close to generosity or grace.

Greece

In 336 BC Greek forces under Alexander the Great took control of the **Persian** Empire, but after Alexander's death in 333 his empire split up.

The largest part, to the north and east of Palestine, was ruled by one of his generals, Seleucus, and his successors. Judah was under its control for much of the next two centuries, though it was at the extreme southwestern border of this empire and sometimes came under the control of the Ptolemaic Empire in Egypt, ruled by successors of another of Alexander's officers.

Israel

Originally, Israel was the new name God gave Abraham's grandson, Jacob. His twelve sons were then forefathers of the twelve clans that comprise the people Israel. In the time of Saul, David, and Solomon these twelve clans became more of a political entity; Israel was both the people of God and a nation or state like other nations or states. After Solomon's day, this one state split into two, **Ephraim** and **Judah**. Ephraim was far bigger and often continued to be referred to as Israel. So if one is thinking of the people of God, Judah is part of Israel. If one is thinking politically, Judah is not part of Israel, but once Ephraim has gone out of existence, for practical purposes Judah *is* Israel, as the people of God.

Judah, Judahites

One of the twelve sons of Jacob, then the clan that traces its ancestry to him, and then the dominant clan in the southern of the two states after the time of Solomon. Later, as a **Persian** province or colony, it was known as Yehud.

Master, Masters

The word *baal* is an ordinary Hebrew word for a master or lord or owner, but the word is also used to describe a Canaanite god. It is thus parallel to the word *Lord* as used to describe Yahweh. Further, in effect "Master" can be a proper name, like "Lord." To make the difference clear, the Old Testament generally uses *Master* for a foreign god and *Lord* for the real God, Yahweh. Like other ancient peoples, the Canaanites acknowledged a number of gods, and strictly the Master was simply one of them, though he was one of the most prominent. In addition, a title such as "the Master of Peor" suggests that the Master was believed to be manifest and known in different ways and different places. The Old Testament also uses the plural *Masters* to refer to Canaanite gods in general.

peace

The word *shalom* can suggest peace after there has been conflict, but it often points to a richer notion, of fullness of life. The KJV sometimes translates it "welfare," and modern translations use words such as "well-being" or "prosperity." It suggests that everything is going well for you.

Persia, Persians

The third Middle Eastern superpower. Under the leadership of Cyrus the Great, the Persians took control of the Babylonian empire in 539 BC. Isaiah 40–55 sees God's hand in raising up Cyrus as the means of restoring **Judah** after the **exile**. Judah and surrounding peoples such as Samaria, Ammon, and Ashdod were Persian provinces or colonies. The Persians stayed in power for two centuries until defeated by **Greece**.

purification, purify, purification offering

A major concern of the **Torah** is dealing with the **taboo** that can come on people and places through the effect of something that is alien to who God is, such as contact with death. There is nothing wrong with being involved in burying someone, but you have to give the taint of death time to dissipate or have it removed before coming into God's presence. A purification rite can bring that about.

Reed Sea

is literally "sea of rushes"; the name is the one that came in Exodus 2 where Miriam left Moses in the reeds by the Nile. It might be one of the northern arms of what we call the Red Sea, either side of Sinai, or it might be an area of marshy lakes within Sinai.

restore, restorer

A restorer is a person who can take action on behalf of someone within his extended family who is in need, in order to restore the situation to what it should be. The word overlaps with expressions such as next-of-kin, guardian, and redeemer. "Next-of-kin" indicates the family context that "restorer" presupposes. "Guardian" indicates that the restorer is in a position to be concerned for the person's protection and defense. "Redeemer" indicates having resources that the restorer is prepared to expend on the person's behalf. The Old Testament uses the term *restore* to refer to God's relationship with Israel as well as to the action of a human person in relation to another, so it implies that Israel belongs to God's family and that God acts on its behalf in the way a restorer does.

spirit

The Hebrew word for spirit is also the word for breath and for wind, and the Old Testament sometimes implies a link between these. Spirit suggests dynamic power; God's spirit suggests God's dynamic power. The wind in its forcefulness with its capacity to fell mighty trees is an embodiment of the powerful spirit of God. Breath is essential to life; where there is no breath, there is no life. And life comes from God. So human breath and even animal breath is an offshoot of God's breath.

taboo

I use the word *taboo* to render the Hebrew word often translated *impure* or *unclean*, because the Hebrew word suggests a positive quality rather than the absence of purity. There are certain things that are mysterious, extraordinary, perplexing, and a bit worrying. Among these are menstruation and childbirth, because they suggest both death and life. These are opposites, and God is the God of life and not of death, yet menstruation (with its association of blood and life) and giving birth (which is both life-giving and very dangerous) bring them into close connection. So contact with them makes people taboo; they cannot go into God's presence until they are **purified**.

Torah

The Hebrew word for the first five books of the Bible. They are often referred to as the "Law," but this gives a misleading impression. Genesis itself is nothing like "law," and even Exodus to Deuteronomy are not "legalistic" books. The word *torah* itself means "teaching," which gives a clearer impression of the nature of the Torah. Often the Torah gives us more than one version of a rule (such as concerning festivals) or more than one account of an event (such as God's commission of Moses), so that when the early church preserved the teaching of Jesus and told the story of Jesus in different ways in different contexts and according to the insights of the different Gospel writers, it was following the precedent whereby Israel expressed its rule of life and told its stories more than once in different contexts. Whereas Kings and Chronicles keep the versions separate, as would happen with the Gospels, in the Torah the versions were combined.

Yahweh

In most English Bibles, the word "LORD" often comes in all capitals, as sometimes does the word "GOD" in similar format. These represent the name of God, Yahweh. In later Old Testament times, Israelites stopped using the name Yahweh and started to refer to Yahweh as "the Lord." There may be two reasons. They wanted other people to recognize that Yahweh was the one true God, but the strange foreign-sounding name could give the impression that Yahweh was just Israel's tribal god, and "the Lord" was a term anyone could recognize. In addition, they did not want to fall foul of the warning in the Ten Commands about misusing Yahweh's name. Translations into other languages then followed suit in substituting an expression such as "the Lord" for the name Yahweh. The downsides are that this obscures the fact that God wanted to be known by name, that often the text refers to Yahweh and not some other (so-called) god or lord, and that it gives the impression that God is much more "lordly" and patriarchal than actually God is. (The form "Jeho-vah" is not a real word but a mixture of the consonants of Yahweh and the vowels of the word for "Lord," to remind people in reading Scripture that they should say "the Lord," not the actual name.)